W9-ASV-452

*Victoria and her daughters*

# *Victoria and her daughters*

*Nina Epton*

W · W · NORTON & COMPANY · INC ·
NEW YORK

Library of Congress Catalog Card No. 70-162796

SBN 393 05445-4

PRINTED IN THE UNITED STATES OF AMERICA

1 2 3 4 5 6 7 8 9 0

# *Contents*

# *List of Illustrations*



Unless otherwise stated the pictures are reproduced by the gracious permission of H.M. The Queen

# *Author's Note*

Victoria and her daughters . . . why? In the course of my travels – Canada, India and Singapore – I have seen the Great Mother figure of Queen Victoria surveying tropical bamboos and northern firs like a goddess dispensing mysterious manna from her orb and sceptre. In an alien land it was somehow reassuring to gaze upon those rotund, maternal and majestic contours, that half-benign, half-chiding expression which seemed to be forever asking of all and sundry: 'My beloved subjects, are you doing your duty? Are you leading useful lives?' Despite myself, I began to look upon her with filial respect, and it was a great shock to find her removed from plinth and lying on her back in the new Republic of Guyana, her hand still caressing the imperial orb designed as a globe, among a tangle of cast-iron lions and crowns. Close by she continues to be remembered by botanists, for there is a pool full of the world's largest water-lily, named after her: 'Victoria Regina'.

I began to wonder what the Queen had been like as a mother in her own home, with her daughters, those five princesses – Vicky, Alice, Helena, Louise and Beatrice – chiefly known to posterity for the dread disease of haemophilia which they transmitted to the royal houses of Europe. What were they like? How did they react to one another? What role did they play in the life of their mother? How typical were they of their age? Was that sugary-sweet song 'Home, Sweet Home' that tinkled in every cluttered Victorian drawing-room a reality in the vast royal palaces? Feminine curiosity and a penchant for Victoriana prompted me to try to find the answers.

# *Acknowledgements*

By far the greatest part of the unpublished material quoted in this book comes from the family papers of Lord Ponsonby of Shulbrede, i.e. the correspondence from Sir Henry Ponsonby to his wife Mary, which provides intimate, first-hand comments and asides on the Queen and her daughters. The author wishes to express her profound gratitude to Lord Ponsonby for his generosity.

The undated letter from Princess Louise to Lady Tennyson on page 222 was kindly drawn to the author's attention by Mr Laurence Elvin, Keeper of the Local Collection, the Tennyson Research Centre, Lincoln. Her Majesty the Queen, to whom the copyright of this letter belongs, has graciously consented to its publication.

The references to Tennyson's visit to Osborne in April 1862, and the extract from Queen Victoria's letter to Lord Tennyson in August 1885 (pp. 175–6) are republished from *Dear and Honoured Lady* (edited by Hope Dyson and Charles Tennyson, and published by Messrs Macmillan in 1969) by kind permission of the editors and publishers and with the gracious consent of Her Majesty the Queen, to whom the copyright belongs.

The various references to Princess Helena's, Princess Alice's, and Princess Beatrice's correspondence with the Duchess of Sutherland are published by permission of the Countess of Sutherland, who directed the author to the collection of her family papers in the care of the Staffordshire County Council Library. The author is indebted to the County Archivist, Mr F. B. Stitt, BA, B LITT, for his assistance in locating the letters.

The letter from Princess Louise to Edward Corbould dated

25 October 1869 (page 135) is quoted by kind permission of the Public Archives of Canada, Ottawa, thanks to Mr W. I. Smith, Acting Dominion Archivist, and Miss B. Wilson, who informed the author of its existence.

The letter from Princess Louise to Miss Josephine Butler dated 27 November 1869 is in the possession of the St Andrew's University Library, St Andrews, Scotland, who provided the author with a copy.

The letters from Princesses Helena and Louise to General Wolseley are in the Wolseley Collection of the Borough of Hove Central Library, and are quoted by permission of the Borough Librarian/Curator, Mr Jack Dove, FLA, FRCO, ARCM, FRSA.

The author wishes to record her appreciation of assistance from Mr A. G. S. Enser, FLA, FRSA, Borough Librarian of Eastbourne; Mr E. Gaskell, Librarian of the Wellcome Institute of the History of Medicine, London; the Royal Commission on Historical Manuscripts, London; Miss B. Greenhill, Assistant Reference Librarian, Brighton Central Library, and Mrs Eleanor Walker, Librarian, Newhaven Library.

For details of the Lornes' and Prince Leopold's visit to Chicago, the author is indebted to Miss Annette Fern, Assistant Reference Librarian of the University of Chicago Library.

The author wishes to thank the copyright holders for granting their permission to quote passages from the books mentioned below. Each book is also included in the Bibliography.

Allen & Unwin: *Queen Victoria at Windsor and Balmoral; Reminiscences of Princess Marie of Battenberg*

Bodley Head: *Unbroken Unity*

Brunswick Press: *Days of Lorne*

Edward Arnold: *Letters of the Empress Frederick*

Evans: *Dearest Child; Dearest Mama*

Faber: *The Empress Frederick writes to Sophie*

Hutchinson: *Embassies of Other Days*

John Murray: *A Victorian Diarist; Daisy Princess of Pless. By Herself; Life with Queen Victoria; Mary Ponsonby, a Memoir; My Dear Duchess; The Correspondence of Sarah*

*Spencer, Lady Lyttleton; The Girlhood of Queen Victoria; The Letters of Queen Victoria* (*1st and 2nd Series*); *Scenes and Memories; Whippingham to Westminster*.

Thornton Butterworth: *Further Letters of Queen Victoria; The World I used to know*

Warm personal thanks are due to Mr Hector Bolitho, Mr Roger Fulford and Mr David Duff, experts on the subject of this book, whom the author pestered at frequent intervals for information, opinions and comments.

# *Section I*

# *The Court is Nesting (1840-51)*

ON 2 May 1840, the *Brighton Herald*, whose readers – influenced by the proximity of the Royal Pavilion and Regency nostalgia – considered themselves to be personally involved with the Court, published an exciting piece of information:

> It is whispered, in circles likely to be acquainted with the fact, that Her Majesty is in a way likely to prevent the succession to the throne from passing into any other than the direct line. The report derives strength from Her Majesty's recent abstinence from her favourite exercise on horseback and also from dancing, in which she is known to take much pleasure.

The news passed quickly round the breakfast tables behind the bow-fronted Regency windows of Brighton's crescents and parades. Gentlemen nodded their satisfaction at the reference to 'the direct line'. That was one in the eye for the ugly old Duke of Cumberland, King of Hanover, next in succession to the throne.

Grandmothers recalled that no direct heir to the throne had been born in England since the year 1762. 'Please God all will go well,' they murmured, remembering the woeful story of the last near miss, when the popular Princess Charlotte, wife of Prince Leopold of Coburg, had died in childbirth after an excruciating labour which lasted over fifty-two hours. The Prince's personal physician, Baron Stockmar, had looked on helplessly while the court doctor, Sir Richard Croft, dieted his patient to the point of starvation and bled her regularly. Croft blew his brains out a few months after the Princess's tragic death. A short time before he had written to Stockmar: 'My mind is in a pitiable state. God grant that neither yourself nor anyone that is dear to you should ever have to suffer what I experience at this moment.'

Leopold was now the King of Belgium, remarried for political reasons to meek little Marie-Louise, daughter of Louis-Philippe, and Baron Stockmar had become his political adviser. The King, who had arranged the marriage between his niece Victoria and his nephew Albert of Saxe-Coburg, was just as anxious as the female readers of the *Brighton Herald* when Stockmar, who had been despatched to the English court, acquainted him with the news; Leopold immediately demanded that daily bulletins should be sent to him from the palace.

Charles Greville, who had expressed misgivings when the newly-weds rose early after their bridal night to walk in Windsor Park, muttering darkly: 'That's no way to produce an heir to the throne', had been proved wrong. The two young people were evidently full of vitality. Lord Melbourne must have smilingly recalled how often his little Queen had complained to him before Albert's arrival: 'I do wish I could have more *young* people round me, Lord Melbourne, young people of my own rank.' The court was full of old dodderers of Melbourne's generation, and sprightly Victoria – as the *Brighton Herald* so pertinently remarked – was greatly addicted to dancing.

That was one of the reasons (which the Queen kept to herself until her eldest daughter was married) why Her Majesty was furious to find herself pregnant so soon after her marriage. She had been looking forward to a year of complete enjoyment with her beloved Albert, to accompanying him everywhere, to dancing and parties. How she had flown through the Regatta Gallop with Albert at Windsor Castle before their engagement! 'Dearest Albert dances so beautifully,' she had noted in her journal,

> It is quite a pleasure to look at him when he gallops and walzes; he does it so beautifully and holds himself so well with that beautiful figure of his. He looks *so* handsome—he has such beautiful blue eyes, a delicate nose, a beautiful mouth with a small

moustache and very slight whiskers. His figure is fine: broad at the shoulders and slender at the waist... I have to keep a tight hold on my heart.

The year before she had danced the *Grossvater* with her Russian visitors, Alexander II and his suite,

> ... which is so amusing; we had such fun and laughter. It begins with a solemn walk round the room which also follows each figure. One figure, in which the lady and gentleman run down holding their pocket-handkerchief by each end and the gentleman jumps over it, is too funny... I never enjoyed myself more. We were all so merry and got to bed at 2.45 a.m. but I could not sleep until 5. I said to Lord Melbourne that all this excitement does me good.

Now, Victoria's satin, slippered feet had to rest upon a footstool during levees and receptions. The newspapers had pounced on that too. One of them heartlessly remarked: 'The Queen was looking less blooming than usual at the last drawing-room of the season ... she spent most of the time seated, her dainty white-slippered feet resting on a gold-brocaded cushion.'

To those who spoke with enthusiasm about how proud a woman should be to give life to an immortal soul, the Queen inwardly replied, and later commented to her married daughter: 'That is all very fine, but I own I cannot enter into that. I think much more of our being like a cow or a dog at such moments, when our poor nature becomes so very animal and unecstatic.' She hated being stared at. And in her present condition she felt that it was positively shocking. The confidences of married ladies who had been through this 'shadow side' of marriage, as she referred to child-bearing, brought a blush to her plump cheeks even at an advanced age. Nor did she have the consolation of being fond of babies, finding them 'quite repulsive' until they reached the age of three or four months, when they became less like frogs in their movements and more like human beings. Pretty babies were rare; as for an ugly one, 'it is a very nasty object'.

As her pregnancy advanced the Queen became restless and

she slept badly. Her doctor – *accoucheur*, Sir Charles Locock, prescribed camphor lozenges; she kept a large supply by her bedside and found them so soothing that she recommended them to her own daughters in later years when they found themselves in the same situation.

When the imminence of a royal birth was made public, Lord Wriothesley, Canon of Windsor, asked Prince Albert whether a prayer for the Queen's special condition should be added to the liturgy to be read out during Sunday services. The Prince replied: 'Oh no, no – you have one already in the litany for "all women labouring of child". You pray already five times for the Queen – it is too much.' A little taken aback, Lord Wriothesley asked: 'But, Sir, can we pray too much for Her Majesty?' 'Not too *heartily*,' said the Prince in his careful German way, 'but too *often*.' Lord Wriothesley later broached the subject of a new anthem which had been specially composed for the christening and wanted to know when it should be sung. 'Not at all,' said the Prince firmly. 'No anthem. If the service ends by an anthem we shall all go out criticizing the music. We will have something we all know – in which we can all join, something devotional. The Hallelujah chorus, for instance – we can all join in that with all our hearts.'

A few days after the royal birth the press reported:

> Her Majesty and Prince Albert went walking in Buckingham Palace gardens and Her Majesty took her seat at dinner and certainly appeared in her usual health, till 11 p.m. when she retired to rest, no suspicion then being entertained of the near approach of those sufferings which providentially have terminated in a manner so satisfactory to every branch of her august family as well as to the delight of her loyal subjects.

This was an indirect way of stating that the birth, which occurred on 21 November, was two or three weeks premature.

It was only in mid-November that the press had announced that Messrs Seddon, the Queen's upholsterers in Gray's Inn Road, had received an order instructing them to design and make the cot and two baths for the expected scion of Her Majesty's illustrious house.

A day or two later a drawing was sent to the palace for inspection. Her Majesty was graciously pleased to signify her approval. The body of the cot was in the shape of a nautilus, the framework in choicest Spanish mahogany, the bottom and sides were quilted in flutes covered with green silk and embroidered with the white Rose of England alternately between arabesques. The cot swings between pillars of mahogany, standing on plinths with richly carved and gilt brackets. The canopy is hung with gold and silver-coloured silk. The whole is gilt and surmounted by the royal crown. This has now been removed to Buckingham Palace together with two baths, lined one with silver, the other with marble.

'Nothing was ready,' the Queen wrote petulantly years after the event. 'My first two confinements, for want of order and from disputes and squabbles, chiefly owing to my poor old governess [Baroness Lehzen] who would meddle, were far from comfortable or convenient and the doctors too had not found out quite how to treat me.'

At 2 a.m. on 20 November the first labour pains began, and at 4 a.m., with great presence of mind, the Queen firmly directed that her attendants should be summoned. Among these were Mrs Lilly, formerly nurse to the Duchess of Sutherland, 'whose experience at once forewarned her of the propriety of calling Her Majesty's personal advisers'. Messengers were sent, according to the primitive custom still in use, to fetch the officials expected to attend the royal birth in the room next to the suffering Queen's. Only a small dressing-room separated the prostrate figure from the embarrassed presence of the Archbishop of Canterbury, Dr Howell, the Bishop of London, the Hon. W. Murray, Comptroller of the royal household, the Lord Chancellor, the Prime Minister, Lord Melbourne, the Foreign Secretary, Lord Palmerston . . .

Prince Albert is reported to have paced up and down the dressing-room, while the Queen's mother, the Duchess of Kent bent anxiously over her beloved daughter. Doctors and ladies of the bedchamber fluttered round the Queen until at ten to two in the afternoon an infant's cry was heard by the expectant male committee, followed by the deep voice of Dr Locock announcing: 'Madam, it is an infant Princess,' to which the Queen's bell-like voice was heard to reply cheerfully: 'Well, never mind, next time it will be a Prince.' Prince Albert emerged from the bedroom with Mrs Lilly, who carefully placed the chubby princess on the table, wrapped in a blanket, for general inspection. The gentlemen gathered round the baby while Sir James Clarke, the attendant physician, 'announced the fact of its being a female'. His words were accepted without question, so that any further unwrapping of the lustily wailing princess was unnecessary. The *Brighton Herald* reported subsequently: 'The loud tones in which she indicated her displeasure of such an exposure rendered it advisable that she should be returned to her chamber to receive her first attire.' So Mrs Lilly, upon a sign from the Prince, picked up her precious bundle, curtsied to the assembly and retired.

This nurse-midwife, who was more experienced if not better trained than most of her colleagues, was to become a palace institution. She attended all the royal births from 1840 to 1857 and in 1850 was immortalized by Thackeray in *Punch*. She received £100 for each attendance, a handsome fee for the times, and for the parsimonious royal purse. Later she was given a pension, died in 1882, and was buried in Highgate Cemetery in London.

Beautiful, plump and healthy as the baby was declared to be by Her Majesty's female attendants, it was so long since an heir had been born that the oddest rumours began to circulate. It was even said that the Princess had been born blind and deformed. This led to the facetious suggestion that she should be displayed under a glass case for so many hours a day and the public allowed to file past and assure themselves that she was normal. (This must have left an impression upon some members of the public. A few years later, in 1845, a Mr and Mrs Horatio Jones wrote to Lord Delaware 'Mr and Mrs Horatio Jones present their compliments and would be much obliged by his sending them a ticket to see the royal children'.)

The Queen, after having 'suffered severely but not felt at all nervous once it [the labour] began', recovered rapidly. Albert hardly ever left her side, 'and was the greatest comfort and support,' she recorded in her journal, but Baron Stockmar wrote him an anxious note of advice:

> Suffer me to remind you that sleep, stillness and rest, and the exclusion of many people from her room are just the all in all for the Queen. You cannot be too guarded on these points. Be therefore a very Cerberus. You ought not yourself to be too much about the Queen or talking with her may be too exciting. Although the Queen is now apparently so well this ought not to lull us into careless security for any agitation may bring on fever and dangerous consequences.

The first member of the public to hear the infant Princess Royal's squeal was the notorious 'Boy Jones'. His exploit in climbing over the palace walls and hiding under a sofa in the room adjoining the Queen's bedroom caused a furore in the press as well as the royal household, whose security measures were revealed to be astonishingly inadequate.

This seventeen-year-old tailor's son was obsessively attracted to the palace. Two years before he had penetrated its inner defences in the guise of a chimney-sweep. Now, he impudently boasted that he had spent three days in the palace hiding under beds and 'helping himself to various soups and other eatables'. He had sat upon the throne (he probably meant the dais in the ballroom), seen the Queen and heard the Princess Royal squall. He was examined by two doctors, who 'were of the opinion that Edward Jones's head was of a most peculiar formation, but they could not give any decided opinion as to his sanity or insanity'. He was declared to be a rogue and vagabond and sent to a house of correction for three months. When he came out, unchanged and unrepentant, he turned down an offer to appear on the stage of a music-hall, was found by the police loitering near the palace and shipped to sea in desperation. A year later, when his ship put in at Portsmouth, he started to walk to London, but was arrested and sent back to the warship *Warspite*.

One night he fell overboard between Algiers and Tunis; he had, he said, wanted to 'see the lifebuoy light burning'. After this incident, which was reported in *The Times*, he disappeared forever from the annals of the press, but not before the anti-monarchical *Punch* had sung his praises:

> Jones is a genius. That of the millions who gaze upon the awful walls of Buckingham Palace, shut out from them as from Paradise, Jones should have been the only daring spirit that conceived a design to pass them—to dip his plebeian fingers in the custards of the royal larder—to creep up the royal chimneys—to crouch beneath the royal sofa, thereby 'causing Her Majesty much alarm'—that he also should have done this make Jones—whatever his real time of life may be—far in advance of his age.

A royal nursery had been hastily arranged on the first floor of the north wing in Buckingham Palace, overlooking St James's Park and Green Park. Up to that time the Queen and Prince Albert had breakfasted in that room and spent much time there together, as it had been Her Majesty's boudoir; they experienced a sentimental pleasure in turning it over to the Princess Royal. 'The little one,' wrote Albert to his brother, 'who has taken possession of her own rooms on the upper floor, looks blooming and grows visibly. . . . Me, the father of a daughter, it will make you laugh! I should have preferred a boy, yet as it is, I thank heaven . . . I have a great deal to do and I hardly ever go out into the open air.' The young papa was already beginning to overtax himself, to take his duties as consort and father with a stern sense of duty, although his position had not yet been made official. The infant was taken to the Queen twice a day, but it was not until she was six weeks old that Mama assisted at the spectacle of her being bathed; it was then, no doubt, that the Queen made her first private comparison between babies and frogs, with their large bodies and small limbs.

As soon as the Queen had sufficiently recovered she removed herself to the healthier atmosphere of Windsor. 'We have arrived here,' she wrote to Uncle Leopold, '*sans et saufs* with our awfully large nursery establishment.' Albert continued to treat her 'almost like a mother' and was constantly at her capricious beck and call. Perhaps, unconsciously, the little Queen was taking her revenge for the sufferings which he had involuntarily caused her, of which she was convinced that 'men could not have the slightest notion'. She asked Dr South, the Bishop of London, if the Prince might read to her, but he objected, saying he was afraid that the Prince might read a novel, which would be too exciting. The Queen solemnly replied: 'Oh no, he would read to me the Lessons for the day, as he has done ever since we were married; it would be particularly gratifying to me now.' Prince Albert was genuinely religious, the Queen less so, but she was so deeply in love with him that she would no doubt have approved of anything he read to her.

At Christmas the Queen and Prince Albert took a childlike pleasure in decorating three Christmas trees. 'Next year, the little daughter will jump about the tree as we used to not so very long ago,' Albert wrote nostalgically to his brother Ernest in far-away Coburg, the sleepy little fairy-tale town nestling among the Thuringian Mountains in the heart of his beloved Germany, which it had been such a wrench for him to leave. The young parents were pathetically anxious to establish a 'home' for themselves and their children; they exchanged confidences about their respective childhoods and discovered that they had both been unhappy – or so they said, noted in their journals and told their children in later years. Albert danced the infant Princess in his arms. 'He makes a capital nurse,' Victoria observed, and she too began to fuss over the child. They had not been treated with such affection in their own infancy, nor were the majority of Victorian children in England or Germany. Victoria had been brought up severely in 'humble' Kensington Palace, as she described it, with the financial assistance of Uncle Leopold (who had then been too much engrossed in the German actress Caroline Bauer to take the personal interest in his niece that he lavished upon her later).

Kensington Palace was then in almost open country; it was badly guarded by old servants, the gardens were not fenced in; footpads haunted the Oxford road, the Serpentine was unbridged. Victoria had not known her father, the bluff, martial Duke of Kent, who had died of pneumonia eight months after her birth. His spirit, however, had been seen since by his Socialist friend Robert Owen, whose philanthropic work was being encouraged from the other world. 'In an especial manner,' Owen wrote, 'I have to name the very anxious feelings of the spirit of H.R.H. the late Duke of Kent (who early informed me there were no titles in the spiritual spheres into which he has entered) to benefit not a class, a sect, a party or any particular country, but the whole of the human race through futurity ... His whole spirit proceeding with me has been most beautiful, making his own appointments and never in one instance has this spirit not been punctual to the minute he had named.' The Duke apparently remained the orderly, methodical commander-in-chief he had been during his sojourn on earth. Victoria had looked for a compensating father-figure in Lord Melbourne and Uncle Leopold, until Albert replaced them and became the epitome of all relationships in his one person: brother, father, lover, husband, counsellor.

The widowed Duchess of Kent had led a hard and *mouvementée* life both as Princess Victoria of Leiningen, bringing up a son and daughter in battle-scarred Coburg, and as the wife of the impecunious Duke of Kent. She had devoted herself conscientiously to Victoria's education but had relied too much upon pushing Sir John Conroy, her Irish Comptroller, who played such a domineering part that he was suspected of having amorous relations with the Duchess. This was probably ill-founded gossip, but the little Princess Victoria resented his overbearing presence and sneering manner, although his daughter Victoire (to whom the Duchess was godmother) was one of her few playmates as a child. The other, closer playmate was her half-sister Feodora, who married Prince Hohenlohe. Feodora agreed with Victoria that their childhood had been painful. 'I was extremely crushed and kept under and hardly dared say a word,' Victoria complained. This probably accounted for the difficulty she experienced throughout her life in making small-talk.

In her loneliness, Victoria turned to her governess, the Baroness Lehzen, for support and encouragement. This German spinster was determined to bring up her protégée 'in English style', although she cannot have known exactly what this implied. Severe though she was, Victoria felt more affection for her than for the Duchess, until Albert stepped in to heal the breach and effect a *rapprochement*. Coming into close contact with his mother-in-law during their frequent tête-à-têtes before and after Victoria's first confinement, they found that they had much in common. They both came from the same country, for which Albert still pined. He had not adjusted himself to the English – he never did – or to their food, their climate; nor had he adjusted himself to his impetuous, hot-tempered little wife. 'I shall never cease to be a true German, a true Coburg and Gotha man,' he wrote to his stepmother when he married.

Albert had had a severe but cherished tutor: Herr Florschütz. The Prince had kept a diary from childhood in which he wrote accounts of his fights with his brother Ernest; Ernest was to take after their libertarian father, the old Duke of Saxe-Coburg, who neglected his young wife and finally drove her into the arms of Baron von Holstein. After his parents' separation, Albert never saw his mother again, but he retained such fond memories of her that Victoria, hard as she was on divorcees, was sufficiently impressed by Albert's description of her to observe: 'She must have been clever and fascinating.' One of Albert's first gifts to her was a little pin which had been given to him by his mother when he was a child. The Prince found maternal affection, to a certain extent, in the loving persons of his two grandmothers, but the Princess Royal told her daughter Sophie years later: 'Papa said he could not bear to think of his childhood, he had been so unhappy and miserable and had many times wished himself out of this world.'

So that when the Queen wrote to Uncle Leopold: 'We must all have trials and vexations, but if one's *home is happy*, then the rest is comparatively nothing', Albert could not have agreed more. These sentiments augured well for the future happiness of the infant Princess, 'the child', whose christening, in robes of Honiton lace (passed in succession to each one of her eight brothers and sisters) took place on 10 February 1841 in the throne room of Buckingham Palace.

Prince Albert wore a Field-Marshal's uniform, all his stars and

Order of the Garter sash; Her Majesty a diadem of brilliants, diamond ear-rings and necklace. The Princess's sponsors were the Duke of Saxe-Coburg Gotha, represented by the Duke of Wellington, the Dowager Queen Adelaide, Uncle Leopold (whose matchmaking mind – he promoted no less than seventeen marriages in his lifetime – was probably already working through the *Almanach de Gotha* for a suitable groom), the Duke of Sussex, the Duchess of Kent and the Duchess of Gloucester.

The ceremony took place at 6.30 in the evening and, according to Albert, went off very well. 'The child behaved with great propriety, like a Christian. She was awake but did not cry at all and seemed to crow with immense satisfaction at the sights and brilliant uniforms, for she is very intelligent and observant . . .' After it was over a dinner followed and the health of the 'little one' was drunk with great enthusiasm. (The gold punch-bowl from the dining-room at Windsor, made for George IV at a cost of £10,000 and designed by Flaxman, was filled with thirty dozen bottles of mulled claret for the occasion.) The christening cake, a masterpiece of confectionery, was topped by a sugar-icing Neptune's carriage, bearing the effigy of Britannia with the Princess Royal in her arms. The event was commemorated by a picture especially commissioned from the Royal Academician C. R. Leslie and, more irreverently, in a popular picture representing the Bishop of London pouring hot water from a little black kettle upon the Princess's head, with the caption:

> This is the Bishop so bold and intrepid
> A-making the water so nice and so tepid,
> To christen the baby, who's stated, no doubt,
> Her objection to taking it 'cold without'.

*Punch* had previously published a satirical cartoon representing Mother Gamp presenting the infant to John Bull, who expressed his disappointment at its not being a boy. He did not have to wait long. A rumour was already spreading in court circles to the effect that the Queen would be attending another christening ceremony in the following year.

As the Queen and Prince Albert bent over the infant Princess's cradle, they must have wondered whose traits she would inherit. Her father's intelligence, surely, which the Queen admired but did not consider so necessary in a woman? Her mother's looks perhaps? The baby was small and plump with a round face and a tiny nose. There was, too, an unfortunate trait of which the royal parents were then unaware, but which was to have a considerable influence upon the European dynasties that were swept away in the twentieth century: the sex-linked inheritance of haemophilia.

It would seem that Queen Victoria was the first royal carrier of the morbid gene. From whom had she acquired it? Professor J. B. S. Haldane suggested that the gene may have originated by mutation in Queen Victoria herself. Such instances of spontaneous mutation are well known in animals and plants. The fact that Queen Victoria was a carrier does not imply that there is any trace of the disease in the present royal family. Queen Elizabeth II is related to Queen Victoria through three generations of male descendants (Kings Edward VII, George V and George VI). Since none of them was haemophilic she cannot have inherited the gene from her great grandmother. According to Professor C. D. Darlington haemophilia is a genetic mutation which is not the result of inbreeding; he believes that its maintenance in royal families is due to their evasion of natural selection along with the unfavourable genes. Similar causes operated in the transmission of the chemical disturbance of the blood known as porphyria, which was carried by Mary, Queen of Scots, reappeared in generation after generation among the Stuarts, Hanoverians and Hohenzollerns, brought the English Stuarts to an end with the deaths of Queen Anne's three children, the only survivors of seventeen pregnancies, and caused such trouble to George III and his subjects on both sides of the Atlantic. Haemophilia was favoured, Professor Darlington writes, by 'traditional coddling and helped to bring the dynasties to an end'.

The Princess Royal, or 'Pussy' as she was called in the family circle soon after her christening, does not appear to have been 'coddled'; the general discomfort of living in Victorian days extended to palaces which – *pace Punch* – were very far from being a 'Paradise on earth'. Squabbles took place in the nursery over the infant's diet. Baroness Lehzen had her own ideas on the subject and nearly caused a rift between the royal parents through her insistence upon the Princess being fed on chicken broth and arrowroot soon after she was weaned in May 1841. This regime caused Pussy, who had grown fat on the rich milk supplied by her wet nurse from Cowes, to lose weight and look pale, although she was taken, propped up on cushions in her carriage, for daily outings in Windsor Park, where the crowds pressed round to get a glimpse of her. She soon realized that people liked to stare at her and that she was an object of interest and attention. In no time she learned to bow to the public. Lord Melbourne had already remarked on the occasion of her christening: 'She looked about her, quite conscious that the stir was all about herself. This is the time that character is formed.'

In this the little Princess was unlike her parents, who were both extremely shy. (She too changed when she grew older.) The Queen wrote to the Princess Royal after her marriage: 'After thirty years in harness I still feel shy and nervous.' Albert hid himself from visitors when he was a child and wept in the presence of strangers. The English found him cold and stiff, but this was probably the result of a supreme effort to maintain his self-control; we know from the descriptions left by the Queen and her elder children that Papa could be gay, that he could turn a pirouette and that he loved to romp with his offspring.

Windsor Park was embarrassingly open to the public. Even before the advent of the Princess Royal, members of the household had complained about the 'Cockney visitors' who went down to Windsor to get a sight of the Queen and pressed round Her Majesty's flowerbeds, trampling the parterres. 'Sightseers,' admonished the *Brighton Herald*, 'should show a distinction between Astley's Circus and Windsor Castle'. (The former, incidentally, was very popular with the queen.) The 'little toy' as the

Queen referred to the Princess Royal during her first year, had to be protected. Threatening letters against her life were received at Buckingham Palace at this time of social ferment and economic distress; most of the letters may have been penned by unstable characters like the 'Boy Jones', but the royal parents were taking no chances. The nursery was fitted with intricate turns and locks; the most important key was never out of the Prince's personal keeping and kept under his pillow at night. As a lady-in-waiting wrote to her family: 'These intense precautions, suggesting the most hideous dangers which I fear are not altogether imaginary, make one shudder.'

On Pussy's first birthday Albert brought her to Victoria 'in such a smart white merino dress trimmed with blue which Mama had given her and a pretty cap, and placed her on my bed, seating himself next to her, and she was very dear and good. And as my precious, invaluable Albert sat there and our little love between us, I felt quite moved with happiness and gratitude to God.'

The rumour alluded to in court circles as early as Pussy's christening was well-founded. To her extreme annoyance, Her Majesty was again *enceinte*. When she had stoutly declared, 'Next time it will be a Prince', she had not actually intended the event to take place quite so soon after her first *accouchement*. Privately she was of the opinion that 'those ladies who are always *enceintes* are quite disgusting; it is more like a rabbit or guinea-pig than anything else and really it is not very nice'. To Uncle Leopold, who had wished her joy and many more children, she replied tartly: 'I think, dearest Uncle, you cannot *really* wish me to be the *maman d'une nombreuse famille* ... men never think, at least seldom think, what a hard task it is for us women to go through this very often.' Nevertheless the Queen, to use her own expression, was 'in for it' again and Edward, Prince of Wales – 'Bertie' in the family circle – was born the year after Pussy thus ending her exclusive reign.

The birth of a male heir delighted the royal parents. The Queen described the new baby to Uncle Leopold as: '... wonderfully strong, with a very large nose and pretty little mouth. I hope and pray he may be like his dearest Papa.' The public, too, expressed its satisfaction, but the anti-monarchical *Punch* published an account of the Prince of Wales's christening 'amid gold plate' alongside an account of the starving masses.

Early in 1842 the royal parents, returning from a visit to the Duchess of Kent at Claremont House, found their daughter, often referred to as 'Vicky', teething and tearful. Prince Albert believed that the infant Princess was being mismanaged by everybody: Dr Baillie, Baroness Lehzen, even her own mother and a first-class family row ensued. The Queen wrote to Lord Melbourne: 'We are much occupied in considering the future management of our nursery establishment and naturally find considerable difficulty in it.' She asked him for his opinion and went on:

> The present system must be changed. Stockmar says our occupations prevent us from managing these affairs as much our own selves as other parents can—we must have someone of implicit confidence, a lady of rank . . . but where to find one ready to shut herself up in a nursery and entirely from society and not accept the office, as in my case and my aunt's and Princess Charlotte's, merely for its title? She ought to be responsible to us parents and we to the country.

Lord Melbourne agreed with the Baron and finally Lady Lyttelton was selected for the delicate and arduous position of nursery superintendent. She had been a lady-in-waiting for eight years, was the daughter of the second Earl Spencer, and possessed infinite tact and patience.

Lady Lyttelton described her new charge as a 'fine, fat, fair, royal-looking baby, sitting bolt upright, and too *absurdly* like the Queen; grave, calm and penetrating in her look, most gentle and sweet-tempered, she surveys us all composedly'. She suspected that the Princess was being 'overwatched and over-doctored. She is always treated with what is most expensive but the quantities are measured out so carefully for fear of overloading her stomach that I fancy she always leaves off hungry.' Baroness Lehzen, however, favoured this regime; she interfered in everything and Albert found her insufferable. But how could the Queen forget that it was to the Baroness that she had directed her first proud smile during her coronation – the Baroness who, as she had written in her journal a few days after her accession, 'would always be her friend'? But then . . . she loved Albert so dearly! That was why she finally agreed that the task of 'nursery reform' should be carried out by an objective go-between: dear Baron Stockmar, who knew so much about everything and in whose judgement both she and Albert had every confidence.

So the Baron was entrusted with this new mission and wrote a rather ponderous survey relating to the nursery and, *en passant*, to the question of royal upbringing in general. He admitted in later years that he had found the reorganization of the nursery one of the most difficult tasks he had ever been set to solve. As for the royal – and indeed any other – education, he firmly believed that it should begin on the first day of an infant's life – in which conviction he anticipated the contemporary American 'forcing system'.

The Queen, who had not been fond of learning as a child, had had her lessons supervised by the Duchess of Kent, 'in view of the station which the princess was likely to fill'; she was examined at her mother's anxious request by the Bishops of London and Lincoln, to whom the Duchess had explained the course she had followed. (In private the little Princess was taught from the very first to beg her maid's pardon for any rudeness or naughtiness towards her. Victoria never forgot this lesson. She always treated her servants kindly – even at times being too lenient with them – and she was distressed when the Princess Royal showed signs of arrogance towards her maids.) The bishops duly examined Victoria and pronounced themselves satisfied (they must have had very vague ideas about a royal education themselves). They reported:

The princess displayed an accurate knowledge of the most important features of Scripture, History and of the leading truths and precepts of the Christian religion as taught by the Church of England as well as an acquaintance with the chronology and principal facts of English history remarkable in so young a person. To questions in geography, the use of the globes, arithmetic and Latin grammar the answers which the princess returned were equally satisfactory.

In addition, of course, Victoria was taught the usual ladylike accomplishments of languages, music, dancing, singing and drawing, in all of which she was proficient. With regard to her own children, her attitude changed with the experience of years, but never for a moment did she agree with easy-going Lord Melbourne's sagacious dictum: 'Be not over solicitous about education. It may be able to do much but it does not do so much as is expected from it. It may mould and direct the character but it rarely alters it.' Such levity would have shocked Prince Albert, who had been educated according to a strict plan with a varied curriculum, devised first by his tutor Herr Florschütz, continued at Bonn University in the company of his brother Ernest and completed by a final 'Grand Tour polishing' under the instructions of Uncle Leopold (in view of Albert's forthcoming career marriage), accompanied by Baron Stockmar. Their aesthetic tour of Italy included 'high society' calls and functions as a prelude to the ceremonial of court life that awaited Albert in England and to which, he had learned with foreboding, Victoria was inordinately fond. 'Albert changed all that,' she told Vicky later.

Albert divided time with a ruler, allocating slots for each type of activity; soon he devised a severe curriculum for Bertie, the unacademic heir to the throne who was so different from clever little Vicky. Stockmar bore some responsibility for this. He warned the Prince: 'Your own interests: political, moral, mental and material, are so bound up with those of the Prince of Wales that every shortcoming in his training and culture is certain to be avenged upon his father.' He also believed that the children should be brought up simply, be as much as possible with their parents and learn to place their greatest confidence in them in all things.

At Christmas, educational problems were momentarily put aside to enjoy the holiday in traditional German fashion. Albert wrote to his father: 'Two children of my own to give presents to at the German Christmas tree and its radiant candles ... it is like a dream!' The New Year was danced in to a flourish of trumpets, another German custom.

The Queen was observed to interest herself less and less in politics. She was a good deal occupied with Vicky, 'who begins to assume companionable qualities'. Lady Lyttelton commented, however: 'Like all very young mothers, the Queen is *exigeante* and never thinks the baby makes progress enough or is good enough. She has her constantly with her and thinks incessantly about her.' As for Albert, he 'tossed and romped with her, making her laugh and crow and kick very heartily'. It was the beginning of a deep bond between father and daugher of which the Queen in time grew a little jealous, for she was of a possessive nature and never entirely freed herself from the doll-grasping stage of her early childhood.

Under Prince Albert's influence, the children grew up surrounded by flowers, trees and a vast collection of dogs faithfully and continually painted by Sir Edwin Landseer, RA, who eventually became an accepted and welcome member of the household, rather like one of the numerous royal pets. Islay, a Scots terrier, was one of his first models. Spaniels, dachshunds, spitzes and collies filled the royal kennels; bloodhounds, mastiffs, wolfdogs, chinese dogs ('the kind the Chinese fatten for eating,' said Lady Lyttelton, 'They have some new kinds every year'). Prince Albert's favourite was the beautiful greyhound Eos, which he had brought with him from his native Coburg. Eos's portrait was commissioned by the Queen as a birthday present for the Prince in 1842. Dogs crept into the pictures of the children in their cradle and, as the years passed, their names, inscribed upon stone, appeared upon canine tombs dotted in the royal parks and gardens in between memorials erected to departed human members of the family.

Sir James Clark, the bluff ex-naval royal physician, having advised a change of air for the royal infants, the royal family and their considerable retinue decided in February 1842 to pay a visit to the Brighton Pavilion. One hundred workmen were employed day and night to make the Pavilion fit for habitation after much neglect; fires were kept burning in all the apartments, carpets were laid, the stables were repaired, the grounds freshly gravelled and the palace baths put into 'a fit state for use'. Quantities of extra furniture were transported from Windsor.

It was discovered, soon after the royal party had settled in, that the chimneys smoked. Few people echoed Mendelssohn's absurd Anglophil sentiment: 'How I love the perfume of English coal!' Her Majesty for one could not bear it and insisted upon having fires of beech logs in her rooms. Was this the 'bracing atmosphere' that Sir James Clark had advised for the infants?

Georgiana Liddell, lady-in-waiting, wrote to her family that her rooms were 'tolerably comfortable, but Lady Jocelyn's smokes so abominably that I am nearly suffocated. The Pavilion garden is odious, low and damp; there is no view of the sea, we might as well pace round Berkeley Square. I suppose it *is* sea air, but so mixed up with soot and smoke that it loses half its value.'

The Queen was familiar with Brighton, but Albert was not, and the Pavilion amazed him. Lord Jocelyn, recently arrived from China, misinformed him that it was a perfect specimen of a Chinese house.

The entire party, which included the Duchess of Kent and Baroness Lehzen, was treated to a municipal display of fireworks, which they watched from behind the windows overlooking the Old Steine. 'Rather pretty,' observed Georgiana Liddell, 'but not sent off quickly enough.' They began with the device 'The Hope of the People', and the initials V and A, 'which did credit to the artist, Mr Jones', according to the *Brighton Herald*. The infant Prince of Wales was represented by a royal star and crown.

Vicky was taken out for an hour's airing in the Pavilion gardens in her pram every day between one and two, as was duly recorded in the *Court Circular*, and accompanied her parents during their afternoon drives up to Kemp Town and along the blustery coastal road to the innocent-looking fishing village of Rottingdean (still replete with smugglers). The Queen went out on horseback ('the first time she has taken equestrian exercise in public since her marriage'), and the royal party attempted to walk up and down the promenade; they were mobbed so unmercifully that the *Brighton Herald* implored its readers to behave better, 'particularly in view of the fact that Her Majesty has declined to sanction the exclusion of the public from the promenade and pier on her account. . . . We trust that the consideration thus shown by Her Majesty for the pleasure of her subjects will induce them to respect her ease and comfort.'

The weather improved, the royal party went out twice a day, the Queen walked along the pier for half an hour in a blue silk bonnet and a long warm black satin cloak described by a maid of honour as 'rather old and shabby'. Prince Albert explored the beach near Kemp Town with two cousins from Coburg and one of them took back to the Pavilion an ear of Indian wheat which had been washed ashore. This was carefully preserved by the Queen in the pressed flower album in which, under Albert's guidance, she had begun to show an increasing interest. Guests came down from London to dine and the artist Hayter was summoned to the Pavilion to paint a picture of Bertie's christening, with the royal model at his disposal. The Duchess of Kent, who lived in a separate house, was brought to the Pavilion in a sedan chair. On 12 March the royal party departed for Buckingham Palace in five carriages, determined never to repeat the experience.

In September the Queen and Prince Albert set off for a round of 'great houses', visiting the Roxburghs, Kinnouls, Abercorns, Buccleuchs and Belhavens, the Duchess of Sutherland and Lord Lorne, at Inverary, where the Queen first set eyes on his fat, fair little son, who was destined to become her son-in-law nearly three decades later.

In November they took the two children with them to be entertained by the Duke of Wellington at Walmer. Lady Lyttelton observed:

> The children will grow up under the strangest delusions as to what travelling means and the usual condition of people in

England ... They must suppose one always finds them shouting and grinning and squeezing, surrounded by banners and garlands ... One hundred and three miles in nine hours; immense crowds, continual cheers, fright lest we should smash hundreds at every turn, and all the excitement of wreaths and bonfires and triumphal arches, church bells and cannons all the way while we kept flying and dashing, our escorts panting, the horses foaming and the carriages swaying with speed.

Once arrived at their destination the royal party had to endure another typically British discomfort: draughts. 'It seems needless to go out for air,' observed Lady Lyttelton. 'The doors and windows all clatter and sing at once and hardly keep out the dark storm of wind and rain which is howling round. Vicky, in Garter blue velvet and Brussels lace, with white shoes, desired to be lifted up "to look at the people", to whom she bowed very actively whether they were in sight of her or not.'

In the evenings the royal parents kept up the reading aloud routine prevalent in so many Victorian homes. They were conscientiously brushing up their knowledge of the British Constitution by reading Hallam's classic tome on the subject and, 'for a light book', Saint-Simon's *Memoirs*, which Prince Albert read to the Queen while she was at her cross-stitching.

The children were becoming obstreperous. On their return journey to Windsor by train 'they were taken with tearing spirits and a rage for climbing, crawling, poking into corners and upsetting everything and – after a little time – being tired, cross and squally for hours.' But Vicky could also turn on the charm. The day before a visit to the palace by Lady Dunmore and her two little daughters, Her Majesty said: 'Two pretty little girls are coming to see baby tomorrow', upon which the Princess got up on tiptoe, put her head down on one side and, with the most extreme slyness of manner, according to Lady Lyttelton, answered: 'Naughty?' 'No, no,' said the Queen, 'They are very good little girls.' 'Kying?' persisted the Princess. 'No, no, they never cry.' 'I can't express,' wrote Lady Lyttelton, 'the drollery of her questions, so meant to be joking and malicious.' Another day, little Charley Edgecumbe came to see Vicky, who turned quite coquettish upon his arrival, hiding behind curtains for him to find her, holding out her frock and dancing up and down before him.

Georgiana Liddell thought that the Princess Royal was 'a darling'. 'She shows off to great advantage, runs about, talks at a great rate and is delighted with two frocks the Duchess of Kent sent her as a Christmas box. She took one first, then the other, showed them to each of us, desired me to put one on. I held it up for her to her great delight; she is very fat, dressed in a dark blue velvet frock with muslin sleeves and yellow kid mittens.'

While the Queen and Prince Albert were spending two months in Scotland, Baroness Lehzen was tactfully 'pensioned off for the sake of her health', so as to avoid an awkward scene. She slipped away without saying goodbye – that would have been too painful – and settled with her sister in Bückeburg, devoting her savings and pension of £200 a year to establishing her brother's children in their careers. The Queen corresponded with her regularly and saw her for the last time in 1862 at Rheinhardsbrunn after Prince Albert's death: 'My poor old Lehzen . . . she is grown so old. We were both much moved.' Lehzen died in 1870, in a room full of portraits and mementoes of the royal family.

One of the immediate effects of Lehzen's removal was an improvement in the relations between the Queen and the Duchess of Kent, who had borne her 'arm's length' treatment from her daughter with patience and fortitude. The Duchess had quite given up the pushing 'public relations officer' role she had assumed when Victoria was a child, probably upon Sir John Conroy's advice. Softened and mellowed, she had developed the middle-age spread of a devoted German *Hausfrau* and rustled comfortably in puce-coloured velvet gowns, with ostrich plumes waving in her thick brown hair. Lady Palmerston found her 'prejudiced, and her antipathies are deep and strong'. She transmitted these traits to her self-willed daughter, but Albert quietly and unassumingly tamed them both and drew them closer together. The Duchess had also moved closer physically. She was now living at Frogmore, a pleasant Georgian house at the end of the Long Walk in Windsor Park, with a loggia and a pond, weeping willows and rhododendrons. The children loved to visit Grandmama, who was surrounded by parakeets, dogs and waxbills and spent so much time preparing presents for them. Portraits of her at this time show a more benevolent expression in her wide face and deep brown eyes. She loved music – she even composed a piece of military music for Bertie's first birthday. It was played by the band of the Grenadier Guards at Windsor as a *Pas Redoublé*, later known as the 'Prince of Wales's Quickstep'. She loved operas, particularly the *Dame Blanche*, knick-knacks, curiosities, prints, political cartoons, Paris (which she visited incognito in the spring of 1844) and dancing. In August 1843 the Duchess's birthday was celebrated by a dance at Frogmore which ended with *Grandpère* or *Grossvater*, the 'follow-my-leader' dance that had amused Victoria so much before her marriage. The Prince and the Duchess led the dance which was pronounced by Georgiana Liddell to be 'great fun, but rather a romp'.

A few days after this 'romp' at Grandmama's, the Princess Royal was taken for a drive near Virginia Water. Noticing some heather growing at the side of the road, she peremptorily asked Lady Dunmore, who was in her carriage, to pick some for her. 'I can't do that, we are driving too fast,' she replied. Vicky gave her one of her stern, princessy looks, then turned to the ladies-in-waiting, Miss Paget and Miss Liddell. 'No, *you* can't' she agreed, 'but those girls might get out and get me some.' The Queen decided that it would be better for the children to be confined to the nursery staff and their governesses, and not to mix with the Queen's ladies, to whom they were beginning to behave as minor royal personages.

They were even beginning to do so to their Mama. The Queen often called the Princess Royal 'Missy' when she took her out riding, but one day the little girl turned to her angrily and exclaimed: 'I'm not "Missy". I'm the Princess Royal!' The Queen went on talking to her ladies without taking any notice of her, so she tried another stratagem to attract attention. 'There's a cat under the trees,' she said, pointing. Then: 'Cat come out to look at the Queen, I suppose?' The amusement caused by her remarks encouraged her precocious ways.

Soon Albert was informing his brother: 'It may interest you to hear that we are expecting an increase in our family, but Victoria is not very happy about it.' (Nevertheless, Mrs Stanley observed in February 1843 that 'the Queen, as usual, talked of nothing but children with Lady Haddo.')

The Queen's second daughter Princess Alice, was born in 1843. 'Victoria suffered much but only for a short time, and now she feels as well as can be expected,' Albert wrote to Uncle Leopold. 'The child is said to be very pretty.' The Duke of Cumberland, King of Hanover, was asked over for the christening ('Our little baby is to be called Alice, an old English name'), but he arrived too late and made a scene because the ceremony had gone on without him. Ten months later the baby was vaccinated; thanks to this royal patronage, Dr Jenner's discovery which had failed to become popular, spread rapidly throughout Britain.

Victoria raged at her constant barrel-like appearance. *The Times* described a recent portrait of her by Parris, tongue in cheek, with an audacious reference to her bosom, 'which has been most delicately handled and has been brought out by the artist in admirable rotundity . . . he has imparted full relief to it.'

On the Queen's birthday (24 May) in 1843, Lady Lyttelton noted:

Princessy [The Princess Royal] looks the image of Mayday in a very fine muslin frock embroidered in wreaths of lilies of the valley and rosebuds, with an apron of light green silk embroidered to match. The presents for the Queen from Prince Albert and the Duchess of Kent were arranged under a bower of magnificent flowers erected in her breakfast room. The chief present is a beautiful sketch by Landseer of the princess Tiny [Alice] in a cradle lately given which belonged to the old Saxon house, watched over by Dandie, the black terrier, with an expression of fondness and watchfulness such as only Landseer can give. It was prepared in secret by Prince Albert, who made his appearance at 8 in the morning in the nursery in a handsome, many-coloured dressing-gown, to fetch the children to Mama... Here we are, very bowery and flowery, nothing but sweet smells and books, muslin and brilliant presents and happy faces.

People wondered how the children ever learned their lessons, as the Queen seemed to run about so much, taking them all with her to Buckingham Palace, Windsor, Claremont and the Isle of Wight, whose air Sir James Clark had been sent over to sample before deciding whether it would be desirable to secure a private residence on the island away from the curious crowds. This thought had been occupying the royal parents' minds for two or three years. 'Windsor is large and beautiful, but it is a *palace*,' the Queen declared, whereas she wanted a *home* which she and beloved Albert, who had *such* good taste, could build and furnish themselves as they liked from A to Z. (Not everybody was so enthusiastic about Albert's taste.)

It was about this time that an inquisitive lady outside the royal circle asked Viscountess Forbes, lady of the bedchamber, what the court was doing, and received the cryptic reply: 'The Court is nesting.' 'What *do* you mean? Not bird-nesting, surely?' 'No, not nesting like the birds – a very different thing.' 'Your remark puzzles me more than ever! The Queen lives in a palace, not in the branch of a tree....' 'Nevertheless, she *nests*. I mean to say that she and the Prince are devoted to the nest and gladly dismiss state cares to think only of the nest.' The Viscountess went on to say that the royal couple reminded her of parent birds: the father gathered fine grass to weave it into a nest and finished it off with wool and feathers and the royal home didn't resemble any other great home in the country in all but its great wealth, but was more like the home of a decent, thrifty, hard-working couple who had married for love and had no reason to regret it.

The death of Prince Albert's father, the Duke of Saxe-Coburg, in 1844, deeply affected both the Prince and the Queen. It was the children's first acquaintance with the paroxysms of Victorian mourning. 'Why do poor Mama and Papa cry so?' Vicky asked, wondering why all the blinds were being pulled down to make the rooms look so gloomy. (The Duchess of Kent, who detested darkness, but thought it right to humour the Queen, did not know what to do until she at last hit upon the expedient of keeping a watch to give warning whenever the Queen was coming towards Frogmore; this was the signal for a general rush to shut blinds and shutters all over the house.) Even Anson, the Prince's private secretary, was so upset by the prevailing atmosphere of grief that he had a violent attack of nervous headache, 'which has quite laid him up,' wrote Lady Lyttelton. Vicky told her: 'Dear Grandpapa is very ill, it makes me so unhappy, Laddle, poor dear Papa and Mama cry so, but he will be quite well in two weeks.'

'Dear Papa's' faults, his libertarianism, his scrounging, were forgotten. Two years before Albert had written to his brother Ernest: 'If you could restrain papa from constantly asking me for money I should be grateful.' Now he wrote to Baron Stockmar: 'My heart impels me to give vent to my tears upon the bosom of a true, loving friend.' He felt, he said, like a deserted child. He had expected the entire nation to mourn with him.

> Here we sit together, poor Mama, Victoria and myself, and weep, with a great cold public around us, insensible as stone. To have some true sympathetic friends at hand would be a great solace. Come to us in this time of trouble if you can. Victoria feels and shares my grief and is the treasure on which my whole existence rests ... The relation in which we stand to one another leaves nothing to desire. It is a union of heart and soul and is therefore noble, and in it the poor children shall find their cradle so as to be able one day to ensure a like happiness for themselves.

Albert went to Coburg to see his brother established as the late Duke's successor, bought toys for the children, sent sugar Easter eggs from Gotha and picked pansies for Victoria. It was their first separation since their marriage and the Queen felt it keenly. Upon his return, Albert noted succinctly in his journal:

*'Great joy'*. Victoria never alluded directly to sex but she did admit to having 'violent feelings' and a 'passionate nature'.

There was another addition to the nursery in August 1844: Prince Alfred, known to the family as 'Affie'. The Queen refused to have regular visits from her doctors before the event, so that the three of them had to observe her from behind the palace windows as she went out and came in from her carriage. It was their only opportunity to do so. Since there was already an assured heir to the throne of England, Albert discussed the future *placement* of the latest born with the Queen and decided to train him for the succession of his native Coburg. 'The little one shall, from his youth, be taught to love the dear small country to which he belongs in every respect, as does his papa.' Also with an eye to the future and to keep foreign relations cordial, the King of Prussia was invited to be Prince Alfred's godfather. The Queen found him small, fat, 'with not much hair and very little whisker', genial and witty.

The children continued to be 'kept away from the Queen's entourage' but in November 1844 Vicky, in honour of her birthday, was allowed to go into the dining room at Windsor and stand by Mama's chair till the first course was over, when Lady Lyttelton took her out of the room to her nurse and then rereturned to her place at table. 'They really looked so nice,' observed Georgiana Liddell, 'coming in to dinner . . . the Queen and the Prince each holding a hand of the Princess Royal.' When it was foggy the children were kept indoors playing in the corridors, where Miss Liddell joined them in a 'game of romps'. In fine weather Vicky went out in the park in her little carriage drawn by a footman, Lady Lyttelton trudging at her side. Every new face was welcome to the children. Vicky asked endless questions when Mrs Stanley first arrived as a lady-in-waiting, wanting to know why she had only three flounces on her lilac gown – ('I said I thought that was quite enough') – asking her name and saying 'Eleanor' very prettily.

Nursery fare for the elder children consisted of 'a bit of roast meat and perhaps a plain pudding,' a servant informed the Prussian ambassador, Baron de Bunsen, adding: 'The Queen would have made an admirable poor man's wife.' The Queen herself ate heartily. Creevey said that she gobbled, and picked chicken bones at table. Sir James Clark ordered her not to eat luncheon any more, only a little broth, but this regime was not kept up for long. It was difficult, of course, when she had such a constant flow of guests. They had their fads; the one the Queen most objected to was an addiction to smoking, an objection shared by many Victorian ladies of lesser rank. When the Grand Duke Michael of Russia visited Windsor Mrs Eleanor Stanley said:

> The smell of tobacco in his rooms beggars description. Bülow, who was in agonies about his smoking all the time he was here, knowing the Queen's dislike to it, was asked to go into them after he was gone and he was quite horrified. They say the Queen will not be able to put anybody into them this year again. It is bad enough all up the Gallery. Even little Princess Royal walked about sniffing the air next his door and said: "Princess smell the Grand Duke", rather clever of her, considering she is not yet three years old.

'Pussy [Vicky],' wrote Albert to Baron Stockmar, 'is now quite a little personage. She speaks English and French with great fluency and choice of phrase.' Her French governess had been teaching her, rather prematurely one would have thought, since she was only four, some poems by Lamartine, which included the line: '*Voilà le tableau qui se déroule à mes pieds.*' A little while afterwards, during a pony ride, the young princess surveyed the landscape from a hilltop and, with a histrionic flourish of her podgy hand, exclaimed: '*Voilà le tableau qui se déroule à mes pieds*'. It was not an easy line for an infant to remember. Vicky adored to show off and was delighted when her governess, Mlle Charrier, repeated the incident to the family. 'Is it not extraordinary?' commented Mrs Stanley, 'it is more like what a person of 20 would say. You have no notion what a knowing and, I am sorry to say, sly little rogue she is – and so obstinate.'

Alice was considered slow at first. Prince Albert referred to her as 'poor dear little Alice', being sent to bed in the daytime, this being the chief form of punishment for the Princesses. Vicky, because of her wilfulness and difficult temperament, spent many hours in solitude in her room. The Queen constantly rebuked her for being 'difficult and rebellious'. Papa, however, was very proud of Vicky. He could not help contrasting her quick brain and interest in everything around her with Bertie's apathy.

Bertie was also a disappointment to the Queen. She did not understand that if Bertie was to become 'thoroughly English', as both parents wished him to be, Albert did not fill the bill at all. Even foreigners agreed on this point. The Marquis de Lasteyrie observed that Albert had a slow mind and that 'he differed as much from most Englishmen as if he came from another planet'. Albert had a German propensity to argue and to require long explanation. On the other hand, those who took the trouble to probe beneath the defensive surface and get to know him better – Sir Charles Eastlake, the royal academician, for instance – liked him very much indeed. At the age of twenty Albert had not been in the least interested in politics. Now, only four years later, he was *en pleine mêlée* and working so hard that Stockmar observed that he 'often looked pale, fatigued and exhausted'. He had not the same robust constitution as his wife, who could not bear overheated rooms and kept their private apartments so cold that prematurely balding Albert was obliged to wear a wig at breakfast while he read *The Times* – a task from which he was on no account to be deflected by trivial conversation.

Although Albert was inclined to scold her – particularly at cards – the Queen was perfectly contented with her family life. 'I know what real happiness is!' she wrote gratefully. And Albert observed the children growing with interest and tenderness.

There is certainly a great charm, as well as deep interest, in watching the development of feelings and faculties in a little child, and nothing is more instructive for the knowledge of our own nature than to observe in a little creature the stages of development which, when we were ourselves passing through them, seemed scarcely to have an existence for us. I feel this daily in watching our young offspring whose characters are quite different and who show many lovable qualities.

Thinking of their future, he added judiciously: 'Education must be consistent with the pupil's *prospects;* nothing is more certain to ensure an unhappy future than disappointed expectations.'

The Queen said: 'A good moral, religious, but not bigoted or narrow-minded education is what I pray for my children. But where to find exactly what one wants?' She now spent less time bathing the infants and visiting the nursery. She believed that she had fussed over the elder children too much and reproached herself for having dandled the Princess Royal on her knee as she was dressing for dinner, making her too excited to sleep; but she enjoyed having the children with her on her walks and visits to the royal farm. Prince Albert took the hands of the girls while the Queen led the boys. The farm was a source of pleasure to the children and of profit to their parents. The Queen had progressed from pressed-flower albums to a practical knowledge and interest in pigs and cattle; she greatly appreciated a gift of Northumbrian black cows from a member of the Grey family, which arrived with a herdsman. The dairy was the Queen's particular domain; it was built according to the latest principles, kept cool by running water and covered with glazed tiles, chiefly in yellow, representing spring flowers. Milkpans in Worcestershire porcelain with gilt rims stood on marble shelves; the floor, too, was in marble. Both the nursery and the royal table at Windsor were supplied from the Frogmore dairy.

Food and drink were still rationed, however; Madame de Bunsen, wife of the Prussian ambassador, observed: 'The wife of a rich man of business would think the meals served up to the Queen's children not good enough for her own nursery.' (On birthdays and anniversaries the children were allowed to lunch with their parents.) Thrift was also observed in the royal wardrobe. The ribbons from the Queen's cast-off bonnets were carefully ironed and served to tie the younger children's sleeves or to dress the Princesses' dolls.

Sir James Clark had reported favourably on the air of the Isle of Wight, which he thought would suit the children's constitution, even though, as a robust Scot, he doubted whether it would be 'bracing' enough. In March 1845 the Prince's private secretary, Major Anson, announced to the household at luncheon that the Queen had concluded the purchase of Osborne House on the island for £26,000. It was first rented from Lady Blatchford for a trial year but it was intended to rebuild the house entirely and lay out the grounds of eight hundred acres, of which five hundred were then pasture. 'How odd,' observed a member of the royal household, 'that the Queen and the Prince should not have chosen Norris Castle, such a splendid place, so regal ... besides, the Queen stayed there as a child and it has so many historic associations. Altogether, a much more suitable place for a royal residence.' 'No, they would have nothing to do with Norris Castle,' Major Anson replied. 'They would prefer – so they said – any cottage-looking thing to a castle.'

The Queen was the first monarch of her race to live on an estate belonging to herself and her husband. An Act of Parliament was presented by Sir Robert Peel, which enabled her to purchase Osborne and any other property she liked. At last she was free of the odious, interfering Commissioners of Woods and Forests, Clerks of the Works and other busybodies ('the plague of one's life'), who prevented the royal pair from doing as they pleased. (In London, a few grimaces were made by disapproving members of the public who believed that 'the object of keeping up a court at great cost to the nation is defeated when the monarch can only be happy by living like a country squire.')

The little Princesses clapped their hands with joy when Papa told them that they were going to have a beach of their very own. 'Now we shall be able to stroll about everywhere without being followed and mobbed,' said the Prince, who had always visited the Isle of Wight in good weather, seen it under ideal conditions and optimistically compared it to the shores of the

Mediterranean. He thought that the Solent resembled the Bay of Naples, 'the sea is so blue and calm'. This inspired him to build a Neapolitan style villa with high towers and a wide loggia. By 1846 the pavilion containing the royal apartments was ready, and the family moved in after a ceremonial house-blessing which the children found very impressive. Papa recited the special psalm used in Germany for such occasions: 'To bless our going out and coming in, our daily bread and all we do; bless us to a blessed dying and make us heirs of heaven.' Miss Paget, the maid of honour, found it 'dry and quaint, being Luther's.' (Albert was born and brought up in the castle where Luther, befriended by the Dukes of Coburg, had written his main works.) All agreed, however, that the Prince 'was feeling it, and truly the entering of a new house is a solemn thing to do', Miss Paget added with prophetic sombreness: 'Especially for those whose space of life in it is possibly not long and who, in spite of rank and health and youth, may be going downhill now.' A pagan rite was then observed on the insistence of the Scottish maid of honour, Miss Lucy Kerr, who threw an old shoe into the house after the Queen as she entered for the first night, 'this being a Scottish superstition. She wanted also to have some melted lead and sundry other charms, but they were not forthcoming.'

The furnishing of Osborne House proceeded slowly – bits and pieces were added to it until the late sixties – but meanwhile the canny Prince, rather than buy an upright piano straight away, hired one by the quarter. The sale of the Brighton Pavilion to the Town Commissioners in 1849 enabled the royal couple to spend £200,000 on furnishings for Osborne. The Queen was appalled to learn from Albert, who examined the accounts with an eagle eye, that the maintenance of the Pavilion since her accession had exceeded £24,000.

At Osborne, the children were taught to swim in a floating bath in the bay devised by Papa, who also showed them how to fly kites. 'He plays with them so delightfully,' the Queen noted in her journal. She could not bring herself to do so with the same joyous abandon. In that relaxed atmosphere the once demure, backward little Alice became – according to her governess Miss Crawford – 'as wild as a fawn'.

The greatest innovation and delight was the purchase by Papa of the 'Swiss Cottage' that was to resound for generations with childish laughter and glee. It was a miniature house, big enough for them to walk into, in black carved wood, with quotations from the Psalms and Proverbs round the walls and outside staircases; there were blue and white tiles in the kitchen and a swinging cradle in the changing-room. The little house was surrounded by plots, one for each of the royal children, where they learned how to grow vegetables, and the girls were taught how to cook them. The cottage was entered by the upper storey and surrounded by a balcony; this was reached by an outside staircase. Albert, an expert carpenter and mechanic, passed his skills on to the boys in a little workshop installed in the cottage. When one of the children produced a good vegetable plot the under-gardener was instructed to present a certificate; this was handed to Papa, who then bought the produce at the current market price. Later, a model fortress with real brass firing canons was constructed by Albert for his sons, similar to one he had built with his brother Ernest when they were both children. The Princesses baked cakes and made dishes for their parents in the tiny model kitchen.

The children were intrigued by Mama's bathing machine with its high, frosted glass windows. It slid down the sloping pier to the beach, where the Queen stepped out on to a curtained verandah and descended the five wooden steps that led right into the sea; once the portly little figure was modestly covered by the waves the cumbersome contraption was removed. 'Delightful!' declared the Queen after her first bathe, 'till I put my head under the water, when I thought I would be stifled.'

The Queen called the Italianate house with its avenue of cedars and ilexes, terraced gardens, two campaniles, clock and flag towers 'Little Paradise'. The ceilings were low, the rooms – compared to those of Windsor Castle and Buckingham Palace – small and snug. Cots with cane sides were installed for the younger children; white fringes provided with strings were sewn on to the coverlets to keep them well tucked in at nights, rush-seated armchairs were placed in the nursery and a favourite hair-covered rocking-horse was brought over from Windsor Castle at each visit. In the Little Audience Room a huge German chandelier of green glass leaves and pink convolvulus flowers reminded the Prince of the wallpaper in Rosenau Castle; bright yellow silk curtains enlivened the sitting-room, the bedrooms were chintzy and gradually filled with bric-à-brac which increased with every anniversary: sketches, statuettes, busts on crimson cushions, marble hands and feet modelled from those of the children. The entwined initials V and A placed over every door (except the smoking-room) symbolized this happy 'nesting' period, when the sea and the sky seemed forever blue and Mama sketched and wrote and rode with Albert, and picked strawberries in season with the children.

The family was never happier, never closer, than at Osborne, where Prince Albert, in his own words, was 'partly forester, partly builder, partly farmer and partly gardener'. 'How happy we are here!' the Queen exclaimed. And, years later, Alice was to write nostalgically about the 'happy days of our childhood at Osborne'.

A great *remue-ménage* was simultaneously taking place in the royal palaces on the mainland, which looked shabby compared with the bright new decorations and furnishings of Osborne.

Buckingham Palace was tackled early in 1845. According to the Queen: 'It was a *disgrace* . . .' There wasn't a hole to put the children into, the nursery was a mile from her apartments so that Albert had to drag the younger children in a basket along the corridors . . . The servants' attics were worse than those of a private house. The drains gave trouble, the doors wouldn't shut, the bells wouldn't ring, and the chimneys never stopped smoking. Prince Albert analysed the palace routine and candidly declared: 'Much as I am inclined to treat the household machine with a sort of reverence from its antiquity, I remain convinced that it is clumsy in its original constitution and works so ill that as long as its wheels are not mended there can be neither order nor regularity, comfort, security or outward dignity in the Queen's palace.'

Once again, he turned to the knowledgeable Baron Stockmar, who produced a lengthy report; on its basis, the 'household machine' at Windsor and at Buckingham Palace was overhauled and set into the groove in which it was to remain until the turn of the century. There was found to be waste and corruption among the staff, but how could the Lord Chamberlain possibly be *au courant* with the maids' requirements? He was in no position to query the purchase of 184 brushes, brooms and mops for only one quarter of the year, nor the twenty-four pairs of housemaids' gloves, the forty-two chamois leathers and three-hundred dusters used up during the same period. Albert looked carefully into the matter of the consumption of candles – two per bedroom were allowed; unburned ends were removed by the servants as part of their perks – and made hotly contested cuts. Servant's wages were good, however, compared to those of other large residences, ranging from £15 15s. to £45 a year. In addition, there were generous tips from guests, and pensions.

The Queen never relaxed her rule that the children must treat the servants kindly, and in this she was supported by her husband. One day, Vicky met Alice in the corridor and they both set out to explore rooms in the castle where they were usually not welcome; many parts of the palaces remained out of bounds to children until Bertie came to the throne. The two little Princesses found a servant in one of the rooms busily engaged in the chore of polishing the big black grate. 'We'll help you,' said Vicky, bending down to pick up the blacking and taking the brush from the servant's hands. The girl did not like to refuse, but before she could even begin to protest the mischievous little girls set to and applied the brushes to her face and clothes. The servant got up and rushed out of the room, which adjoined Prince Albert's apartments, so that before she could wash her face she had to pass in front of Papa, who, looking up from the papers on his desk, was astounded to see what appeared to be a female chimney-sweep. Then, hearing the Princesses' suppressed giggles, he hurried to tell the Queen what had happened. Her Majesty was not at all amused. Calling to the Princesses to go to her at once, she crossed the courtyard to the servants' quarters, holding a culprit in each hand, and asked to see the grate-cleaner. The girl ran up with a curtsey – and a clean face. Then Her Majesty, regarding Vicky sternly, asked her to beg the maid's pardon, after which it was Alice's turn to do so.

With her 'ladies', however, the Queen, at least at the beginning of her reign, was more constrained. This may have been due to shyness. Upon her arrival at Windsor, Lady Lyttelton found the Queen 'perfectly kind and civil and good-natured; at first, however, the restraint and peculiar frame of society here was very disagreeable to me but I have, I think, got into it and feel settled into a proper stiffness. There is such heartiness and seemingly endless good temper about all the royal family to judge from their manner and looks. It is so nice to see them . . .'

After a time, Osborne was found to be too relaxing and also still too near Whitehall to be entirely comfortable. Ministers – though reluctantly – crossed over too frequently. Sir James Clark repeatedly advocated the brisk, invigorating air of his native Scotland for the whole family. The Queen and Prince Albert paid three visits to Scotland and on each occasion were more impressed with its grandeur and the hospitality of the people. Albert thought that Edinburgh was one of the finest cities he had ever seen; the countryside reminded him of the mountains near Rosenau, and had not Mr Mendelssohn, whose music both he and Victoria so admired (and who had admired Victoria's interpretation of his songs) been inspired by this magnificent scenery? At that very moment he was working on 'Fingall's Cave'.

The children did not accompany their parents on their first visit to Scotland in 1848. On her return to Windsor the Queen found 'our dear little Victoria so grown and improved, speaking so plain and become *so* independent. I think really few children are so forward as she is. She is quite a dear little companion. Bertie is sadly backward but also grown and very strong.'

Vicky accompanied her parents on their second visit. A little boy stepped forward at Blair Athol to present her with a basket of fruit and flowers. The Queen was most amused and remarked to Albert that she could 'hardly believe our child was travelling with us, it put me so in mind of myself when *I* was "the little princess" '. Albert observed, a trifle pedantically, that it was always said that parents lived their lives over again in their children, 'which is a very pleasant feeling'. The Highland air did them all good. 'Pussy's cheeks are on the point of bursting, they have grown so red and plump,' Albert wrote to his brother. 'She is learning Gaelic, but makes wild work with the names of the mountains.'

Daily life at Windsor Castle – in the royal apartments and in the nursery – followed a carefully worked-out schedule. The royal couple rose at 6.30 a.m. in the summer and 7.30 a.m. in the winter. A morning service was held in the chapel with the household after a breakfast of coffee, bread and butter, eggs or cold meat. This was followed by a walk in the gardens and a visit to the home farm. Then the parents inspected the nurseries to see the older children at their lessons; this was dreaded by Bertie, who was not of a studious disposition, and by Alice, who was still a little slow, but Vicky looked forward to these visits. Albert asked for the tutor's daily reports to be sent to his study before luncheon; he went through them at table, administering scoldings or praises as the case demanded, a procedure which often ended in childish tears. After the visit to the nurseries Albert went to his study to finish *The Times* and the *Morning Post*, which he had begun to read during breakfast, and the Queen received the Master of the Household in the library to discuss the domestic arrangements for the day and give commands about guests, who were usually invited for three days.

The Queen made time in the afternoon to play with her children. She was just as entertained as they were when Georgiana Liddell showed them how to 'imitate a little mouse with her fingers and make it crawl over their forearms', and she joined in the fits of laughter when Bertie and Vicky 'spun the ivory counter and it turned for them'. The Queen took harp and piano lessons and had a sweet soprano voice. The children were often brought in to attend these music sessions. Vicky and Alice loved them, but Bertie was inclined to fidget. 'The Princess Royal,' observed Miss Liddell, 'is wonderfully quick and clever; she is always in the Queen's room when we play or sing and seems especially fond of music; she stands listening most attentively without moving.' When she grew tired, she played bo-peep with the Queen's scarf. Lady Lyttelton described her at this time as 'all gracefulness, very fat and active, running about and talking a great deal. She is over-sensitive, affectionate, and rather irritable in temper at present, but it looks like a pretty mind, only very unfit for roughing it through a hard life, which hers may be.' Prophetic words!

The Queen and Prince Albert often paid a visit to the children's apartments before dressing for dinner with their household. One evening they arrived while Lady Lyttelton was teaching Vicky her prayers. The Queen could not understand Lady Lyttelton's insistence on making the Princess kneel to say them, for she – and the Prince – had been brought up in the 'dry' Lutheran manner of saying them seated. Albert found that the gesture of kneeling was 'stiff and cold – a peculiar feature of English religion. In Germany,' he said. 'kneeling went out with the Reformation. I do not like it.' Lady Lyttleton retorted that she thought sitting was 'highly irreverent'. The Queen began to fuss. What should she do? She wrote to her half-sister Feodora to ask what she did and received the following mildly surprised reply:

My dearest Victoria,

You ask in your letter about the manner in which my children say their prayers. They say them when in their beds, but not kneeling; how absurd to find *that* necessary, as if it could have anything to do with making our prayers more acceptable to the Almighty, or more holy. How really clever people can have these notions I don't understand. I am sorry it is the case there, where there is so much good and, I am certain, real piety . . .

In spite of this, however, Albert and Victoria, after further deliberation, agreed that 'as the Princess was to be brought up in England, her prejudices must be those of the English church' and so she continued to kneel. Lady Lyttelton had won her point.

The Queen liked her religion plain and Lutheran. She enjoyed a good but not a lengthy sermon; in no way was she mystical. Her transports were reserved for Albert and – following his example – nature and music. She gave much thought, however, to Vicky's religious teaching and noted in her diary:

> I am quite clear that she ought to be taught to have reverence for God and for religion but that she should have the feeling of devotion and love which our Heavenly Father encourages His earthly children to have for Him, and not one of fear and trembling, and that the thoughts of death and an afterlife should not be represented in an alarming and forbidding view and that she should be made to know *as yet* no differences of creeds, and not think that she can pray *only* on her knees, or that those who do not kneel are less fervent and devout in their prayers.

The royal children had few playmates, but the nursery, full of brothers and sisters, kept them in constant high spirits.

On 25 May 1846, the day after her own birthday, the Queen gave birth to her third daughter, Princess Helena, called 'Lenchen' in the family circle, who disgraced herself at her christening by sucking her thumb and crying lustily; yet this was the daughter who was destined to give the Queen less trouble than any of the others. Buckingham Palace was illuminated by gas for the first time for this occasion, and 'ventilated by Professor Faraday's ingenious system of drawing the noxious fumes down the stems of the ormolu candelabras'.

Entertainment came from various sources. Whenever the circuses of Astley or Wombswell were within reach, the children were taken to see them. Wombswell was commanded to Windsor several times to exhibit his animals in the royal quadrangle. Tom Thumb was introduced to the royal household by Comptroller Murray, who had travelled in the United States and met the diminutive celebrity in the house of the American ambassador in London. Tom paid two visits to Windsor, sat on a sofa beside Vicky and Bertie in the Yellow Room and 'played with them without servility'. The Queen, who shared the contemporary interest in freaks, presented the tiny visitor with a gold pencil-case and his coat of arms engraved on emeralds. Other entertainments were unwittingly provided by visiting Ojibbeway Indians at Osborne, a Chinaman with two dwarf small-footed wives, and three Highland dwarfs, two of them brother and sister, being only forty-four inches high.

In September 1846 a State visit with far-reaching consequences for Vicky was paid by the Queen Dowager and Princess Augusta of Prussia, who stayed at Windsor for a week, long enough for the impressionable Queen to be 'delighted' with Augusta (who was the daughter of the Grand Duke Charles of Saxe-Weimar).

Augusta was a vivacious brunette who had received an unusually liberal education for a German Princess; Goethe had lived at her father's court and she had come under his influence. Now she was married to the soldierly Crown Prince of Prussia. She was too clever for him and he resented it. Victoria found her

> . . . so amiable, so well-informed and so good; she seems to have some enemies for there are whispers of her being false but, from all that I have seen of her, from her discretion, her friendship through thick and thin to her own detriment for the Queen Dowager, who has known her from birth, I cannot and will not believe it. Her position is a very difficult one. She is too enlightened and liberal for the Prussian Court not to have enemies, but I believe that she is a friend to us and our family and I do believe that I have a friend in her who may be most useful to us.

The last words of that diary entry are revealing – the outcome of talks with Albert about Vicky's future. It was a 'useful' friendship indeed. Victoria kept it up by a regular correspondence. She 'needed a close woman friend badly,' she confided to 'dear Augusta'; she had had none since the death of Louise, Uncle Leopold's wife, whose name was later bestowed upon her fourth daughter. Augusta, too, kept up the friendship. At Christmas she sent to Windsor a large case of toys, which contained four little 'shops' for Vicky with fruit and vegetables like those in the Berlin markets and five boxes of toy soldiers for Bertie.

The following year 1847, each of the children had a little table laid out with their toys and they ran about in great glee showing them off. 'Prince Alfred,' wrote Mrs Stanley,

> ... in a glorious tinsel helmet that almost covered his face was shooting us all with a new gun and Princess Alice was making us admire her dolls. They had one Christmas tree among them like us, but the Queen, the Prince and the Duchess of Kent had one each. The Queen made them laugh at dinner talking about the Thorburn drawing. The first time the Prince had a great deal of trouble about the attitude in which Princess Alice, sitting on the Queen's lap, should be in, as they didn't like Thorburn's idea to have her arms spread out so that the child was in the shape of a cross; when the picture was finished and they observed this to him, he said: 'Yes, I meant it to be allegorical, to represent the Church leaning upon the bosom of the State, so I thought the Church was better represented by a cross.'

In 1848, as Prince Albert wrote to Stockmar 'all social conditions were shifting and tottering.' Karl Marx had written his *Manifesto*, the Emperor of Austria was forced to abdicate, the Milanese revolted, the Venetians established a republic. 'What dismal times are these!' Albert exclaimed to his brother.

> Augustus, Clementine de Nemours and the Duchess of Montpensier have come to us one by one like people shipwrecked; the king of the French and his Queen are still tossing upon the waves or have drifted to other shores; we know nothing of them. France is in flames. Belgium is menaced. We have a Ministerial, money and tax crisis, and Victoria is on the point of being confined. My heart is heavy ...

On 18 March a 'spot of light appeared on the gloomy scene': the birth of Princess Louise. Albert now wrote more cheerfully: 'I have good news for you today. Victoria was safely delivered this morning and though it be a daughter, still my joy and gratitude are very great, as I was often full of misgivings because of the shocks which have crowded upon Victoria of late.

Victoria and the baby are perfectly well . . .' 'Our new baby,' wrote Lady Lyttelton, 'is right royal; very large, extremely fair, with white satin hair, large, long blue eyes and regular features, a most perfect form from head to foot. The Queen is extremely proud of her; hitherto she is as placid and happy as possible, cries very little and begins to laugh and even crows, which at six weeks is early.'

The old Duchess of Gloucester attended the christening, but she was becoming senile and had been to so many functions that she could no longer remember what was expected of her. Quite forgetting what this particular one was about, she got up in the middle of the service and knelt at the Queen's feet: 'Imagine our *horror*!' Victoria confided to her journal. Family celebrations were apt to be so trying; one never knew what one's eccentric relatives would be up to next.

The Prince of Prussia and Louis-Philippe of France sought political asylum in England, where Louis-Philippe joined the special constabulary formed to check the Chartist riots, and the Queen and Prince Albert lodged him and his wife Amélie at Claremont House. Anything could happen to anybody; the highest in the land could not be sure about their possible future. The Queen wrote anxiously in her diary on the subject of her children: 'I always think and say to myself: let them grow up fit for whatever station they may be placed in, high or low. I never thought of this before, but I do always now.' And Albert wrote to his brother:

> The education of six different children, for they are none of them the least like the other in looks, mind or character, is a difficult task. They are a great deal with their parents and are very fond of them. I don't interfere in the details of their upbringing but only superintend the principles, which are difficult to uphold in the face of so many women, and I give the final judgment. From my verdict there is no appeal. Unfortunately, also, I am the executive power and have to carry out the sentence.

It was due to Victoria's influence that the rod was not spared.

It was a relief to go to Osborne with the new baby Princess and forget tiresome politics. Albert, too, found consolation in domesticity. Lady Lyttelton observed:

> The whole royal family seems to be out all day long. I don't believe the Queen thinks of reading a despatch or of doing anything in the way of business further than scribbling her name where it is required; she told Lady Canning that she had not read out of a book since February. She draws a good deal and walks about and enjoys herself. The children dine and tea in the garden and run about to their heart's content and, yesterday evening—assisted by their august papa and sanctioned by the prescence of their royal mama, who was looking-on washed a basketful of potatoes and shelled a ditto of peas, which they are to cook for themselves today if they are good. Did you ever hear of such happy children?

Vicky was overheard arguing with Bertie during a cruise on the royal yacht – (they were both sick at first, which the Queen thought was good for them; after that they bore it well) – as to which of them was the owner of the Scilly Isles; each claimed ownership. The governesses did not like the children to be taken on cruises; this departure from the strict nursery routine made them 'so petted and neglected and irregular and idle, in spite of much trouble taken by the Queen, that it takes long to recover orderly ways at Windsor'. Vicky was also heard telling Bertie what she intended to do when she was Queen. She was the eldest, so she would be Queen – just like Mama. She had started to take piano lessons for half an hour every day. She tried Lady Lyttelton sorely many a time. 'I am sorry, Laddle,' she would say, 'but I intend to be just as naughty next time.' One day she 'quarrelled with her bonnet at the last minute' and, in a rage, tried to bite the poor lady's hand. On another occasion, after she had been sent to her room for misconduct, the governess, Miss Hillyard, overheard Alice exclaiming plaintively: 'Oh, Vicky, how *can* you be so naughty?' 'I can't help it,' came a sobbing reply. 'But Vicky,' Bertie chipped in, 'I am afraid Miss Hillyard is gone down to call Papa and dear Papa will be so sorry – *do* stop.' And she did, at once. None of the children ever wished to upset 'dear Papa'.

'The Princess,' observed Lady Lyttelton, 'begins to try one's depth and talk blue: "Poor Roger Bacon, it's so hard upon him to have been thought wicked because he was so clever as to invent gunpowder." ' When talking of the canal she was asked whether she understood the word 'Caledonian'. 'Oh yes,' she replied immediately, 'Caledonia meant formerly Scotland, so it is only a more elegant way of saying Scotch.' 'No ridicule or foible escapes her,' wrote Lady Lyttelton after recounting the 'pony whip' incident. Apparently the French governess Madame Rollande was a rather 'uppity' lady and when Miss Hillyard suggested to Vicky that Madame Rollande should use the broken whip which she herself took with her when she rode the old pony with the younger children, the Princess said, in her sharpest, sly way: 'Oh no, that whip won't do at all for her; she is much too grand to use what you use. You are only Miss Hillyard – *she* is Madame Rollande de la Sauge.' 'She is as satirical as a young lady of 20.' But a few moments later, when the pony broke into a canter and Bertie was thrown from the carriage, she became a tearful, affectionate little girl and screamed: 'Oh, can't they stop him? Poor dear Bertie', and burst into tears.

She could be tender-hearted with others too. One night she heard a Windsor Palace guard coughing beneath her window. Tiptoeing across the room she opened the window, leaned out and whispered: 'Guard, guard, you *do* have a horrid cold! Go home to bed.' As the guard showed no signs of obeying, Vicky addressed him in her 'royal' voice: 'I am the princess, guard – don't you realize that? You *must* obey me.' A few days later she passed the same guard when walking with the Queen; she heard him cough again and asked her mother to get some medicine for him. The Queen gave her two sovereigns to hand to him 'to help cure his cold'. (The children were given very little pocket money. Vicky received about a shilling a week, out of which she bought a penny trumpet for little Affie's third birthday, which he preferred to more expensive presents.)

Vicky never suffered fools gladly and she could be high and mighty with her own brothers and sisters. One day Bertie took a Bible picture-book and showed Alfred a portrait of Samson. The child had not yet heard of him and Bertie was too lazy to bother to reply to his repeated query: 'Who *was* he?' Vicky left the piano on which she had been practising and walked across the room. 'You are quite right, Bertie dear,' she said sententiously, 'don't explain to him. We must never do too much with little minds.' The Queen often read passages from the Bible to her elder children. After she had quoted the passage: 'God created man in His own image', Vicky – thinking of one of her mother's very ugly secretaries – piped up: 'But Mama, surely not Dr Praetorius!' This kind of remark took the Queen aback: 'I hate to explain anything to a child – one does not often know what to say to them,' she confessed. She complained that Vicky was unmanageable, but Lady Lyttelton observed at the end of 1848: 'There is a blessed improvement. the Princess Royal is becoming capable of self-control and principle and patience and if her wonderful powers of head and heart continue she may turn out a most distinguished character.' She still continued to fight with Bertie, however, and teased him when he stammered. 'There was a tremendous fight in our room which was really *too* absurd,' the Queen wrote in her journal after she had been reading history to Vicky, 'her strongest subject'.

When Dr Brown entered Prince Albert's service the children, hearing their father address him as 'Brown' did the same, until they were sternly told to call him '*Doctor* Brown'. All of them obeyed except Vicky, who was threatened with bed if she transgressed again. The very next day, as soon as the Doctor came in, she said loudly: 'Good morning, Brown.' Then, seeing her mother's eye fixed upon her, she rose, curtsied and said: 'Good night, Brown, for I am going to bed', and walked away to her punishment.

In 1849, Vicky and Bertie, now aged nine and eight made their first public appearance at the opening of the new Coal Exchange, one of the least ugly of the new Victorian buildings; it was designed by the City Corporation architect James Burnstone Bunning, who had had the novel notion of using cast iron and glass in the rotunda behind the masonry façade. The Queen was unable to attend: she was suffering from chickenpox. Everybody at Windsor Castle had been vaccinated in consequence, 'as it had been dinned into the Queen's head that they have got a bad kind of smallpox in Windsor. I hope we won't catch it,' wrote Mrs Stanley, 'but I think there is much more chance of it from those tiresome little brats [referring to the royal children] that roll about everywhere and wrap themselves up in all the curtains to play at hide-and-seek than there ever was from the Queen herself.'

Vicky was delighted to be allowed to accompany papa to the Coal Exchange in Lower Thames Street and to be the 'only great lady present', as she informed her dresser, Miss Lindfield, after the event. She left the Palace at noon, seated in a State carriage next to Prince Albert, with Bertie facing them, wearing a green silk frock with white stripes and three flounces, a black velvet mantle drawn in at the waist, a pink quilted satin bonnet with a small pink feather at the side and 'pale boots'. At 12.30 they descended the Whitehall stairs and climbed into the antique gilded royal barge (this was to be its last State voyage) manned by twenty-seven royal watermen. Dressed Admiralty boats, the Lord Mayor's State barge and the barges of the livery companies stood out in the fairway. More than a million Londoners with banners and flags jostled each other on the banks to watch the water procession gliding down to Customs House Quay, where the bewigged City Recorder bellowed out an address in which he made a reference to Bertie: 'Your Royal Highness, the pledge and promise of a long reign of kings.' The abashed little boy started back. 'Bow to him,' hissed Vicky audibly. 'Poor Princey did not seem to guess at all what he meant,' remarked Lady Lyttelton who was standing behind the children.

Vicky felt like a little Queen – such a fuss was made of her, from the Lady Mayoress to 'ever so many ladies whose names I didn't hear or remember'. The only drawback was that, owing to some unaccountable confusion, there was no separate lunch for the children, who had to be served in a back room.

Vicky complained that she got no pudding, 'which was very hard'. After lunch, Vicky took Bertie by the hand and, amid a salvo of clapping, led him to her father; he took them to the middle of the hall and Vicky curtsied again and again on their way out.

The elder children were involved in theatricals, which had begun to be taken seriously at the Palace since, as the Queen wrote to her friend Augusta:

> Chevalier Bunsen the Prussian ambassador has been helping us in an attempt to revive and elevate the English drama, which has greatly deteriorated through lack of support by society. We are having a number of performances of classical plays in a small, specially constructed theatre in the Castle ... The stage has been erected in the Rubens room and I never enter it without the most vivid recollections of your dear visit seven years ago ... May it soon be repeated!

It *was* repeated – on the historic occasion of the opening of the Great Exhibition in 1851, which was preceded by the visit of Augusta's daughter Louise, the future Grand Duchess of Baden. But it was more important for the royal couple's premature matrimonial plans that Augusta's seventeen-year-old Fritz should come to England. Victoria wrote purposefully to Augusta in April:

> As regards your son, we think that whatever plans may be made for the future it would be best if you brought him with you now. It would then be much easier to discuss the best way of meeting your wishes foı a prolonged stay with us. The young Prince should certainly not miss the Exhibition and once he has made the acquaintance of England it will be easy for him to make another long visit, perhaps in the autumn ...

What she really meant was that the young Prince should make the acquaintance of eleven-year-old Vicky, who had taken to wearing her hair 'all twisted into a large curl tucked into a dark blue or black silk net, which keeps it all very tidy and neat ... and white lace gowns over white satin with pink bows and sashes,' wrote Lady Augusta. The young people met for the first time in the Chinese drawing-room at Buckingham Palace. Fritz spoke to Vicky in English, while she answered in fluent German.

At Christmas, when the elder children were allowed to stay up until ten as a special treat, Vicky wrote to Fritz on the new gilt and illustrated notepaper she had been given as a Christmas present, describing a parade: 'The music was very beautiful and the cavalry horses trotted so well in time that they were a pleasure to watch. I am telling you this because it will interest you for you are a soldier yourself. Goodbye, dearest Fritz, from your loving and devoted Vicky.' He replied: 'I keep thinking of beautiful Osborne and London where I spent so many happy hours with you. Your loving Frederick William.'

At a dance in a fellow student's house in Bonn, Fritz confided that he was very happy after his trip to England. When his friend (Eberhard von Claer) asked why, the Prince suddenly became serious and whispered: 'If you give me your word of honour that you won't repeat anything, I'll show you something.' Eberhard assured him that he could rely upon his discretion. After looking round cautiously the Prince pulled out a gold locket concealed near his heart, pressed a spring and showed him the portrait of 'an extremely youthful but charming girl. He kissed it, then shut the locket and put his finger to his lips.'

The happy family celebrations at Windsor crowned a splendidly successful year. People were beginning to appreciate Prince Albert. The Queen was all smiles. There were now seven in the family, ranging from one-year-old Arthur, born in 1850, to eleven-year-old Vicky. It had been a happy decade on the whole, despite the lamented deaths of Albert's father and various other relatives. The Queen told Lady Barrington that she had been nine months in mourning each year for the last three or four and had lost ten uncles and aunts since her marriage. Lady Barrington confided to a friend afterwards that she had felt inclined to ask: 'And pray, Ma'am, how many more have you got to lose?'

# *Section II*

# *Growing Up (1852-62)*

THE elder children had reached an age when they needed playmates outside the family circle. The Queen had played with few children of her own age when she was little, and Albert had detested parties, but they decided that it would be a good plan to organize children's balls at Buckingham Palace to which a chosen few would be invited. It would also encourage the children to practise their dancing steps.

Invitations were duly sent out and were followed by a frantic appeal from their recipients for the services of Monsieur Delplanche, Master of Ceremonies, dancing professor *par excellence,* who supervised the royal children's lessons. Monsieur Delplanche was invariably summoned on the eve of a court ball to make sure that everybody knew their steps and would not disgrace themselves before the eagle-eyed Queen who – on the slightest sign of hesitancy – would skip down from her dais, take the children's hands, and show them what to do. Lord Ronald Gower, who attended some of these functions in his childhood, described the formidable Monsieur Delplanche as having 'the manners and appearance of at least one if not several ambassadors and plenipotentiaries. He made his half-dozen pupils in the Stafford House gallery go through all the figures of a quadrille with the ceremony and decorum of a *menuet de la cour.*'

> When the night of the ball arrived and we performed at the palace under the eye of the terrible Delplanche, we almost lost all enjoyment and trembled to think that we were insufficiently turning out our toes or that we had hopelessly forgotten the next figure in the quadrille. They were rather awful festivities.

Her Majesty, an excellent dancer herself, was critical and, when dancing with a Princess and knowing that Delplanche's eagle eye and the august eyes of royalty were following our gyrations, the honour of the dance was hardly compensated for by the dread of failure.

The Duchess of Gloucester's and the Argyll children were invited to play in the gardens of Buckingham Palace, and the Duchess of Gloucester gave balls at which the Queen 'frisked about her small subjects' finding them partners. Helena and Louise were now old enough to take part in them and they were also allowed to attend a fancy-dress ball given by Queen Amélie at Claremont. The postilions lost their way between Claremont and Windsor and the royal children did not get home to the castle till past three in the morning, but such exciting occurrences were exceptional.

It rained so hard in the late autumn of 1852 that Windsor was flooded, yet no water came into the castle because the engine that forced the water up to the reservoir of Cranbourne Tower was out of order. Prince Albert decreed that nobody could have their usual baths or tubs. The ladies were shocked. Mrs Stanley said:

> We all rebel and declare we would rather walk down to the numerous pools or great lake that occupies the place where the Home Park ought to be below the North Terrace, with a bucket in each hand, than go dirty, which the Prince and Colonel Biddulph seem to think the easiest and most obvious way of managing the difficulty . . . indeed, if it goes on raining as it has done this morning we need only put the tubs outside the windows for a few hours and they will soon be quite full!

The entire royal family went over to the riding school to attend a distribution of beef, plum-pudding and blankets to the local flood victims. 'The Queen, Prince, and seven children look such a flock when they are all together,' observed Mrs Stanley.

The 'flock' was increased in the following year by the birth of the Queen's last (and haemophilic) son, Leopold, on 4 April 1853.

In the same way that she had previously given an impetus to vaccination, the Queen now set a further example to the nation's womanhood by allowing chloroform to be administered to her during the birth. With characteristic forthrightness she stated that the new baby was extremely ugly, an opinion which she adhered to for most of his short life; he was frail, stooped, and walked with a limp.

Victoria continued to write to her 'dear friend' Augusta and presumed to offer her advice on the subject of Fritz's education (of a nature never applied to her own sons): 'For your dear son, it would certainly be necessary to secure a wider intercourse with men of distinction, and also that he should get away from Potsdam a little. Some travel in summer and autumn would be most desirable.' She wrote this with Balmoral in mind.

The foundation stone of Balmoral Castle was laid on 28 September 1853; the Rev. Anderson, Minister of Craithie, prayed for a blessing on the work. This did not prevent the workmen from striking, an activity which Albert described as 'being all the rage now', and which he attributed to the opening of Australian mines and the consequent emigration. The Castle, nominally designed by William Smith of Aberdeen, was actually – as the Queen declared proudly in her diary – 'my dearest Albert's own creation, own work, own building, own laying-out, as at Osborne'. Albert also designed the Balmoral tartan of black, red and lavender on a grey background which was freely used in curtains and upholstery and led to the royal couple's being accused of 'tartanitis'. (Lord Rosebery thought that the ugliest rooms he had ever seen in his life were those of Osborne, until he saw Balmoral.)

Balmoral was beautifully situated in a long, wooded valley on the south side of the river Dee between Ballater and Braemar, whose games and gatherings were encouraged by the royal family, to the irritation of the members of their household and many guests. Five miles away, Abergeldie Castle was held on lease, first for the Duchess of Kent and later for distinguished visitors.

On the day of the inauguration, a parchment was signed by

the Queen, the Prince, the Duchess of Kent and all the royal children. (It was Louise's first important signature.) This was placed in a bottle with coins of the reign, sealed, put in a cavity under a stone which the Queen struck with a mallet upon its bed of mortar; she then poured oil and wine upon it to the accompaniment of bagpipes – a truly medieval ceremony, appropriate to the Gothic setting and the turrets of the new 'baronial hall' type of dwelling which, for Albert, represented a plunge back to his childhood at Rosenau.

The little Princesses loved Balmoral. This was 'Home, Sweet Home', which Vicky and Alice would emulate later in their respective palaces in Berlin and in Darmstadt. Louise was more critical.

Theatricals were one of their chief amusements. The royal children performed before their parents, the household and a few select guests. 'I never saw anything so pretty as the children's little play on Friday evening,' wrote lady-in-waiting Mary Bulteel [later Mary Ponsonby] in February 1854.

> So nicely acted, and the little stage and all the dresses so beautifully got up. Of course regardless of expense. Some of the Hood and Van de Weyer children and little Sybil Grey [the Comptroller's daughter] were called in for the minor parts and really the whole thing was most beautiful. As to Princess Alice, her acting and her little songs introduced were charming; she is quite aware of it and very proud of her success. But I do think she is rather old to be dressed like a little boy, which she is in this play, her part being a little Savoyard such as we see in the streets [they performed the function of chimney-sweeps in their own country *and* in England]. There was a dance on Friday, the two elder children dancing with us for an hour or so, then off to bed.

A week later the children performed in a tableau representing the four seasons. On this occasion, wrote Mrs Stanley, Princess Alice

> ...came out as Spring, scattering flowers and speaking an appropriate little speech out of Thomson's *Seasons*. The curtains then fell and presently rose again, showing Prince Arthur in a

very short and scanty blue frock asleep on the ground, and the Princess Royal as Summer in a rosy light; she too spoke a little speech out of the *Seasons* and we then after a short interval had the third scene: Autumn. Prince Alfred as Bacchus in a leopard skin and crowned with grapes, and then Winter: the Prince of Wales as an old man warmly dressed and icicles hanging about his coat and hat, and Princess Louise also dressed in character and very prettily but her's was a dumb part, and then came the closing scene showing them all in a group with Princess Helena appearing in clouds in a white robe, holding a cross. She spoke a speech composed for the occasion, told us she was Christ-loving Helena who had appeared to bless this auspicious day [their parents' wedding anniversary] and tender their homage to their parents . . . it was the prettiest thing possible and the parents might well feel proud and happy with their group of eight round them.
After all was over the Prince called out to them to come out and jump down from the stage among us, and the curtain was drawn up, but one of them piteously remarked: 'We can't get through the atmosphere,' (the gauze behind which they act). However, the 'atmosphere' was somehow pushed aside and they came down, when the Queen was so shocked at Prince Arthur's scanty attire (though his nurse assured her he had 'flesh-coloured decencies' on) that she sent him away to be dressed, but when he came back all the difference I saw was a pair of socks that hardly came above his ankles.

The performance was followed by a dinner-party for the adults at which Vicky, Bertie and Alice were allowed to eat the first two courses. Lady Augusta Bruce was still of the opinion that the children 'never ate their fill'.

As time went on more ambitious spectacles were produced, such as Racine's *Athalie* and Molière's comedies ('after the coarsest passages had been deleted'). There were times, however, when the royal parents were more broad-minded than the members of their household gave them credit for. When *The School for Scandal* had been selected, and 'some of the improper bits had been cut out', the Prince, upon being shown some of the doubtful passages, said with a smile: 'Oh no, let that stand, we are not quite so squeamish as all that!'

The Queen continued to send progress reports to Augusta about Vicky, inserted between general comments on the domestic scene. In August 1854,

> ... the birthday of my beloved husband, which we celebrated peacefully and happily in the bosom of our family [at Osborne] the children did all they could to make their dear adored father happy; they drew, worked, recited, wrote compositions, played on the piano and Affie the violin [Objective outsiders said that he played execrably.] ... I have been lately suffering a great deal from nervousness ... Vicky is growing fast and her figure is developing; she is taking swimming lessons from a Frenchwoman whom we have brought over from Boulogne. [The chauvinistic household disapproved of this. Why bring a Frenchwoman? Couldn't the Queen have found an Englishwoman?] The boys have already learned to swim, it is so useful ...

Alice was now old enough to begin to appear in public – one of the most memorable occasions being the opening in 1854 of the Crystal Palace, which had been transferred from its original site for the Great Exhibition of 1851 to serve as a permanent concert and exhibition hall. The young King of Portugal and Prince Albert with the two Princes (Bertie and Affie) sat on one side of the Queen's solitary gilt chair upon its crimson platform, the Duchess of Kent with Princess Vicky and Princess Alice on the other. Clara Novello intoned 'God Save the Queen', and her splendid voice 'filled the whole space to the uttermost parts'. It was like a Palace tableau but on a grander scale.

Eighteen-hundred and fifty-four, was, however, a sad year. For the first time since the Queen's accession, England was at war: the Crimean War, with all its horrors and sufferings and bumblings. The balcony at Buckingham Palace was used for the first public appearance of a sovereign when the Queen walked out upon it to watch the last Guards battalion march out of the courtyard on its way to the East.

Wounded troops began to fill the hospitals and Vicky and Alice accompanied the Queen on her visits to them. Victoria felt moved. To her – as Florence Nightingale commented:

'They [the soldiers] were *men*, and not machines.' When Lord Raglan paid a flying visit from the front to Buckingham Palace, Vicky seized his arm and entreated him, with tears in her eyes: 'For Heaven's sake hurry back to Sebastopol and take it or else you will kill Mama.' The fall of Sebastopol was celebrated at Balmoral with bonfires, dancing, the imbibing of whisky by the ghillies and the construction of the first of the commemorative cairns that began to disfigure the surrounding hills and countryside during Victoria's long reign. On a commercial level, a best-selling picture displayed in many shops showed a scene in Buckingham Palace with the Queen and Vicky in bonnets and crinolines chatting to a wounded soldier while others craned forward, anxious to catch Her Majesty's eye and ear, and another warrior showed Vicky the bullet-hole in his coat.

The elder Princesses, who had 'taken in poverty', now 'took in' physical suffering and mutilation. It was not to be the last time: a decade later both were to be personally involved in scenes of a similar nature. Their imagination – and that of the Queen – was fired by the accounts of the wonderful work being accomplished for wounded soldiers by the indomitable Miss Nightingale, whom the Queen presented with a medal and later invited to Balmoral. To Vicky and Alice Florence Nightingale became a shining example and – several years later – a teacher at whose London house Vicky called, flinging off her bonnet and shawl and asking humbly for advice on her nursing projects for Germany.

In April 1855 Napoleon III and the Empress Eugénie arrived in England for their long-expected State visit.

When they reached the coast of England, the imperial couple were greeted by a typical British fog. The Queen and the children were waiting for them anxiously at the castle where 'all was bustle, excitement and expectation', the Queen fussing over her dresses, bonnets, caps and mantillas of every sort made for the occasion. She did not usually 'trouble herself' about fashion, but – the Empress had such a reputation for taste in dress; her dressers had arrived the day before and even *they* looked almost as elegant as royalty! Everyone agreed that the new Empress was striking. Lady Ely, who had seen her in Paris, was full of her praises. The girls had never seen Mama so agitated over a foreign visitor, but then they had never received such a glamorous one.

The Queen, 'in a light blue dress with shaded trimmings and a pearl necklace' (she made a careful note of the dresses she wore on every occasion) went into the gallery with Vicky and Bertie, the latter in Highland dress. Then, as guns were fired and the first grooms clattered into the forecourt and cheers were heard from the crowds outside the gates, the Queen moved towards the staircase. The band struck up *'Partant pour la Syrie'* (a tune composed by Queen Hortense, the Emperor's mother, with words by her son), trumpets sounded, the carriage doors opened. Accustomed as she was to meeting foreigners, Victoria found such occasions 'always very agitating'. They embraced the Emperor, the Empress looked nervous, Vicky's eyes were 'quite alarmed' and she bobbed up and down making curtsies to cover up her confusion.

Up the grand staircase to the Throne Room to present the other children – then the imperial pair were conducted to their apartments. The Empress, in a plaid silk dress and straw bonnet, had recovered her composure and was 'most pleasing, charming, and full of kind expressions'. The fog had been fearful, she said, the passage dangerous . . . the *Austerlitz* had gone aground and the English fleet stationed near to receive the august visitors had not been seen . . .

Vicky appeared after dinner in a light blue dress, 'her hair out of her face, looking very nice, and dancing began; Vicky danced with the Emperor, which frightened her very much . . . she continued to make beautiful curtsies and was very much praised by the Empress, whom Vicky raves about.' Even Albert liked and admired the Empress and the Queen was gracious enough to note in her diary that she was delighted 'as it is so seldom that I see him do so with any woman'.

While the men engaged in *conférences de guerre* in Albert's apartments, the children gathered round a table to admire the presents from France: soldiers for Arthur, a panorama, games and a piece of Gobelin tapestry depicting a dog for Vicky (the Empress must have been told that she could not fail to please English royalty if she took them presents involving dogs or representations of them), and two beautiful models of nine-pounders 'which the Emperor himself had invented and which he showed off with great pleasure'. Next day the Empress gave Vicky a watch of rubies and diamonds and was 'touched to tears' when the Queen reciprocated by giving the Empress a bracelet containing a sample of her hair, a characteristically Victorian gift but not a very lavish one. The Queen was never generous about presents or tips, and Vicky took after her.

There was music (the Emperor, however, did not much care for it), visits to the opera and of course the Crystal Palace. The Emperor wrote in Vicky's autograph book and all the children cried when the pair finally drove away to the tune which had heralded their arrival, and which, the Queen observed drily, they had heard fourteen times the day before.

The return visit to Paris in August of the same year was an even more spectacular affair, as the imperial couple put themselves out to dazzle Victoria and Albert. They succeeded very well. The Queen described every detail of the visit in her Journal with her usual vividness and girlish enthusiasm. In her eagerness to see everything, Lord Clarendon (who formed part of her retinue) complained that she 'knocked up everybody ... the Emperor went in great distress for the last league ... no royal person ever yet known or to be known in history comes up to her in indefatigability.'

Miss Mary Bulteel and Miss Hillyard were in charge of Vicky and walked her through the Elysée gardens. 'The Queen, I regret to say,' wrote Miss Bulteel, 'is badly dressed in early Victorian gowns with a penchant for "the lilac cravat" as she calls it.' So surely the Emperor must have had his tongue in his cheek when he solemnly assured the Queen at the end of her visit that 'he remembered every single dress she had worn'? She herself recalled every one of Eugénie's 'creations' and wrote admiringly that 'she looked like a fairytale queen ... even the Emperor exclaimed when she appeared for dinner resplendent in white and diamonds: *"Comme tu es belle!"* ' Vicky agreed; she had developed a childish crush for Eugénie.

Vicky's and Bertie's rooms were immediately below those of their parents in the beautiful Palace of Saint-Cloud, guarded by handsome Zouaves, which had been placed at the royal family's disposal. They breakfasted ('Excellent coffee,' remarked the Queen) *en famille* at 9 a.m. and then drove in the gardens with the Emperor. The Parisians dubbed Queen Victoria *'la bonne mère de famille'*. But this 'good wife and mother' was shrewder than they imagined. 'All seems now so prosperous, the Emperor seems to fit his place and yet how little security one feels for the future,' she observed in her journal.

Vicky was allowed to be present at the great ball at Versailles, but she was not permitted to dance until the Emperor himself walked up, bowed gravely, and led her in a dizzy waltz down the Galerie des Glaces. Later that evening Count Otto von Bismarck, Prussian ambassador in Paris, was presented to her parents. The Empress Eugénie looked pale; she was expecting her first and only child: the future Prince Lucien Bonaparte. Who could then have foreseen the débâcle of Sedan, the flight from Paris, exile in England, the death of the future Prince Imperial in Zululand? Who could have foreseen the antagonism that was to estrange the starry-eyed little waltzing princess from her own son because of that cold, blue-eyed Count von Bismarck? Who could have foreseen that, in that very same hall, a quarter of a century later, Vicky's father-in-law would be proclaimed the first Emperor of Germany and that Paris would be bombarded by men under the command of Vicky's husband?

Vicky 'melted in tears, *selon son habitude,*' observed the Queen during the final adieux from beautiful Paris. 'She is much devoted and attached to the Empress.'

The royal yacht, 'a most glorious ship, fitted up in brass and mahogany like a huge toy,' according to Mary Bulteel, sped back to dear, familiar Cowes. 'Incredible,' exclaimed the Queen, 'to be transported in one night from that gay, brilliant scene.' Affie and the other boys were waiting on the beach near the house with Helena and Louise and inside the house 'poor, dear Alice', who was quite upset at seeing them again after this first family separation. All the children were recovering from scarlet fever. Both the Queen and Vicky were too excited and bewildered to do anything but talk all day about their Parisian experiences, recalling every incident. The Queen had driven incognito and seen the shops and the cafés, comparing them favourably with English shops – but, as Miss Bulteel remarked, she had no idea what English shops looked like.

Papa wrote proudly to Baron Stockmar: 'You will be pleased to hear how well both the children behaved. Nothing could be more unembarrassed or more friendly. They have made themselves great favourites, too, especially the Prince of Wales, *qui est si gentil;* as the French are sarcastic and not readily partial to strangers, this is so much the more important.' The Queen, too, was pleased with the children's behaviour. Vicky had not resorted to any of her 'disagreeable tricks' such as standing on one leg, laughing violently, waddling as she walked and cramming in her food for which she was constantly reproached at home.

Life soon resumed its normal pattern, divided between Osborne for Christmas and in the early summer, Balmoral in the late summer and autumn, Windsor in between and Buckingham Palace for most levees and state occasions.

Mary Bulteel found that Alice was 'becoming obstreperous . . . as I was resisting her whims, she said: "Really, Mary, don't you know you must do what I tell you?" Such little royal airs!' Louise was even more temperamental, but her character developed slowly. She was one of the 'in-betweens' as far as age was concerned, and inclined to be withdrawn with her sisters. She was clever with her fingers and an excellent baker of scones and cakes which, *faute de mieux*, she cut out with a teapot lid in Swiss Cottage, but she preferred sketching and painting. Later she took up sculpture and longed for the day when she could have her own studio. Helena attached herself to

Alice, to whom she was utterly devoted, while Vicky, being the eldest and most imperious, ruled the little roost.

The royal household became fascinated by the current craze for table-turning, which Vicky and her sisters practised in their rooms. One evening the whole family – the Queen, the Prince, the children, Lady Ely and Mary Bulteel – 'whirled a table round upstairs and then took it downstairs to continue the experience in the drawing-room'. The Queen was quite provoked by Colonel Grey's incredulity. Level-headed Miss Bulteel believed the cause of the phenomenon to be 'the unconscious pressure that each person gives the table in one direction, when it is well *ébranlée* by the vibration of the fingers, which sends it round'.

The greatest event of the year, for Vicky, took place in September at Balmoral, where young Prince Frederick William (Fritz) of Prussia had been invited to join the royal party. Vicky was not supposed to be aware of what lay behind the visit, but it was naive of her entourage to imagine that that sharp young lady had not guessed their designs long before.

Fritz travelled by rail, to Aberdeen, in the company of General von Moltke, from where he proceeded via the little Dundee railway to the nearest station to Balmoral. Prince Albert and Colonel Grey awaited him with a carriage which rumbled across the white bridge of Craithie to the gates of the royal estate. The gates swung open, displaying an avenue of dancing fires: ghillies, shepherds and gardeners lined the drive with blazing pine torches, pipers emerged from behind the shadows of the trees and marched before them to the porch, where the family and their suite stood ready to greet the young lover from across the sea. The hissing torches were thrown into a heap and formed a magnificent bonfire, the pipers struck up a reel and pranced round the flaming pile in a wild dance. Fritz, who shared Albert's love of Nordic sagas, was enchanted by the primitive spectacle. What more romantic setting could have been devised for the beginning of a love affair? Everything had been planned with consummate showmanship, but now that the crucial moment had arrived the Queen began to have misgivings; she may have been feeling guilty at the prospect of forcing her little Juliet so early into the arms of this Prussian Romeo and 'the lion's den of Prussian politics'. 'The visit makes my heart break,' she wrote – a little exaggeratedly – in the diary which so often stood her in lieu of a confessional – 'as it may and probably will decide the fate of our dear eldest child'.

Vicky admired Fritz's 'high forehead, noble brow and clear blue eyes'. According to the Empress Eugénie, he was 'tall, handsome, slim, fair, with a light yellow moustache – in fact a Teuton such as Tacitus described; chivalrously polite and not without a resemblance to Hamlet.' Papa carried him off deer-stalking immediately after breakfast the day after his arrival; he shot a stag and at dinner talked animatedly with Vicky and praised her sketches. Dear Papa, who engaged Fritz on a variety of topics, found him straightforward, frank and honest, free from prejudices and well-intentioned; he did, however, appear to be a trifle slow-witted, and caused the Queen endless amusement by never understanding the simplest rules of *vingt-et-un*, which was explained to him by Prince Albert with Teutonic thoroughness. Vicky looked at Fritz most lovingly at dinner, but Lord Clarendon fancied that now and then 'the thought flashed across her very intelligent face that he was a shade slow'. He was bound to add, however, that 'all the remarks I heard from Fritz were sensible and in excellent English'.

Vicky observed Fritz closely and her father admitted in a letter to Stockmar: 'I will not answer for it that the clever child may not have noticed that something is in the wind; but I can say that I know that Fritz is not displeasing to her.' On his side, four days after his visit, Fritz wrote to his parents that Vicky had pressed his hand very hard when they were alone and that night he could not sleep. Thus encouraged, he decided to speak to her parents in the best Victorian tradition. He braved them alone and asked whether he might be permitted to talk of 'belonging to the family'. The Queen squeezed his hand and whispered how happy they would be, but suggested that he should wait until after Vicky's confirmation the following Easter, when she would still be only seventeen. This conversation took place on 20 September. Nine days later the young Prince, unable to bear the suspense (or pretence) any longer, begged the royal parents to allow him to speak to Vicky. They agreed.

Fritz resorted to the convenient language of flowers, which dispensed with the embarrassment of stammered words. During a ride up Craig-na-ban in the afternoon of 29 September the young couple lagged behind on their horses and then dismounted. Fritz picked a piece of white heather growing by the path and shyly presented it to Vicky. She preserved it to her dying day. 'This,' wrote the Queen, who was told all the details that evening during an emotional family scene (Vicky hid her face and sobbed on her mother's bosom) 'enabled him to make an allusion to his hopes and wishes as they rode down Glen Girnoch, which led to the happy conclusion.'

Fritz reported to his parents that the Princess 'possesses great feeling and intelligence and has a lively interest in art and literature, particularly that of Germany. Without exaggerating, I think I may say that we will be well suited to each other.' Albert noted soberly: 'My feeling was rather one of cheerful satisfaction and gratitude to God for bringing across our path so much that was noble and good.' He was convinced that 'the young people are ardently in love with one another and the purity, innocence and unselfishness of the young man have been on his part equally touching.' Fritz expressed himself with more warmth to his English tutor Mr Perry: 'It was my heart ... *on devine ceux qui aiment*.'

On Fritz's departure 'an abundance of tears were shed ... while deep visible revolutions in the emotional natures of the two young people and of the mother took place,' according to Albert, 'by which they were powerfully agitated.' Vicky's happiness overflowed in ecstatic letters to Fritz addressed to 'My precious, madly-loved Fritz, from his own Vicky'. 'If you only knew how your love moves me, how happy it makes me and how much I return it, I do not deserve so much. Dear, dear Fritz, I think of you day and night.' Albert told him a little sadly: 'From the moment you declared your love and

*top* The Queen at Windsor Castle in February, 1854, surrounded by four of her children. Left to right: Bertie (The Prince of Wales), Vicky (The Princess Royal), Alice and Affie.

*bottom* The Royal children taking part in a 'tableau of the seasons', February, 1854. Left to right: Alice, Arthur, Vicky, Helena, Alfred, Louise, Bertie.

Osborne House, Isle of Wight, the Royal Family's first real, personal home.

Swiss Cottage, the Royal children's playhouse at Osborne, a gift from Prince Albert.

The family at Osborne in 1857. Left to right: Affie, Prince Albert, Helena, Alice, Arthur, baby Beatrice, the Queen, Vicky, Louise, Leopold and Bertie.

*left* Vicky (now Princess Frederic William of Prussia) and Fritz on their honeymoon at Windsor, January, 1858.
*right* Alice and Louis of Hesse in garter robes at Bertie's wedding in 1863, looking grander than they actually were. They led a frugal life in Darmstadt.

The Queen in 1867, at Balmoral with her dog Sharp.

embraced her, the child in her vanished ... I hope the long period of waiting won't make you impatient.'

The engagement was intended to be kept secret until the following year, but it proved impossible to prevent the news from leaking out. '*The Times* is deeply offended that its permission has not been asked,' Albert informed Fritz. Indeed this newspaper, which never ceased to advise the royal family with the candour of Uncle Leopold, thought that the proposed marriage was to be deplored and that Fritz was 'only a paltry German prince'. It could not, however, suggest an alternative groom.

Victoria fulfilled her matchmaking role by sending a progress report on Vicky to 'dear Augusta'. She had not, she stressed, discussed Vicky with her before 'partly because it seemed immodest to mention her gradual development or to praise her unduly, and also because she was so largely the object of our secret hopes and desires'. Fritz must have told Augusta a great deal about Vicky. The Queen merely wanted to add that she had 'developed amazingly of late, and her visit to France proved beneficient in every way'.

> She is now slightly taller than I am and grows visibly. I find her very good company and this important event in her life has now brought us even closer together. I experience everything she feels and since I myself still feel so young, our relationship is more like that of two sisters. Her health is excellent. Early this year she went through a critical time and did not suffer even the slightest indisposition. But she is still half a child and has to develop both physically and morally before the marriage takes place in two years' time ... I admit it is rather long for dear Fritz to wait but I hope he will often visit us here alone to see his Vicky.

Fritz came back in the following spring. He visited Mme Tussaud's with Vicky to inspect their effigies in wax, Vicky in a light blue silk flounced dress ornamented with lace and pearls, and the Prince in the fusilier uniform of the Prussian Guards, with a tall cap. He paid yet another visit in November 1856, when it was observed by their entourage that although the Princess Royal looked very happy, 'the young couple were not allowed much lovemaking: a little walk with the royal parents and one hour a day in tête-à-tête in the room adjoining the Queen's sittingroom, with the door open. Vicky was shy in Fritz's presence and kept blushing when he looked at her and glancing the other way. Sometimes the walks were pleasant, other times less so.' One afternoon the two royal couples, old and young, started out but alas, as Vicky complained afterwards: 'Papa and the Prince followed us, talking politics, and when we got to the farm they stayed there and mama and I came home in the carriage, so we saw almost nothing of him.' The court ladies were unanimous in thinking that it was most unfeeling on the part of the parents and they all felt sorry for the Princess Royal.

During this visit, the Duchess of Kent's only son by her first marriage, Prince Leiningen, died in Germany and on 17 November, while the Queen was consoling her mother at Frogmore, the Princess Royal remained with the two Princes (Fritz and his Coburg cousin) and the elder Prince, the cousin, went to sleep. This, thought Miss Bulteel, would be a grand opportunity for the young couple to have a flirtation: 'But I stood corrected, for the Princess said: "Oh no, we could not talk for fear of disturbing him, it might have woke him; we sat very still and looked up at the ceiling and Prince Frederick turned over a book of photographs very gently." ' Miss Bulteel wickedly asked if that was not a little dull, 'when I was assured that nothing could be dull when *he* was there'.

*He*, however, found his sojourn frustrating, as he saw so little of his fiancée and had nothing to do. On 19 November the Princess, too, was sad about seeing so little of Fritz. 'It seemed that the tête-à-tête could take place at no hour but 6 as Prince Albert won't spare them his little study next to the Queen's room at any other hour, and the doctors have ordered the Princess to dine at 6, so she does not see him at all in private.'

This was really too hard. Had Albert forgotten his own tête-à-têtes with Victoria in her little blue drawing-room, where – as he had written during his engagement, 'he had so often warmed her little hands'? Or was he secretly jealous of Fritz? And what about Victoria? Had she forgotten her tête-à-têtes with 'dearest, beautiful' Albert? Or was she agitated at the prospect of yet another confinement; it was destined to be her last. Perhaps, too, the Queen sensed and resented Albert's ambivalent feelings about Fritz. She referred in her diary to 'the rare happiness of being alone with her beloved Albert' when Vicky left them after dinner, at 10 p.m. But Albert was tired and irritable. He scolded her more than ever when they played cards together.

Fritz now complained to his mother, who passed on his comments to Victoria. The Queen replied indignantly that Augusta's fears that Fritz saw Vicky only with the younger children were quite unfounded. The latter appeared at breakfast and luncheon and 'leave immediately afterwards'. Vicky always went out with Fritz and her parents in the afternoon; she also saw him every day between six and seven and ate with him in the evening. The royal couple had had the opportunity of getting to know Fritz closely: 'We regard him quite as a member of the family; in London during the season it would have been impossible for then one never sees people quietly and alone and there is no opportunity for intelligent and serious conversation.' At the same time the Queen wrote to Uncle Leopold: 'I must chaperone this loving couple, which takes away so much of my precious time.'

When Fritz went back home Vicky found solace in collecting specimens of flowers and grasses to enclose with her letters. 'A very amusing way of showing her affection,' thought Walpurga, Lady Paget, her future lady-in-waiting, when she was told about it and shown the collection in later years. Fritz kept every one of these sentimental mementoes. 'You can imagine what a heap there was after three years' engagement,' exclaimed matter-of-fact Walpurga.

It was only after Vicky's confirmation that her sisters were informed of her engagement. The Queen wrote to Augusta: 'Alice, who had no suspicion of such a thing, was told first. She shows a touching love for her sister and tears come into her eyes when she speaks of it. Then the two boys and Lenchen were told. Louise and Arthur are to know nothing about it at present as they would not understand.' On the same day, Alice wrote to Fritz: 'Dear Fritz, I cannot tell you what great pleasure and surprise it has given me to hear from my dear parents that you are henceforth to be so nearly connected with our dear Vicky and that we may think of you as a brother. We are all so fond of you and are convinced that Vicky will be exceedingly happy with you. We shall of course be sorry to part with her as she has always been the kindest sister to us.' From Balmoral she wrote to him again: 'You cannot imagine how much I enjoy going out shooting with my parents'; and in December she sent Fritz a gift of handkerchiefs from the four younger children.

Fritz returned to England in June 1857 to attend the christening of his future mother-in-law's latest born: Princess Beatrice, the last of the Queen's five daughters. On this occasion he was formally introduced to the British public and officially treated as the Princess Royal's fiancé. He was escorted by special train to Windsor, went to Ascot in the first of the eleven royal carriages and dressed like a young Englishman as a compliment to the people among whom he had come to seek his bride: he wore a hat with a small flat brim and a blue check cravat. He attended the Handel Festival at the Crystal Palace, leading the Queen by the arm, and both he and Vicky beat time with their music scores. The young couple also went out riding together in Rotten Row.

The public was entitled to have a good look at Fritz. The Queen had already asked Parliament to make a financial provision for the marriage – an annuity of £8,000 was voted (with fourteen nays) and a dowry of £40,000, which was passed without opposition. *Punch*, however, reminded its readers that there remained eight brothers and sisters to be provided for.

The first brush between the German and English courts occurred before the wedding, which the Prussians believed should take place in Berlin. The Queen was furious and wrote off to her ambassador that she could '*never* consent to it both for public and for private reasons; the assumption of its being too much for a Prince Royal of Prussia to come over to marry the Princess Royal of Great Britain is too absurd, to say the least. . . . Whatever may be the usual practice of Prussian Princes, it is not every day that one marries the eldest daughter of the Queen of England; the question therefore must be considered settled and closed.'

In Germany, Count von Bismarck, who disliked Victoria and Albert, observed to General Gorlach:

> You ask me what I think of the English marriage. I must separate the two words to give you my opinion. The 'English' in it does not please me. The 'marriage' may be quite good, for the Princess has the reputation of a lady of brain and heart. If the Princess can leave the Englishwoman at home and become a Prussian, then she may be a blessing to the country. If our future queen on the Prussian throne remains the least bit English then I see our Court surrounded by English influence.

Bismarck proved to be only too right. Not only the Princess, but her father in the background were determined to exert a 'liberal' influence on the rigid Prussian caste system and the anachronistic German princelings who revolved like slow-moving satellites round her. By the way of preparation, Albert began to 'groom' Vicky for her future role, to lecture her on history and constitutions, to set her essays on political subjects, so that she would be well equipped to face 'the labyrinth of Berlin'. He was pleased with the results of this crash course, for Vicky was an apt pupil. What he omitted to inculcate in her was a sense of tact.

The wedding was to be on 20 January 1858. As the date approached, the Queen became more and more nervous and despatched more and more letters to Augusta. 'Vicky will depend so on her environment . . . I am depending on your good advice and your sweet maternal nature for support, otherwise it would be too risky to send a totally inexperienced 17-year-old child who has been used to parental care into a strange country to live among complete strangers.' This was true, but not the most tactful way of putting the case to a future mother-in-law. No doubt Albert had been discussing the matter with the Queen and recalling his own reactions before his marriage, when he had written so appealingly: 'Think of my position, dear Victoria: I am leaving my home with all its old associations, all my bosom friends and going to a country in which everything is new and strange to me: language, customs, modes of life, position. Except yourself, I have no one to confide in. . .' The Queen had never had to undergo a similar ordeal, but it was beginning to dawn upon her that a fearful trial lay in store for Vicky, who had dined outside the palace for the first time in 1856 and that in the house of her cousins the Cambridges! The self-confidence she displayed in public was at a distant remove and never involved any dialogue with ordinary people or with strangers.

An objective description of Vicky on the eve of her marriage was penned by Walpurga, Countess Hohenthal, the future Lady Paget, who was sent over from Berlin a little before the wedding. She had been chosen by Princess Augusta because of her excellent knowledge of English and Anglophil upbringing. Walpurga found Vicky charming and talkative. 'If she is like that at Berlin, everybody must be pleased and will even think she is pretty, although she has a tendency to roundness all over.'

> Her eyes are what struck me most. The iris was green like the sea on a sunny day and the white had a peculiar shimmer which gave them the fascination that, together with a smile showing her small and beautiful teeth, bewitched those who approached her. The nose was unusually small and turned up slightly and the complexion was ruddy (like the Queen's), perhaps too much so—but it gave the idea of perfect health and strength. The fault of the face lay in the squareness of the lower features and there was even a look of determination about the chin, but the very gentle and almost timid manner prevented one from realizing that at first. The voice was very delightful, never going up to the high tones but lending a peculiar charm to the slight foreign accent with which the Princess spoke both English and German.

(Many people remarked that the Queen, too, spoke with a slight foreign accent.)

Alice, Helena and Louise were delighted with their bridesmaids' dresses of emerald green poplin tissued in gold shamrocks, with embroidered sleeves and collars, ordered from the Shanballymore Female Industrial School for Poor Girls. Owing to the poverty prevalent in the country at the time, it was decided that the wedding should be a simple ceremony at the Chapel Royal of St James's, without pomp or circumstance. The chapel was too small to admit the ten press reporters and extra gilt chairs had to be provided in the forecourt for some of the guests.

Before the wedding the Queen inspected the rooms set aside for the young couple's brief honeymoon at Windsor. 'I do feel for Vicky so,' she wailed, comparing her daughter to a lamb being led to the sacrifice. Meanwhile Fritz wrote gaily to his fiancée from Berlin to report on the preparations being made there for their reception. He had 'sat down for a moment in the gilded monkey cage in which we will make our State drive; it shakes and sways like a ship at sea'.

The first guests arrived on 16 January and once again the Queen referred to the 'bustle and excitement' going on at Windsor and at Buckingham Palace. Albert helped to entertain the flock of German cousins and Hohenzollern relatives. Between eighty and ninety guests sat down at the royal table daily. 'It seems as though preparations were being made for an operation,' observed Victoria grimly, and she referred to Fritz as 'the kidnapper'. Her half-sister, Feodora, fully entered into her sentiments. 'Alas,' she wrote sympathetically, 'the sweet blossom coming in contact with rude life and all its realities so soon are changed into mature and less lovely persons, so painful to a mother's eye and feeling. . . .' A wedding party at Buckingham Palace on the nineteenth included the old faithfuls, Uncle Leopold and Baron Stockmar, besides all the petty German royalties and courtiers. Further celebrations included a command performance of *Macbeth* at the theatre, followed by the farce *Twice Killed*, a gala performance of the *Rose of Castile*, a State banquet, a performance of 'Mr Leslie's celebrated choir' and an exhibition of 'Mr Rarey's infallible system' of training wild horses, all of which occasions were attended by a 'row of royalties'. The wedding presents were laid out personally by the Queen and Prince Albert on tables in the drawing-room. Many of them were destined to be put up for sale at a London auction room, several decades later . . .

The night before the wedding Vicky gave her mother a brooch enclosing a strand of her hair, to wear next to her heart. On the actual wedding day, the Queen felt as she had on her own wedding morning, 'only more nervous', so much so that she trembled when she was being daguerreotyped with the bridal pair and came out as blurred as a ghost. Vicky came into her room while she was dressing in a peach velvet dress with a long train and told her that she had slept better than of late. The Queen gave her a prayer-book called *The Bridal Offering*.

It was a brilliant morning and church bells pealed joyfully in the crisp January air as the carriages left the palace, Albert and Uncle Leopold with the eldest boys in Highland uniform, Lady Lyttelton with the three girls dressed in pink satin, the Queen with Vicky beside her. In the dressing-room at St James's chapel the bridesmaids picked up their bouquets of pink roses and white heather. Lord Palmerston, bearing the Sword of State, led Her Majesty across the forecourt into the Chapel Royal with the two smallest boys on either side and the three girls behind, which 'had the most touching effect'. Drums and trumpets played. Fritz was pale and agitated, but 'behaved with great self-possession, bowing to the Queen and then kneeling down in the most devout manner'.

Then came the bride's procession.

Our darling flower looking very touching and lovely with such an innocent, confident and serious expression, her veil hanging back over her shoulders, walking between her beloved father and dearest Uncle Leopold, who had been at her christening and confirmation . . . My last fear of being overcome vanished on seeing Vicky's calm, quiet manner. It was beautiful to see her kneeling with Fritz, their hands joined and the train borne by seven young ladies who looked like a cloud of maidens hovering round her as they knelt near her. Dearest Albert took her by the hand to give her away . . . The music was very fine, the Archbishop very nervous. Fritz spoke very plainly, Vicky too. The Archbishop omitted some of the passages.

After the service the Queen left her seat to kiss the dry-eyed bride, who kissed Grandmama Kent ('looking so handsome in violet velvet trimmed with ermine'). The Queen kissed Fritz, Vicky kissed her parents-in-law. Mendelssohn's 'Wedding March' struck up (for the first time on such an occasion) and the bridal couple walked hand in hand to the throne room to watch the signing of the register according to highly delicate and complex rules of precedence.

On the arrival of the bridal pair at Windsor station, some boys from Eton loosened the traces, ran the horses and riders away through the mob and pulled the carriage from the station to the castle. There were no policemen or troops about to prevent this enthusiastic demonstration of youthful loyalty. The young couple sat down on a sofa in their honeymoon suite; overcome by emotion and Victorian prudery, they 'didn't know what to say to each other'. But the embarrassment was momentary and Vicky was soon tightly enveloped in Fritz's arms. Windsor was associated with Vicky's happiest memories and she was to allude to it over and over again in her letters home, provoking the exasperated Queen to exclaim: 'How *can* you like Windsor?'

There were more state banquets for the guests, fireworks, free meals for the poor throughout the country: bread and beef to the two hundred poor of the parish of St Pancras, coal and a shilling to the five hundred poor of Dover, beef, plum pudding, ale and tobacco at Birmingham. In London, Albert was kept busy assisting the agitated Queen to entertain, as he wrote to Duchess Marie of Saxe-Coburg and Gotha:

At Buckingham Palace we had thirty-five royal personages to house, to fête, to show England to, to exhibit the bride to the people, to receive the bridegroom, to marry the young people, to prepare their brief honeymoon, to induct our son-in-law into the Order of the Garter . . . Today [30 January] is devoted to receiving addresses and to a monster Drawingroom. The marriage ceremony was very solemn and affecting. I send you a programme and with it a piece of wedding cake and some orange blossom from the bridal dress . . .

On the snowy morning of 3 February the young couple prepared to leave England. 'Treat her well or we'll have her back!' shouted the draymen from Barclays Brewery to Fritz as the open carriage passed through the city on the way to the waiting ship at Gravesend. 'A dreadful moment, a dreadful day,' said the Queen, who for days could not bear to go near Vicky's old corridor at the castle. In spite of the snow and biting wind, thousands of people gathered outside Buckingham Palace and many of them began to cry. 'I parted from Vicky downstairs in the hall and I also wept as much as I could,' wrote the Queen, as if a flood of tears were part of her maternal duty. 'Alice sobbed loudly, and so did the little ones.' (As soon as the Queen began to cry the others almost invariably followed suit.) 'Albert and the boys went on board with Vicky and there the final parting is said to have been really terrible.' Vicky did most of her crying on board at Gravesend; after the last farewells she went down to her cabin and did not appear on deck again. Albert exercised self-control, but he told her in his first letter that, although he was not demonstrative by nature, he had felt the parting keenly.

There were more tears upon the return to the Palace, except for a moment of light relief when young sailor-to-be Affie remarked between sobs: 'And Vicky was so fond of the Navy!' The Queen sat down almost immediately to begin the first of thousands of letters to her daughter demanding detailed accounts of her life and movements. Eventually the British ambassador in Berlin was obliged to restrain Her Majesty, with the utmost tact; as if Vicky had not more than enough to cope with adjusting herself to her alien life at Berlin! The Queen abhorred Windsor because of its formal etiquette (to which in time she became resigned and even contributed), but that of the Prussian court was infinitely more rigid and Vicky never became attuned to it.

All began well. 'The whole royal family is enchanted with my wife' Fritz telegraphed after their icy procession through the streets of Berlin, in open carriages, Vicky in obligatory *décolleté,* to the palace, where her in-laws and the Prussian court were standing stiffly to welcome them. 'Are you not terribly cold?' asked Princess Augusta affably, to which Vicky replied: 'I have only one warm place left – that is my heart.' If she had been able to keep up this courtier's diplomacy throughout, her life in Berlin might have turned out differently, but she was her mother's child: impetuous, self-willed, unable to conceal her thoughts and unrepentantly insular. Berlin hoped she would become Prussian. Britain hoped she would remain British. *The Times* exhorted her not to forget her ancestry and country. She complied with too much fervour. 'I am a freeborn Englishwoman!' she exclaimed on one occasion – she, the sheltered princess who had known so little freedom!

Mama had written to her newly married daughter from Buckingham Palace only a few hours after her wedding, 'Let it be your study and your object to make your husband's life and his home a peaceful and happy one and to be of use to him and to be a comfort to him in every possible way.' It was difficult to create a home atmosphere in the musty old *Schloss* allocated to the young couple, which had not been lived in for years and where – in a gloomy room through which the Princess had to pass to reach her bedroom – Frederic the Great had died. Astonished to discover that there was no bath in the *Schloss,* she immediately ordered one. The Grand Master of her household, Count Redern, objected: 'I do not think His Majesty will agree to alterations – he sets a high value on the ancient splendours of the *Schloss.*' 'You must agree, Count,' Vicky retorted sharply, 'that the *Schloss* is almost medieval in its internal arrangements. At home, at Windsor, the castle is just as old but all our living-rooms have been modernized.'

Redern was right. Old King William I would not hear of a bath being installed. Then he repented, recalled Redern and ordered a stone bath to be put in one of the rooms adjoining the Princess's suite, but no hot or cold water system was laid on. Water had to be brought in buckets; the bath, placed on the floor without supports, rocked when the bather moved in it; and the floor of the room was icy cold. Fritz made a personal appeal to his grandfather and persuaded him to allow Vicky to have her way. She was delighted. Then one day, upon her return from a State function, she met the workmen carrying her new enamel bath out of the palace entrance, while others were busy removing the pipes. His Majesty had changed his unstable mind. Eventually the bath was reinstated for good.

Vicky caught cold soon after her arrival and sneezed while she was standing near old Queen Elizabeth's chair. A lady-in-waiting, one of the court martinets known as the 'Hallelujah Aunts' because of their austere piety, hissed into her ear: 'In Prussia, you do not sneeze in the presence of the sovereign!' Vicky spun round in astonishment and exclaimed: 'But I have a bad cold, Ma'am!' 'That makes no difference.' 'I'm sorry, Ma'am. I did not know. We don't have customs like that in our court at home.' Her hearers were scandalized at what was considered her impudence, as well as at her reference to England as her home.

Her mother-in-law, Princess Augusta, warned Vicky that the English character of her household was unfavourably commented upon at court, but Vicky tossed her head defiantly. She called her dogs and ponies by English names and told people whom she thought were broad-minded that in her opinion Prussia ought to adopt a form of government with a real parliament modelled on Westminster. Now that she was free to have guests of her own choice she followed her father's inclinations, thwarted by Victoria: she and Fritz invited artists and scientists to supper and enjoyed their lively and erudite conversation. The first words of the Princess to Professor Schelbach, who had taugh Fritz mathematics, were: 'I love mathematics, physics and chemistry.' This was an unusual remark for a lady to make in that century – let alone a Princess. Even Princes, as Victoria had remarked, rarely wished to learn and hear.

Inwardly, as Vicky confided years later to her daughter Sophie, she felt shy and uncomfortable. She always 'suffered very much from this malady', which all Victoria's daughters inherited from their parents. Vicky was pleasant with distinguished intellectual guests, whom she found congenial, but *gauche* in public; more and more she came to realize that she lacked social talent. 'The perfection of a hostess was the Empress Eugénie,' she once said, 'no one ever came up to that – with the exception of Bertie.'

Papa impressed upon Vicky that it was most important for her to establish a budget and make room in it for those 'uninvited guests – the extras'. He volunteered to look through her accounts. Mama demanded to be told the colour of Vicky's curtains, how each piece of furniture was placed in her rooms, etc. so that she could picture her everyday life. Both parents were insufferable. They would not let go. . . .

The royal parents' affection was now concentrated upon the last arrival, Beatrice; but even to look at her made the Queen melancholy as she remembered how fond of her Vicky had been.

Nevertheless, Beatrice was 'the new toy' in the nursery and the Queen found consolation in her company. She was spoiled as the first-born had been; she sat upon Vicky's little chair, tapping on the table where her eight brothers and sisters had played before her. 'She is a great darling.' She was fair and plump with round blue eyes and a gay disposition. (Her clothes do not sound very attractive. The Queen, describing a visit to Grandmama Kent at Frogmore with 'baby', told Vicky that Beatrice was dressed in a blue satin bonnet and a little black coat with ermine.) On her first birthday a table was decorated with a giant B in flowers surrounded by candles. Vicky sent her a woolly lamb and a brooch in the shape of a rose set in precious stones. Prince Albert sat her on his knee while he played the organ. He wrote to Baron Stockmar: 'Little Beatrice is an extremely attractive, pretty, intelligent child – indeed the most amusing baby we have had.' He recounted all her sayings in his weekly letter to Vicky.

Only three months after Vicky's marriage the Queen was fretting because there were as yet no signs of an heir, and she began to plan a visit to Germany. Both she and Albert longed to see their eldest daughter and to visit her and Fritz in their little Gothic castle of Babelsberg near Potsdam, which they used as their summer residence. Vicky had set about planting rare trees in the gardens and English chintzes in the rooms.

When the royal parents arrived they were delighted to see the young couple looking so happy and – by then – signs that a grandchild was on the way. Victoria felt a little young to be a grandmother at thirty-nine but she began to prepare for her new role with her customary mixture of zeal, meticulousness and meddlesomeness, determined that everything to do with the confinement would be English, for 'they can't manage these things so well in Germany'. Vicky's physician, Dr Wegner, would have to go over to Windsor to be vetted. This naturally caused resentment in Berlin. The nurse and the layette would be provided from England too and, of course, chloroform would have to be administered during labour.

The Queen clasped Vicky to her heart and 'felt she was her own again'. Papa played duets with her on the piano. They visited the royal palaces; the Queen expressed a preference for Sans Souci and observed that Queen Louise's rooms in the *Schloss* looked all 'sad and cheerless for the colour is gone out of everything and the whole is oldfashioned'. Even the present king's rooms she found 'not very comfortable'.

Albert's birthday was celebrated during their visit. The Queen presented him with a life-size picture of Beatrice by Horsley, photographic views of Gotha specially taken for her by a Mr Bedford, and a paperweight of Balmoral granite and deer's teeth designed by Vicky, who had ordered a birthday cake 'with as many lights as Albert numbered years, which is the Prussian custom' – as yet unknown in England. All the children had written letters for 'this dear day'.

'Stockmar promises to watch over our precious child,' the Queen noted with relief before her tearful departure. Albert went to Coburg to revisit the scenes of his childhood – always a sad mistake when years have elapsed, blurring and transmuting memories, relatives have died and childhood companions grown up and changed; he complained bitterly, he who had pronounced himself to be a 'true Coburger and German', that now he felt 'like a complete stranger'. The sadness produced by this realization, Vicky's absence from home and overwork combined to sap his physical and moral energy. He was declining and gradually losing the will to live. The vacuum left by the departure of his favourite daughter and closest companion played an important role which historians appear to have overlooked. Many people, including the Queen, laid much of the blame for Albert's premature death on wayward Bertie, but the main, unconscious cause was in Berlin.

The Queen, engaged with Parliament and politics, was frantic not to be able to be present at her daughter's first confinement; she now began to realize how unpleasant it was to have one's married children living abroad. William ('Willy', as he was called in the family), the future Kaiser Wilhelm II, was born on 27 January 1859, after a difficult labour during which his left arm was permanently damaged. This planted the first seeds of Vicky's prejudice against German doctors, which was to have disastrous consequences in later years. At the news of Willy's birth, Prince Arthur ran round Windsor Castle shouting: 'I am an uncle! I am an uncle!' as if some grand title had been conferred upon him. When an order was issued to all the 'royal children in the schoolroom', eleven-year-old Louise cried out: 'We are not "royal children", we are uncles and aunts.' They had not been given details about the birth of their nephew for, as the Queen observed, 'these things are not proper to be told to children, as it initiates them into things which they ought not to know of till they are older'.

She was horrified to hear that Willy's christening, in accordance with German custom, was to take place soon, with Vicky reclining on a *sofa* in a *dressing gown*. Could she not postpone the ceremony and hold it in the more becoming English way? 'No,' Vicky replied firmly, for once prepared to bow to local usage. 'What would you say if a German Princess in England wished to adhere to *her* customs?' For the moment the Queen was silenced, although she did not think it was 'quite the thing' for Vicky to write to her 'Dear Mama' so peremptorily.

By this time – 1859 – Alice had blossomed into a sprightly girl of sixteen. 'Dear, good Alice has improved so much,' the Queen wrote to Vicky. 'She has a sweet temper, is industrious, and has made good progress. She takes lessons of an evening with papa, who says she is very attentive, whereas Bertie is stupid and inattentive.' Prince Hohenlohe, who had a lively conversation with Alice in this year found her 'very well-informed for her age, quick and gay, and her face, in spite of a long nose, which she herself regards as a calamity, is very pretty'.

At times, Alice felt like a bird in a gilded cage and she longed to spread her wings. What fun it was to leave the Palace in May for an overnight visit to the newly built Royal Pavilion at Aldershot, the work of dear Papa! Mrs Stanley accompanied the Princesses and remarked: 'Princess Alice was forever in and out of our room – very affectionate – I went last night into their bedroom, saw Princess Helena sound asleep in her little camp bed, her little brown capless head looking rather nice on the white pillow. Great was Princess Alice's indignation at her having selected the largest bed for herself. Indeed, she threatened to wake up the child and make her change.'

Alice, like her other sisters, was taught to ply her needle from an early age and now she joined the Queen and Lady Caroline Barrington in making short stripes for the valances of a set of curtains to be sent as a present to Vicky for her new drawing-room. The Persian pattern, traced in black, filled with yellow, blue and red, on coarse canvas, was thought to be very smart.

Alice accompanied her mother on a visit to Netley Hospital, where the Queen had inspected the Crimean wounded with Vicky. The Queen had made some pertinent comments at the time and it had been vastly improved. 'Oh, to be able to devote myself to the poor and sick!' the Queen exclaimed, during one of her frequent bouts of self-delusion. Alice, walking quietly at her side, took in everything. She was to make good use of all she saw, in very different circumstances, a few years later.

Vicky paid a visit to England in the summer of 1859, leaving Willy behind; it was feared that he was too frail to stand the Channel crossing, even in the relative comfort, for the times, of the royal yacht *Victoria and Albert*. Vicky herself was advised by mama to take a lump of sugar with a few drops of chloroform on it to prevent seasickness. A touching family reunion took place upon her arrival. Dear Osborne – dear Windsor – dear England – dearest family who nearly choked her with their affection!

Albert was pleased with Vicky. She had acquired more poise since her marriage, he thought, although she was still childlike in many ways. They discussed the war pending between France and Sardinia and Austria. Vicky was full of military ardour. On a more personal level she confided her 'in-law' problems to her parents. The Queen sympathized with her daughter. She knew what it felt like to 'be on pins and needles with the family,' she said; she had scarcely been on speaking terms with the members of her family in her childhood, because of her mother's squabbles with William IV, of whom she disapproved. Victoria had been between 'two fires, trying to be civil and then scolded at home afterwards. Oh, it was dreadful! That was what had given her such a horror of Windsor, which constantly reminded her of all that early domestic friction . . . such as the dinner-party at which King William IV had admonished her mother and she had burst into tears. . . .'

Yet, but – Vicky reminded the Queen gently – Victoria had been an innocent, uninvolved child. In-law trouble was very different; there was no growing out of it. Victoria seemed surprised. She had always believed that Augusta was so pleasant. 'You have never lived near her,' Vicky said. Augusta was an embittered woman who, in the absence of her husband's love, sought to dominate him. She was so restless, it was exhausting to be with her for any length of time. and she was always fault-finding. Vicky could never do anything right in her eyes.

Albert remarked that one should try to be conciliatory in an alien milieu, but his advice went unheeded. The Queen was fully aware that Vicky, too, could be trying and obstinate; she had not been an easy child to bring up. 'Oh yes, I know I was a plague to you – I never thought you would miss me so much,' Vicky admitted candidly.

In a letter to Fritz Vicky described Beatrice as '*à croquer* ... anything as sweet, apart from our little one, I really have never seen. She looks like a little fairy ... so clever and amusing, by far the prettiest of us all.' Beatrice supped with the family and enlivened them all by reciting little pieces of nursery rhymes: 'Twinkle, twinkle, little star' – 'Little Miss Muffet' – 'Humpty Dumpty' and others, 'speaking remarkably plainly and nicely,' wrote Mrs Stanley, 'but showing a considerable degree of character in her choice of the poems and her claiming of the reward (biscuits) for repeating them. She is a most amusing little dot, all the more so for being generally a little naughty.' 'Baby musn't have this,' the Queen scolded, as Beatrice stretched a chubby hand towards a forbidden dish. 'But she likes it, my dear,' Beatrice replied in her mimic grown-up voice that never failed to provoke mirth – and how the infant Princess knew it! 'Darling Beatrice' also came to lunch *en famille* for the first time, in short clothes, with 'darling little stockings and pink satin shoes ... it was the dress she wore at Vicky's wedding, only shortened,' wrote her governess. (No wonder the thrifty Queen was able to leave a handsome nest-egg for her children when she died.)

The Queen, on her side, confided some of her troubles to Vicky. Bertie, at the age of eighteen, was still so immature, she complained. He read novels bought at railway stations, but then most young people did so nowadays. He really should be married off to a pretty Princess ('He would never marry a plain one.') Marriage might help to 'settle' him. Could not Vicky help to find one among the German princesses? She was at the centre of the eligible girls available. Vicky promised her anxious parents that she would make inquiries upon her return to Berlin, for she was devoted to Bertie and eager to make him happy. Once married, he would no longer have to live under his parents' roof and that would make life much easier for them all.

Then there was Alice's matrimonial future to think of, although she was still only sixteen. Vicky found her very elegant, well dressed and coiffed, 'quite a young lady'. What about the Prince of Orange for her? The Queen wondered. There had been rumours about his flightiness, so perhaps it would be wiser to ask him over to Windsor to be 'inspected' at close quarters. Vicky remarked that he was said to be very plain. 'Beauty I don't want,' the Queen replied, 'though I should be glad of it when it was there, but a nice, manly, sensible, healthy, gentlemanlike appearance is essential.' After Vicky had left the Queen wrote to the Queen of Holland. Both Queens had Princesses Helena and Alice in mind for 'Citron', as the Prince of Orange was called. When this came to Alice's sharp ears she told Lady Ely 'she should die no other death than her sister being preferred to her and that she wanted to be Queen of Holland'. But Mme Bülow thought that Citron was thoroughly ungentlemanlike and low-living. 'He has no sense of what is decent and proper, and unless he mends very much I do not think it would be safe for the little duck Alice to marry him, seeing what a ragamuffin he is. His father was one too and the *existence manquée* of his mother in consequence!'

Citron was invited to Windsor in February 1860, but he was so shy that he turned his back on Princess Alice. The Duchess of Cumberland took him to the ballet and remarked that he 'didn't look much and was quite quiet'. 'Can't you hear her saying this?' Lord Clarendon wrote to the Duchess of Manchester, 'with a look of surprise as if she had expected him to jump out of the box on to the stage!'

Alice was ripe for any prince who might be presented to her. In May 1860 Lord Clarendon wrote to the Duchess of Manchester:

Our little friend Alice is so full of lark that she admits she doesn't know what to do with herself. Last night, she said to my wife: 'Now let's off to your house and take the girls by surprise,' so, after ascertaining that the Queen had given permission, Lady

Barrington had to bring her home, when she told the servant merely to 'show her the way to the young ladies' room and not to announce her'; You may imagine their surprise just as they were about to dress for dinner and there she would remain till long after the time she was due at home. She was only prevented from coming to me by the girls telling her I was in my dressing-gown and so she managed to tell us all her little amourettes and discussed quite seriously whether it would not do for her to marry the royal boy who was quite ready for it. Of course she made us swear never to mention it as she probably has done to all the other people she makes similar communications to. She said she had been to St George's Chapel, Windsor, for the purpose of not going to the royal seat but by herself among the public, as it was such fun sitting *between anybody*.

By the following month a more suitable young man than Citron was being discussed. Uncle Leopold – that inveterate and able matchmaker – had brought Prince Louis of Hesse over to Windsor for an inspection by the royal parents, the pretext being the races at Ascot. Louis hailed from the sleepy, music-loving little town of Darmstadt, capital of the small German state of Hesse-Darmstadt. He was handsome, Protestant, and pure. On the debit side, he did not have much money and Alice would never be a queen, as Vicky had every chance of becoming one day, but he would no doubt make her happy. In June, Alice confided her feelings to her great friend Constance (Lord Clarendon's daughter) during a two-hour drive:

She talked almost exclusively of her anxieties and sufferings from her excessive love for Prince Louis of Hesse-Darmstadt. He is now the 'one being', the only man she ever did, shall, can or will love and Mama knows from *his* mother that she is the only girl he could ever bring himself to marry, so we expect it all to be arranged when we go abroad in September. She is just like a bird in a cage, beating its wings against the bars and if she could get out, wouldn't she go it! It is lucky for her that she has not the same liberty as her stout cousin princess Mary of Cambridge . . .

A visit to Coburg in September 1860 took in Berlin, a visit to Vicky and the presentation of 'that sweet child Willy' to his fond grandmother. His deformed arm was not alluded to in the Queen's journal. Vicky was still trying to find a cure. The poor little boy was subjected to all manner of tortuous treatments in an effort to develop the maimed limb.

Vicky now had a daughter: Charlotte was born in 1860, the year after Willy, but Vicky did not have many close friends and often felt lonely. She took Miss Bulteel aside at Coburg and begged her to pay her a long visit in Berlin although she knew it would make her Prussian household frantically jealous. She said that she so wished for a walk sometimes in Berlin, where she was shut up from October to May. 'Sometimes I can not help sitting down to cry, and I wish I could walk up and down the walls like a fly.'

In Coburg Prince Albert walked with his brother through their old childhood haunts; suddenly he broke down and exclaimed prophetically that he would never see his native land again.

As soon as Vicky returned to Berlin from the family visit to Coburg, she began to make inquiries about Prince Louis of Hesse as a possible fiancé for Alice. Nobody had a word to say against this rather undistinguished young man, so she was able to forward a favourable report to Windsor. Letters were exchanged between the respective future in-laws and the Prince was formally invited to England in November to make his proposal.

Albert told Louis on their return from a visit to Aldershot in November 1860 that it had been arranged that he should be given the opportunity to speak to Alice after dinner. It was the Queen who, becoming agitated as usual, had pressed Albert to bring matters to a head. She could not bear the uncertainty any longer. 'Dear Papa,' she wrote to Vicky plaintively, 'in his very quiet way, thought he might wait till today or tomorrow, as if people violently in love could wait for a stated time.' Nevertheless a 'time' had to be settled, since otherwise it would not have been proper for the two young people to be together alone. The contrived tête-à-tête must have been embarrassing for all concerned. After dinner, Louis and Alice purposefully moved towards the fire that useful winter focus for sentimental scenes – and the alerted guests melted away as if by enchantment, while the Queen gaily chattered from a position where she could watch their progress. After a suitable interval she made for the door, the guests fell back on either side of her like the waves of the Red Sea and she brushed past Alice, who whispered to her that she had received a proposal from Louis and begged for her mother's blessing. The Queen squeezed her hand and said: 'Certainly', and that she would summon Louis to her room later. She took up her crochet to calm her nerves and then wrote a letter to her great friend and confidante Augusta.

A characteristically Victorian scene then took place: Albert asked Louis to his study while Alice simultaneously received a summons from Mama. She was, the Queen observed ambiguously, 'agitated but quiet'. Then a message came from Papa's study, where the Queen and Alice repaired for 'joyous tears' and mutual congratulations. Louis was so overcome by emotion that he was unable to say a word. He seemed quite overpowered, the royal parents remarked. Alice was a good deal upset too but (as usual) 'very quiet and sensible and reasonable'. It was decided that Louis would stay in England until Christmas and that the wedding must not take place before another year; Everybody hoped that Parliament would vote the proposed dowry of £30,000 and the annuity of £6,000 without a murmur. The Queen was positive that charming, persuasive Mr Disraeli would see to that . . .

The Queen was quite taken with Louis, whom she found 'so natural and unaffected, so quickwitted and he takes an interest in everything and I think him so goodlooking'. (His teeth, however, were bad, so by royal command were taken care of by Sir James Clark and Dr Saunders.) He was 'quite shy and blushing and bashful when one spoke to him alone about Alice'. The young couple seem to have had more opportunities to be together than Fritz and Vicky during their engagement, but Mama always hovered watchfully in the background. Louis and Alice went walking in the gardens – with a chaperone – and when, as frequently happened, it was wet, they sat looking at picture-books in the Queen's room. There was already a steadily mounting collection of albums of sketches, daguerreotypes and family photographs all carefully labelled and captioned by the Queen and Prince Albert. The latter could not resist the heaven-sent opportunity of Louis's visit to 'talk to him a little about German politics which will, I am sure, be very useful'. 'Oh!' exclaimed the Queen, if only our darling Lenchen is as lucky – it would be *so* nice if she could settle in England.' That was the worst part of a daughter's destiny: she was obliged to leave home, unlike the boys, who came back to it.

The young people behaved as people in love were expected to in that sentimental age: Alice told her friend Constance that when she parted from Louis they exchanged pocket-handkerchiefs which were quite in a sop with their tears and 'she wears night and day a little miniature of him tied with a bit of velvet which she fears won't last as she is always rubbing it. If her august parents try to make her wait for another year, she will be off to Darmstadt or Potsdam on her own hook.'

Vicky was delighted to hear that Alice's match had been settled. Of course, as she wrote a little sanctimoniously to her mother: 'Her position won't be as fine as mine, but she will have more freedom.' She would also be living fairly near, so that they could visit each other informally without the fuss that was made at the Prussian court whenever Vicky planned to visit 'home'.

'Oh, if you and Fritz and the children were only with us!' lamented the Queen on New Year's Day 1861, when Vicky's 'fine position' moved a step higher upon the death of the ninety-year-old King Frederick William, father of her father-in-law. Vicky was now the Crown Princess, but the coronation of her father-in-law, King William I, did not take place until October. Fritz was so taken up by his military duties, councils, audiences, the sorting of the late King's papers, that he did not breakfast or take walks or drives with Vicky any more. 'We might as well not be married at all,' she complained bitterly.

At the end of the winter the Duchess of Kent fell seriously ill.

Alice tripped across to Frogmore from Windsor Castle almost every day to play the piano to the old lady, who was approaching her seventy-fifth birthday. There was something very sweet and consoling about Princess Alice; she had the inborn 'nurse's touch' that calmed and soothed. The sick, the unhappy felt easier in her presence.

The Queen could hardly believe the doctors when they warned her that the Duchess's end was approaching, but she immediately went over to sleep at Frogmore. Lady Augusta Bruce described how one night the Queen 'stole downstairs in her white dressing-gown and knelt beside the Duchess, kissing her hand and whispering "Mama" so lovingly and earnestly, as if the sound must rouse her'.

When the end came on 15 March the Queen gave way to such a paroxysm of grief that Albert was alarmed. 'Go and comfort Mama,' he bade Alice, knowing that she was the comforter *par excellence*; his role, he believed, was to try and control Victoria's overflow of feelings, as he had done with a great deal of success in many different circumstances since their marriage.

The Queen could not face her family, and for some weeks took breakfast and lunch alone in her room. The bright presence of Beatrice consoled her a little. 9 April, she noted in her diary, 'was dear little Beatrice's birthday'. (She was four years old.) The Queen was delighted that she continually spoke of her Grandmama, 'how she is in heaven, but hopes she will return. She is a most darling, engaging child.' On 10 April the Queen lunched for the first time since the Duchess's death with her elder daughters. She could not bear the presence of her boisterous sons. Every day she paid a visit to the mausoleum at Frogmore, which had been designed by Albert at the Duchess's own request and was almost completed at the time of her death.

Vicky came over for the funeral and stayed on. The Queen rebuked her for appearing to be 'in such very high spirits', and poor Bertie – who could never do anything right – gave great offence by not crying when he arrived from Cambridge in

April. ('If he had cried, he would probably have been reproached for increasing his mother's grief,' observed Lord Clarendon.) Vicky tried to improve relations between her mother and Bertie; she was actively concocting a meeting between him and the beautiful Princess Alexandra of Denmark, who had been suggested as a possible bride by Walpurga, Countess Hohenthal, Vicky's lady-in-waiting.

In August 1861 the Queen had rallied sufficiently to undertake a visit to Ireland with Albert, Alice, Alfred and Helena, to see how Bertie was acquitting himself of his military duties there. Albert found, as he had feared, that the officers were too keen on sport and relaxation. German officers were much more earnest.

Ireland had not been favoured with royal visits; the family never took to it as they did to Scotland, despite Lady Augusta Bruce's repeated attempts to convert them. Alice, however, thought that Killarney was the most beautiful place she had ever seen. During their visit Albert found time to reply to a letter dictated to him at home by Beatrice. 'My darling little Baby,' he replied to her on broad, black-edged mourning notepaper, 'thank you for your delightful letter.' He went on to describe the mountain scenery and to tell her to eat well in the bracing air of Balmoral where they would soon be reunited, and he signed himself: 'Your ever loving Papa.'

The royal parents did not seem to understand Louise so well as their other daughters. 'Louise was so pleased to be taken a little notice of,' wrote Lady Augusta when the warm Irish commented on the Princess's attractiveness, for she was the most striking of the sisters. As for Helena, who was going through a pious phase, she was pleased to observe Alice absorbed in a sermon on the theme 'Prepare to meet Thy God.'

Upon their return to Windsor the Queen indulged in a fresh bout of grief over her mother's death, while Albert pursued his strenuous self-appointed round of duties to such an extreme that Victoria complained to Uncle Leopold that she saw very little of him during the day. The children did not provide her with the company she needed, she missed a woman's society and sympathy, but she felt bound to add that 'dear, good Alice is full of intense tenderness, affection and distress for me'. She must be allowed to come over frequently from Darmstadt after her marriage, and spend long periods with Mama who, the doctors all agreed, should not attempt to make too much effort. Long conversations, loud talking of many people together, she still could not stand.

The Queen looked at Prince Louis of Hesse with a kindly eye when he visited Balmoral later in the year, and Albert began putting arrangements in hand for the wedding, rejecting the first designs submitted by Honiton for the bridal veil. He wanted the pattern to be more symbolic. Victoria wrote to Uncle Leopold that she found Louis 'good, amiable, honest, warm-hearted, high-principled and unassuming'. Not an exciting list of qualities, perhaps, but it suited the Queen's purpose. 'I cannot say what happiness and comfort it is to me . . . I feel my dear child will first of all have a peaceful, quiet, happy home without difficulties and, secondly, that she will not be entirely cut off from us and monopolized as our poor Vicky is.' Alice, she added, 'though radiant with joy and much in love, is as quiet and sensible as possible'.

While Alice's romance was progressing at Balmoral, Bertie was – more or less graciously – submitting to Vicky's matrimonial scheme for him in Germany, where a confrontation with Princess Alexandra had been planned in the course of an allegedly casual sightseeing tour of Speyer Cathedral. Vicky, spying from a distance, on the pretext of looking at frescoes with the Bishop, noted every detail of the encounter with the meticulousness of a paid detective: 'The young couple exchanged photographs, they shook hands twice the second time. . . .' Although Bertie found the Princess's forehead too low and her nose too long, he pronounced himself pleased with the proposed marriage. The Queen could not be grateful enough to Vicky and dear Fritz for 'the well-organized, tactful and suitable manner in which they had managed the delicate affair'. She did not, however, believe that Bertie was or ever could be really in love.

Vicky, mission accomplished, turned her attention to designing Augusta's coronation robes and the dresses and trains of all the court ladies to be worn on 19 October 1861. This feminine pastime did not deter her from forming firm views about politics. Lord Clarendon, who assisted at the coronation of William I, was astonished by Vicky's knowledge of the internal and foreign policy of Prussia and of the duties of a constitutional king. Both she and Fritz were shattered by the King's reactionary coronation speech, in which he proclaimed the archaic belief that he had received the crown from the hand of God. As Albert wisely commented: 'The days are past when a single man can expect millions of educated, thoughtful people to trust their entire welfare and existence to the judgment and hands of one man, be he personally ever so excellent, be he more than a monarch by the grace of God, yes, even an angel descended from heaven!'

Meanwhile, in England, an avalanche of troubles preceded the final tragedy in the royal household in that fateful year of 1861: Prince Leopold who was haemophilic had had a bleeding attack and was sent to the South of France to recuperate. Then Victoria's and Albert's cousin, King Pedro V of Portugal, upon whom Albert centred his hopes for the 'restoration of a nation that had fallen very low', died of typhoid fever while his two younger sons were on their way home after a visit to Windsor. This shook Prince Albert deeply.

On 12 November 1861 Albert received a letter from Baron Stockmar warning him that there was a rumour going round Europe to the effect that twenty-year-old Bertie was having an affair with an actress. The Queen hinted in a letter to Vicky that Papa had had 'dreadful news – but don't ask me what it is'. For four days Albert ate alone in his room, pondering what to do. What if the news leaked as far as Copenhagen? Prince and Princess Christian, Alexandra's parents, were almost as strait-laced as Albert and Victoria.

Albert sent his erring son a letter of reproach, followed up a fortnight later by a personal visit to Cambridge for a heart-to-heart talk. This was soon after his inspection of the new Staff College at Sandhurst in pouring rain, during which he got wet through. He developed rheumatic pains, was sleeping badly, felt shocked and exhausted. He had reached the end of his nerve, his convictions, his motivation. He shuffled from room to room in his dressing-gown at Windsor Castle, pale, nervous, restless. His last work was to revise and tone down a truculently worded despatch to the United States on the *Trent* episode. 'It is too much – you must tell the Ministers,' he finally murmured, too weary to lift his pen. Gastric fever was diagnosed, but the Queen could not believe that he was dangerously ill. 'Her little knowledge of nursing,' remarked Lady Augusta Bruce acidly, 'made her rather not the best nurse in the world.'

Albert appeared to be quite himself when she went in to see him on the evening of 5 December, after Alice had been reading to him. 'He was most dear and affectionate when I went in with little Beatrice whom he kissed. He quite laughed at some of her new French verses which I made her repeat. Then he held her little hand in his for some time and she stood looking at him. He then dozed off, when I left, not to disturb him.' The next day he was up, but exhausted, due to overwork and worry. The Queen could not think of Bertie without shuddering, for she blamed him, first and foremost, for Albert's illness.

Finally, Albert chose to lie down in the Blue Room, where George IV and William IV had died. Alice tiptoed in and he asked her to read to him, then to play the piano. She wrote to Berlin about her father's illness. 'What did you tell Vicky?' he wanted to know. 'That you are very ill,' she said, with tears in her eyes. He looked at her steadily. 'You did wrong. You should have told her I was dying,' he whispered. Frightened, Alice sent off a telegram begging Vicky to come, but she was pregnant and the doctors insisted that her health was not up to a journey in winter. On 13 December Alice took it upon herself to send a telegram summoning Bertie from Cambridge. 'Suddenly Princess Alice seemed to be a different creature,' wrote Lady Augusta.

Still the Queen refused to believe that the end was near. It was unthinkable. Albert ... why, he was only forty-two! He would, he *must* rally ... he was not as ill as he imagined. Why did he seem so ready to believe that he was seriously ill? The doctors had to break the news to her. Albert's short, hectic life was drawing to its premature close. They tried to keep the Princesses from the patient's room for fear of infection, so Alice waited patiently by the door while Albert called out her name so often.

At 9.30 p.m. on 14 December the Queen, who had been kneeling grief-stricken by her husband's bedside for hours, left the room for a few moments, overcome by emotion, to talk to the Dean of Westminster. Alice turned to comfort Helena, then she glanced at the bed and whispered to Lady Augusta: 'That is the death rattle', and ran to warn her mother. The Queen hurried back and they both knelt on either side of Albert with the other children. The end came, quietly, at 10.50 p.m.

The Queen fell upon her husband's body, calling him by every endearing name, and then sank into the arms of Alice and Lady Augusta, who led or half-carried her to the adjoining room, where she lay on the sofa. Then the Queen drew herself up, summoned her children round her to clasp them to her heart and assure them that she would endeavour, if she lived, to live for them and her duty and to appeal to them 'from henceforth to seek to walk in the footsteps of him whom God has taken to Himself'. Then she broke down and wept and talked to Alice for the rest of the night.

Louise was not told about her father's death until early next morning. 'Oh, why did not God take me? I am so stupid and useless!' exclaimed the poor child.

Alice had her bed moved in next to the Queen's in a closet near the Blue Room. She wondered, she said later, how she and her mother came through the ordeal intact. Perhaps the most moving words that Victoria ever uttered were the heartfelt cry: 'There is nobody to call me Victoria now!' She was incapable of attending to business. The doctors, fearing for her reason, advised her to leave for Osborne. But first she drove with Alice to Frogmore and walked round to select a spot for the mausoleum – for Albert and later – she hoped it would be soon – for herself.

Alice took her mother's orders, carried messages between her and her ministers and altogether acted with great presence of mind, zeal and intelligence where all was consternation and confusion. 'There is not such a girl in a thousand,' wrote Lord Clarendon enthusiastically, 'I never met one who, at her age – seventeen – has such sound principles, so great judgment and such knowledge of the world, yet she has been boxed up in a gilt cage all her life and has not had the advantage of interchanging ideas as other girls have.'

Little Beatrice, dressed in mourning from top to toe, was brought down from the nursery every morning to see her distracted Mama, who could bear to see only her and Alice. 'I had such a funny thought today, just for my own amusement,' Beatrice confided to Lady Augusta, 'but it turned out an improper thought so I would not let it think.' 'No doubt' wrote Lady Augusta, 'the poor child was going to play, or some such diversion which didn't suit a house in mourning.'

Uncle Leopold offered guidance, but the Queen wrote firmly: 'I am determined that no one person, may he be ever so good, ever so devoted, is to lead or guide or dictate to me! No human power will make me swerve from what *he* decided and wished, and I look to you to support and help me in this and apply this, particularly as regards our children.'

# *Section III*

# *Divided Loyalties (1862-71)*

THE royal family, immured within the thick walls of Windsor Castle, or concealed at Osborne behind the shrubs and trees so lovingly planted by the Prince Consort, was stricken with a grief which the general public could not begin to understand. How could they know that the Queen's life and thoughts depended entirely on Albert.

My own ambition was to please him, to be worthy of him. The burdens, worries and difficulties of my position, which never had an attraction for me, were made bearable through his goodness, his wisdom, his guidance; one has to thank him, and him alone, for all that is done. He supervised the children's education, he managed our household and home, in short he was the life and soul of everything. And moreover the most loving, tender husband, the most delightful and instructing companion there has ever been. As for me, I depended on him body and soul. And now I am left alone with my poor children . . .

Vicky rushed over to Osborne as soon as her health permitted, to try and calm her mother, although she herself was in the depths of despair, having lost 'the best counsellor I ever had'. She wept copiously over mementoes, including a strand of her father's hair. At Osborne she found 'everything so different – everyone lives for himself and is depressed and sad'.

Darling mama, it is so touching to see her. She looks so young and pretty with her white cap and widow's weeds. [Little Beatrice called her mother's mourning cap 'the sad cap'.] She always sleeps with papa's coat over her and his dear red dressing-gown beside her, and some of his clothes on the bed. Poor mama has to go to bed, has to get up alone—for ever. She was as much in love with papa as though she had married him yesterday. Mama had so longed for another child. The central point is missing. We wander round like sheep without a shepherd.

What Vicky was delicately touching upon was the Queen's sexual solitude and loss. She realized that her mother was, on her own account, a woman of violent emotions. Her reference to the longing for another child was a veiled allusion to the physical presence by her side in bed which was denied to her at a difficult age, forty-two, in the life of a passionate woman. The Queen wrote frankly that she was being 'driven mad with desire and longing'. Only Vicky could understand and sympathize with that intimate aspect of her mother's widowhood. Alice – loving, tender Alice – probably guessed but as yet had no experience of the close physical contacts of married life. She was looking so thin and worn after all she had been through; her fiancé, Prince Louis of Hesse, feared that the engagement might be broken off, but there was no question of that. The Queen pulled herself together sufficiently to declare that both Alice's and Bertie's weddings would take place as and when planned: Alice's in 1862, Bertie's in the following year. That was what Albert would have wished, what he had arranged.

The Queen confided to Augusta, who had written to her sympathetically, and who *understood*: 'How weak and shaken I feel with my poor vitality wasting gradually away.' The children were good and loving but she did not find their company the same and it was no support. 'I can only have two with me at a time and I still take my meals in my own room.'

Lord Tennyson, who had written some 'glorious lines' for the Queen – she much admired his *In Memoriam* – was invited to Osborne in April. He found the Queen's face 'beautiful – not the least like her portraits. She talked of all things in heaven and earth, laughed heartily at many things that were said, but shades of pain and sadness passed over a face that sometimes seemed all one smile. Princess Alice joined pleasantly in the conversation. One feels that the Queen is a woman to live and die for.' The poet had seized on the intangible quality which Victoria's daughters, in their different ways, felt so keenly all their lives in their relations with their mother. There was a strength, a power, a mesmeric quality about Victoria which emanates from great leaders of men, and, at another level, from 'stars'. It is the intangible quality that is capable of bringing out devotion and fanatical allegiance. Severe, nervous, excitable, hot-tempered, selfish as she could be on occasion, these defects were passing clouds upon an infinite horizon that was shot through with a peculiar radiance. That was what made the Queen's subjects, from her courtiers to her children, kiss her plump, dimpled little hand with reverence, respect and love.

Preparations soon began to be put in hand for Alice's wedding in July 1862 which, in view of the recent bereavement in the family, was to be held in absolute privacy. But this did not stop the mother of one of the bridesmaids from arranging most expensive presents.

> What do you think of the Duchess of Buccleuch [Lord Clarendon wrote to the Duchess of Manchester] having taken upon herself, without any consultation with the mothers of other bridesmaids, to send on the part of the latter a list of presents to Princess Alice, who selected a gilt breakfast service? This, the Duchess of Buccleuch says, she will have selected and thinks that £50 from each bridesmaid will be enough. I call this very cool; in the first place £50 is a great deal more than need be given for young ladies who have no intimacy with Princess Alice and it is great want of courtesy of the Duchess not to mention the matter previously to the mothers, one or two of whom had just as good a right as her to put themselves forward.

A few days later, the gossip-mongering Lord added that Princess Alice had intimated to Lord Methuen that they should all make separate presents, 'a dodge, of course, to get them more valuable. With respect to the bridesmaids, Lady Mount Edgecumbe will only give £25 and Lady Elgin £30.'

Prince Louis of Hesse arrived at Osborne, overjoyed at the prospect of his marriage, but the Queen eyed him a little more critically than before. She detected 'a lack of refinement in him' and decreed that he must not bring any of his young officer friends into Alice's society and intimacy, 'for that would be most dangerous'.

The Queen slept little the night before the wedding. Alice went in to see her on her wedding morning and received, as Vicky had done before her, a prayer-book similar to the one given to the Queen by her mother 'for her own happy marriage'. They breakfasted together and went to look at the dining-room, which had been converted into a chapel for the occasion referred to by the Queen as 'poor Alice's wedding – it was more like a funeral', because of her unshakeable morbidity.

A family picture by Winterhalter had been placed over the altar, the dominating figure being Albert with a hand outstretched as if in blessing. Only a few relatives had been invited: Louis's two brothers and his father, (his mother was dead), Ernest of Coburg, Prince Augustus of Saxe-Coburg, Princess Feodora Hohenlohe, the Queen's half-sister, Fritz. Vicky, who was expecting the birth of her second son, Henry, was once again prevented from assisting at an important family event.

Alice was dressed in her wedding gown with its flounces of Honiton lace and a corresponding pattern on her veil designed, as we have seen, by her late father; Helena, Louise and Beatrice also wore Honiton lace and veils designed by Albert, whose ghostly presence seemed to fill the quiet room, so that the uneasy guests did not quite know how to behave. The Queen was led in before them, flanked by her four sons, and she took her seat in an armchair close to the altar, so that nobody could see her face. The men were in black evening coats, white waistcoats and grey trousers, the ladies in grey or violet mourning dresses. Ernest of Saxe-Coburg gave the bride away during a service from which 'the worst coarsenesses had been purified' by the officiating Archbishop of York. He read it with tears running down his face, for he had lost his wife four years before. Alice was looking calm and beautiful, her voice very sweet. Affie, always emotional, 'sobbed all through the service and afterwards – dreadfully'. He was not alone. The Queen, too, broke down after she had embraced Alice and she retired upstairs to lunch alone with the bridal pair in the Horn Room, a repository of stags' antlers – trophies of many a Balmoral chase by her beloved Albert. It could hardly be called a festive occasion.

The only consolation for the Queen was that Alice promised to return 'home' in the autumn. Princess Charles, Alice's sister-in-law, jibbed at this; Victoria thought she was 'most unamiable'. Louis, however, was more understanding. Alice, dedicated to looking after dear Mama ever since the death of her father, took a firm stand with her mother-in-law. For the second time in her life, Victoria was determined to rule her daughter's roost and ride roughshod over in-laws.

The usual brief three-day honeymoon took place in Harcourt, the castellated mansion lent by Colonel and Lady Vernon, where Victoria and Albert had stayed when they were looking for a home on the Isle of Wight. The Queen drove over to tea on the second day, making a detour so as not to be seen by stray members of the public, and found the young bride looking 'serious and older than her husband', although he was in fact six years her senior. She reflected that it was not surprising, considering what poor, dear Alice had been through. Actually, Alice was extremely happy, but she said later that she was careful not to upset her mother, who had already written melodramatically in her diary that 'she felt as though a dagger had pierced her heart'. The Queen's attitude was common knowledge, and *Punch* published a full-page picture of the couple leaving Osborne in which Mr Punch himself bowed to the Princess, saying: 'Bless Your Royal Highness, I am glad we are not going to lose *you* . . .'

The journey to Darmstadt took five days. Bells and bands welcomed the bridal pair and a mounted escort drove them along the Wilhelminstrasse, the Rheinstrasse and into the Luisenplatz, dominated by a statue of the Grand Duke Louis I. The little town, with its white houses, avenues of chestnut trees and many gardens full of laburnums, looked most *gemütlich*.

Although it could not be compared to Berlin, where Vicky lived, Darmstadt was not a backwater. The art-loving Grand

Dukes encouraged music and literature. The grand ducal opera was famous for the technical perfection of its spectacles and the court theatre of the Baroque period mounted elaborate productions. It was well known to the English, who found it more economical to send their sons there to learn German than to the larger cities. Sir Charles Hallé had studied counterpoint there with the celebrated organist Rinck in 1836. He observed, in a letter home, that the seventy members of the court orchestra practised daily; it was almost their only occupation, 'For in quiet Darmstadt, nobody appeared to have anything in particular to do and nothing could exceed the stillness of its vast and regular streets'.

What kind of a family had Alice joined? Like most old families, its members had their little eccentricities and they were fairly stiff. Etiquette demanded that at a reception people stood around speechlessly and stared at the Princess. Alice had been carefully trained in the art of '*cerclé*-ing' (walking round a room and addressing pieces of furniture as if they were real people, switching frequently from English to German and French). But what could she do when real people answered her in monosyllables? She found public life exhausting and wearisome. Finally, she concentrated on the middle classes and the British families living in Darmstadt. But this was resented just as Vicky was criticized in Berlin for inviting scientists and *literati*. It was the same story over again, as Princess Marie of Battenberg (later Countess Milford-Haven) recounted in her *Memoirs*:

> She was a foreigner from distant England and as I soon remarked, did not fit in at all with the Darmstadt connections. I often felt sorry for her, she was so kind and so congenial to us, more than our Hesse relations, and in a different way.
>
> In our circle but little was known in those days of England and English customs; of its luxury and practical, solid enjoyment of life, and it was a long while before the really very great difference between the modest little house in Darmstadt and the castle at Windsor was appreciated.
>
> Alice was for me a most attractive and arresting personality,

her voice particularly, and her pretty mouth with its even teeth aroused my admiration, as did her clothes which had a distinctive and to me an unfamiliar style. I liked too the way in which her rooms were arranged and the real luxury she developed in the New Palace which she built, pleased me greatly. It interested me also to hear people speaking of the complete absence of court usages in her house and of her intercourse with people of the middle classes who were 'not eligible' for presentation. A new spirit came in with her which was not altogether in keeping with the old castle and its traditions . . . she dined at 2 p.m., for instance, instead of 4 p.m. which irked the Grand Duke.'

Princess Marie omitted to add that those 4 p.m. luncheons were formidable affairs taken in evening dress and consisted of innumerable courses. Tea was taken at 8 p.m. Alice could not accustom herself to the habit and began by eating luncheon in her own house at 2 p.m. and having tea at 4 p.m. as in England. Her first house, in the old part of the town, was very hot in the summer, but she drove through the parks and woods and eventually the Grand Duke had the pretty Renaissance-style hunting lodge of Kranichstein repaired for her use. It was situated only a few miles from the town, among low wooded hills.

'I do earnestly strive and cheerfully to do my duty in my new life and to do all that is right which is but doing what dear papa would have wished,' she wrote to her mother like a good child, but her entourage did not think that she was adapting herself enough to local customs. When the Queen asked Alice point-blank whether she was happy, she replied with characteristic delicacy and thoughtfulness:

You tell me to speak to you of my happiness, our happiness. You will understand the feeling which made me silent towards you, my own dear, bereaved mother, on that point, but you are unselfish and loving and can enter into my happiness though I could never have been the first to tell you how intense it is when it must draw the painful contrast between your past and the present existence. If I say I love my dear husband, that is scarcely enough; it is a love and esteem which increases daily, hourly, which he also shows me by such consideration, such tender, loving ways . . . What was life before to what it has become now? There is such blessed peace being at his side, being his wife. There is such a feeling of security and we too have a world of our own when we are together which *nothing* can touch or intrude upon. How he loves you, you know, and he will be a good son to you.

Dear, tactful Alice, bringing Mama into the picture of her domestic bliss!

The Queen insisted that Alice's first child should be born at Windsor, and there she went, well in advance of the event, and of Bertie's wedding in 1863. The daughter born to her was dutifully christened Victoria and eventually married her first cousin Prince Louis of Battenberg (later Marquess of Milford Haven), the brother of Princess Marie of Battenberg who so admired Alice upon her arrival at Darmstadt (although she became a little less enthusiastic as time went on).

At Bertie's wedding Alice wore a violet velvet dress trimmed with ermine which had belonged to the Duchess of Kent and which the latter had worn at Vicky's wedding. (Queen Victoria kept every single one of *her* dresses, labelled, to remind her of the occasions on which they had been worn.) Vicky came to the wedding, leading Willy by the hand. 'Such a dear, *good* little boy!' the Queen remarked approvingly. She had not seen him biting his Uncle Arthur in the leg and throwing the dirk from his Highland stocking during the wedding service. (A few months later, at Balmoral, the 'charming child' referred to his English relatives as *Stumpfnase*: 'pug-nosed'.)

The Queen retired after the service; Vicky and Alice tried to kiss away her tears but she would not be comforted. 'Here I sit, lonely and desolate,' she wrote in her journal, 'who so need love and kindness, while our two daughters have each their loving husbands and Bertie has taken his lovely, pure, sweet bride to Osborne.' She lunched alone with little Beatrice and afterwards drove to the mausoleum with Helena to pray. It was not surprising that when the painter W. Frith went to

Windsor to complete his picture of the wedding and asked six-year-old Beatrice whether she would not have liked to be one of the bridesmaids she replied: 'Oh no, I don't like weddings. I don't like weddings at all. I shall never be married. I shall stay with mother.' Weddings, as she had observed, were terribly tearful occasions.

As the Queen's eldest daughter, Vicky held a 'Drawing-room' on her behalf for the guests. There 'was not a hole to spare' in any of the palaces, she had been warned before her arrival, so would she please not bring any of the 'dear children' except Willy. Accommodation was always a problem on these royal occasions and it gave the Queen a headache to contemplate the succession of 'busy, dreadful days'. It was so necessary to have a daughter permanently around. In a year or two it would be Helena's turn to marry. She told Uncle Leopold: 'Lenchen is so useful and her whole character so well adapted to live in the house that unless Alice lives constantly with me, which she won't, I could not give her up without sinking under the weight of my desolation.' She decided that a man of good sense and high moral worth should be looked for. He need not belong to a reigning house. Indeed, it would make matters easier (for her own comfort) if he did not, so that he could take up residence at or near Windsor. 'A married daughter I must have living with me and must not be left to look about for help, and to have to make shift for the day, which is *too* dreadful.'

When Alice went back to Darmstadt in May the Queen lamented: 'It is a great loss and adds to my loneliness and desolation, she is a most dear, good child and there is not a thing I cannot tell her. She knows everything and is the best element one can have in the family. Louis, too, is quite excellent, *un coeur d'or*. He has no duties to perform at present, no house to live in . . . they ought to be with me as much as possible.' Upon her return, however, Alice wrote to her mother several times to explain why she could not go to England more frequently. Darmstadt was her husband's home and heritage; he had to take his seat in the Chamber, he should have done so before, had he not had to go to England. They both had to attend official entertainments and they were busy over their new house, which Alice had planned beyond the scope of her finances, so they would have to cut down on expenses. The Queen turned a deaf ear to this hint. She expected her daughters to manage on the annuities and dowries wheedled for them from the British Parliament, supplemented by her occasional presents: a couple of ponies for the children, a donkey, turkey pies and toys at Christmas, a weekly consignment of pastries from Swiss Cottage for both Vicky and Alice, made by the younger sisters, rose cuttings from the gardens, sometimes accompanied by one of the Queen's own gardeners.

Alice's letters home were full of trivia whcih delighted the Queen: the baby was sick crossing over to Antwerp and all over the new Indian shawl given to it by its grandmama; she had decorated a Christmas tree for the servants, buying their presents and hanging them herself; baby had a small tree of her own; she and Louis were giving a dinner-party in honour of the turkey pie sent from Windsor; they had had such a long frost and she had skated with the only other lady in Darmstadt who knew how, but was a poor performer; hearing of a poor woman who had just had a baby, she went out incognito with a servant, cooked for the woman and tidied the house 'being careful to keep the visit secret as Darmstadt society might think it a strange adventure for a princess', but she felt that she *must* occasionally get out of that cold circle of court people and see poverty and help it else her good feelings would dry up and her self constantly turn up like a bad sixpence. She thought frequently of her beloved Mama.

Other things have taken me from being constantly with you, but nothing has lessened my intense love for you and longing to quiet every pain which touches you and to fulfil, even in the distance, *his* request. Oh, darling Mama, were there words in which I could express to you how constantly my thoughts and prayers are yours, I would write them. The sympathies of our souls can only tell each other how tender my love and gratitude to you is and how vividly I feel every new trial or new thing with you and for you!

In the summer of 1863 a first clash took place between Crown Prince Fritz (encouraged by Vicky), his father King William and Chancellor Bismarck, who had become the power behind the throne. Soon after the publication of a royal decreee suppressing the liberty of the press, Fritz made a speech at Danzig against his father's decision and came forward openly as a leader of the liberals. The King threatened to compel his son to resign his military appointment, offices and place on the Council. Bismarck was more subtle and did not wish to provide the cause with a martyr.

Queen Victoria, feeling obliged to pour some oil upon the troubled family waters, wrote to King William 'entirely on my own impulse; the children have not made even the remotest suggestion and know nothing whatsoever about it'.

> Should a serious discord arise between you and Fritz owing to a yet more intensive opposition, it might end perhaps with a deplorable election and would also menace our daughter's happiness. My apprehensive heart seeks for ways and means of averting such a disaster. I do not want to discuss whether your son's opinions are right or wrong, but I can well imagine that the manner in which they were publicly announced must have been injurious to you. If Fritz has been very rash in this respect you might indulgently call to mind what daily experience teaches us, namely, that those very people who are used to repressing their own opinions in public often do not know the best way to act merely because of their inexperience.

She concluded by advising the King to give Fritz 'reasonable and necessary freedom . . . Let him decide his own mode of living, let him choose his own residence.' Like other propounders of good advice, she did not apply it to herself. Bertie was looked upon with disfavour for his mode of living, and the Queen greatly deplored the way in which he and Alix – who was growing pale and thin, she said – gadded about at parties and went to bed so late.

Bismarck posed hypocritically as a mediator between father and son and then felt free to proceed with his plans for the expansion of Prussia. He judged that the Crown Prince was not an important person; he had no real strength of character and no great following in the country. The known fact that he was assisted by his English wife sufficed to alienate him from the proud Prussian people. According to Bismarck, Fritz was vain and not very intelligent.

An even deeper rift between the English and the German members of the royal family occurred only a few months after the 'Danzig episode'.

Vicky and Fritz were on their way to England on 15 November 1863 when they heard that King Frederick VII of Denmark had died. Princess Alexandra's father ascended the throne of Denmark as Christian IX. He immediately ratified the new Constitution drawn up by his predecessor, incorporating the adjacent Duchy of Schleswig, which had been guaranteed independence by the London Protocol of 1852, together with the Duchy of Holstein. Fritz's friend, Duke Frederick of Augustenburg, stepped forward to lay claim to Holstein; Denmark was brought into conflict with the German Confederation. The wrangle suited Bismarck's purpose admirably. He declared later that he 'had had annexation of the Duchies before his eyes all the time'.

The issue was so complicated that nobody really understood it, least of all the Queen, who wrote: 'I am miserable, wretched, without my Angel to stand by me and put the others down.' The quarrels between Bertie, Alix, Vicky and Fritz became so intense that the Queen finally put her foot down and refused to allow the subject to be mentioned in her presence.

Finally, a combined Prusso-Austrian army marched into Denmark under the command of Marshal Wrangel, well supplied with Krupps artillery and needle guns. Fritz took part in the brief campaign and, according to Vicky, 'spared many lives through his kindness and generalship'. At the peace conference in Vienna in October 1864 Denmark was obliged to give up the duchies to Austria and Prussia, but Bismarck planned to force Austria to hand over her share of the spoils.

'My Angel always wanted my children to be gay and happy,' said the Queen as she tactfully advised Vicky not to ask Bertie to be godfather to her new baby, Sigismund. Bertie and Alix avoided Berlin and Vienna that year but they did meet Fritz and Vicky incognito at Cologne in the summer, when Bertie was offended to see Fritz wearing a Prussian uniform, 'flaunting before our eyes a most objectionable ribbon which he received for his deeds of valour (? ?) against the unhappy Danes'.

Princess Helena (known as Lenchen) had been rather neglected during these family squabbles, which took up so much of her mother's time. She was a good, model Victorian child upon whom the Queen felt she could always rely, although she does not seem to have bestowed overmuch affection upon her. Lenchen was closer to affectionate Lady Augusta Bruce who, to everybody's astonishment, married Dean Stanley of Westminster in November 1863. Her departure from the intimacy of the royal family circle was greatly lamented by the younger Princesses, to whom she had been an understanding confidante. Lenchen wrote to her almost despairingly: 'I have always looked up to you for comfort and advice in all my troubles and difficulties and you always helped me – pray always remain the same to me, for what should I do without you, my ever dear kind friend?'

The Queen now began to look around for a 'tame' husband for Helena, one who would agree to live in England. She had had enough of family rows over foreign issues. Uncle Leopold was sounded, and so was Vicky. Both agreed that Prince Christian of Schleswig-Holstein was a most suitable candidate. He was the younger brother of Duke Frederick, one of the claimants for the Duchies. Austria and Prussia having appropriated their territory the brothers had been left without a country, and Bismarck had deprived them of a commission in the Prussian Army. Vicky sent one of her detailed 'private detective' reports, informing the Queen that Prince Christian was often at her home in Berlin, that he was 'the best creature in the world, amusing when he felt inclined, bald, had a good military figure, was fond of children and of speaking English'.

The Prince was invited to Windsor and the Queen told

Augusta that he had made the most favourable impression upon Helena, 'and so has she upon him. Since then he has expressed through his brother his lively desire to get to know Lenchen better in the hope of winning her love, and I have invited him to Osborne for the end of December . . . No engagement can take place till they get to know each other better, yet I may regard the matter as pretty well settled, and that sets my mind at rest.'

In 1865 a grand family reunion of Queen Victoria's nine children took place at Coburg for the unveiling of a gilt bronze statue of Albert. The Queen, Helena, Louise and Beatrice broke the journey for two nights at Darmstadt and occupied the castle of Kranichstein. Prince Christian was asked over and the Queen found him 'pleasing, gentlemanlike, quiet and distinguished'.

The engagement was finally announced from the Highlands at the beginning of 1866. It was feared that unless the Queen came out of her seclusion and opened Parliament in person, the usual dowry-cum-annuity asked for the Princess might well be refused. So, very reluctantly, for the sake of her 'dear Lenchen', the Queen agreed, though she compared her ordeal to an execution and could not understand why the public 'wanted the spectacle of a poor, broken-hearted widow, nervous and shrinking, dragged in deep mourning, alone in state, as a show to be gazed at without delicacy or feeling'.

When, on the bright morning of 6 February 1866, she left Windsor for London with the children, she was so agitated that she could hardly touch her luncheon. She entered her carriage to the accompaniment of the band, with Helena and Louise facing her. 'They were a true help and support to me – they so thoroughly realized what I was going through.' Both windows of the carriage were open in spite of the high wind and the crowds cheered this unusual spectacle of a public appearance by the 'widow of Windsor', who was wearing an evening dress trimmed with miniver, a cap with a long flowing tulle veil, a small diamond and sapphire coronet and diamonds outlining the front of her cap.

The Queen said later that she thought she would faint when,

with all eyes fixed upon her, the House fell silent as she took her place alone on the throne. Not quite alone – her family sat round her and Albert's robe lay half across the chair on which he used to sit beside her. She leaned a little towards it, observed an eye-witness, 'and touched it, as a Catholic might a relic. An image of a Byzantine saint couldn't have looked more fixed, unmoved, indifferent from the pageant, yet her nostrils quivered and tears gathered round her drooping eyelids and rolled down her cheeks.'

Alice sent her warm congratulations. 'It was noble of you, my darling Mama, and the great effort will bring compensation. Think of the pride and pleasure it would have given darling Papa! The brave example to others not to shrink from their duty, and it has shown that you felt the intense sympathy which the English people evinced and still evince in your great misfortune.' She went on to recall how bright and young and handsome she had thought her parents looked on their wedding anniversary days. 'As I grew older it made me so proud to have two such dear parents and that my children should never know you both together will remain a sorrow to me as long as I live.'

Alice had not been able to 'make a fine show' on her allowance. She had no business head, nor had Louis, who was obliged to borrow money from the famous bankers Coutts of London to pay for their new house. 'We must live economically, not going anywhere or seeing many people, so as to be able to spare as much a year as we can. England cost a great deal, as the visit was short last time. We have sold four carriage horses and have only six to drive with now, two of which the ladies constantly use for the theatre, visits, etc so we are rather badly off in some things. But I should not bore you with our troubles, which are easy to bear. . . .' Alice designed the details of her new house herself, as Vicky had done, on a grander scale, in her Berlin palace. 'If I have any taste, I owe it all to dear Papa, and I learned so much by seeing him arrange pictures, rooms, etc. The house and all its arrangements are so English. When can we hope to have you here? Your rooms are on the east side and very cool, as you always go abroad when it is hot and suffer so much from the heat.' How fortunate that she had been taught how to use her needle! Alice said she had made seven walking-out dresses during the summer, with paletots for the girls, 'not embroidered but entirely made from the beginning to end and likewise the necessary flannel shawls for the expected new child'. 'I manage all the nursery accounts myself, which gives me plenty to do, as everything increases and on account of the house we must live very economically for these next few years.'

At the end of 1866, both Vicky's and Alice's knowledge of nursing was put to a practical test.

Prussia and Austria had agreed to govern the Duchies of Schleswig-Holstein jointly until these states were fit to govern themselves. Since then Bismarck and the Prussian press which he dominated had been finding fault and meddling with Austria, who called a meeting of the German states at Frankfurt in the autumn of 1866 to discuss a revision of the German Confederation. Bismarck would not allow Prussia to attend a meeting presided over by Austria and he finally mobilized the army, Fritz being placed in command of one of the three corps.

In his absence, his little son Sigismund died of meningitis. 'I think my heart will break,' Vicky wrote to him when she broke the news. She had a wax figure modelled and placed in the baby's cot, with a ball and rattle on the floor where he had been in the habit of flinging them out when he was alive, and she placed a pair of slippers at the foot of his cot with his favourite toys. She could be as morbid and macabre as Queen Victoria where death was concerned. But she pulled herself together, organized hospitals and began to find fault with the Prussian surgeons, although she declared herself to be 'every bit as proud of being a Prussian as I am of being an Englishwoman – the Prussians are a superior race'.

Saxony, Hesse and Hanover sided with Austria; Coburg, Anhalt-Mecklenburg were neutral. The seven-week war ended with the Austrians' defeat at Königgratz on 3 July. The Prussians crossed the Hessian frontier and guns were heard in Darmstadt. No serious resistance was possible. The Hessians lost eight hundred men. There were wounded to be looked after in Darmstadt, where Alice founded hospitals and begged her mother for coarse rags and linen.

> ...They are the things of which one can't have enough for the hospitals. In your numerous households it is collected once a year and sent to the hospitals. Could I beg for some this time? Lint has been ordered from England, bandages too through Dr. Jenner. Could you procure them? We are making four dozen shirts in the house. The horse you gave Louis rode in different engagements—it stood the fire quite well, but not the bursting of the shells close by.

Cholera and smallpox were rife. Alice now had two daughters, Victoria and Ella, whom she sent to Windsor. Her nerves were terribly strained. In the middle of the war she gave birth to her third daughter, Irene. 'Poor, dear Alice – what a position for her!' exclaimed the Queen as she listened to the little girls scampering up and down the corridors. 'As your children grow up and marry, you feel you can be of so little use to them, and they to you ... especially in the higher classes.'

'What would you like to give Lenchen for a wedding present?' Vicky asked Louise. 'Bismarck's head on a charger', she replied tartly.

When the war was over the Queen again appealed to the King of Prussia, reminding him of what Albert had once said and of what he himself had written in an album of Fritz's: 'May Prussia become merged in Germany, not Germany in Prussia.' She entreated him not to make too exacting peace terms.

In the Bohemian Campaign Fritz had commanded the Second Army which played a decisive part in the victory of Königgratz. Vicky, flushed with pride, wrote harshly: 'The victor must make his own terms and they must be hard ones for the enemy. We have made enormous sacrifices and the nation expects them not to be in vain.' Alice wrote resignedly when peace had been concluded:

> The terms are not too bad. We lost the hinterland and domains

there, the whole of Hesse-Homburg, 64,000 souls. We must pay three millions besides having kept the Prussian army six weeks for nothing. This is costing the country 25,000 florins daily. Half the army is under Prussian command. There is dreadful confusion on the railroads; the posts and telegraphs are to become Prussian. They demand art treasures, old pictures, books and manuscripts . . .

She thought it would be better for the other German sovereigns 'in spite of all' to unite with Prussia so as to make her unite with Germany, otherwise they would be annexed at the next opportunity. 'Whatever comes, our position and that of the small sovereigns must undergo a change which, for the older ones, will be very hard and which they will ever feel. Even dear Louis, who is so sensible and reasonable, says he has been brought up with particular rights which for centuries have been ours and he feels sore that he is never to inherit them.'

She hoped to be able to spend three months in England, perhaps part of the time with Bertie, 'if he can have us'. She and Louis had been through a great deal that summer and she was getting thin again after her confinement, but she carried on with her 'good works'; she presided at the Ladies' Union at Darmstadt to organize nursing in times of peace and war, to train nurses for the poor and rich, she launched a scheme to help poor unmarried women and to promote girls' education, with the assistance of an authoress, Fräulein Louise Buchner, a champion of women's rights. An 'Alice Bazaar' was held in the palace grounds for the sale of needlework and other products of 'female industry'. Prince Alfred, who was in Darmstadt on one of his frequent visits, took personal charge of one of the stalls. Alice also organized lectures at her home; a Swedish art historian Van Molin, talked about Venetian art to a room full of people, artists and professors. 'All the natural cleverness and sharpness in the world won't serve nowadays unless one had learnt something. I feel this so much and just in our position it is more and more required and expected, particularly in a small place where so much depends on the personal knowledge and exertions of the Princes.'

Alice's little daughters Victoria and Ella, aged three and two were taken to Windsor where their mother attended the wedding of her sister Helena to Prince Christian in 1866. Helena, according to a description left of her by her younger daughter, Princess Marie-Louise, had 'lovely wavy brown hair, a straight little nose and amber eyes'. She played the piano, had an exquisite gift for drawing and watercolour, and a clear soprano voice. Her outstanding gift was her loyalty to friends. She had a good head for business and a direct, authoritarian manner of expressing her opinions. On one occasion a special prayer of intercession was composed to be read in all churches to settle a dock strike. Leaflets with this prayer were distributed in the pews of Windsor Park chapel; Princess Helena picked one up, scrutinized it and observed in the penetrating royal family whisper: 'That prayer won't settle any strike', and put it down again.

Prince Christian (again from his daughter's description of him) had a pointed beard, blue eyes and an aristocratic face. He was a splendid shot, a keen horseman. He had, she wrote, a profound knowledge of forestry, and the Queen – to give him something to do – made him Ranger of Windsor Park. He loved poetry and passed his literary taste to his children, teaching them German by means of German fairy-tales told to them as they gathered round his armchair of an evening before going to bed.

Helena was the first of the Queen's daughters to enjoy her honeymoon abroad, after a dutiful visit to the Queen at Osborne. Paris, Interlaken, Genoa . . . freedom at last! But not for long. Upon their return the newly married pair took up residence at Frogmore, close to Mama and later at Cumberland Lodge, a warm red-brick building covered with virginia creeper and honeysuckle. The prince had inherited a love of flowers and gardening from his mother. When the Duchies were invaded in 1864 the ducal family had left in a hurry, piled into large travelling coaches between pet pigeons, doves and rose trees which were planted in their new home in Silesia. Prince Christian brought a couple of the doves to England when he married and established them at Cumberland Lodge.

The Queen soon discovered to her horror that her son-in-law smoked. This he was permitted to do at the palace only in a small uncomfortable room adjoining the servants' quarters – as an indication of the low esteem in which the abominable habit was held. In Balmoral Castle, too, a special room was allocated for the purpose.

Life soon resumed its even tenor. Prince Christian was not very amusing and both the Queen and the Princesses welcomed the few guests invited from the outside world. Sir Charles Hallé was one of them. He had often been summoned to Windsor, Balmoral and Osborne by the Queen and Prince Albert to play to them and give them instruction. He was asked to Osborne at the end of December 1867 and was immediately seized upon with glee by Helena, Louise, Beatrice and Leopold who made him sit down and play to them from 5.30 to 7 p.m. and the next day he played duets with Helena. 'The Queen takes most kindly to music,' he wrote to his family, 'she has suggested many of the pieces I played, but . . . when shall I get away from here? That is the rub. The Queen speaks, and Princess Helena speaks, as if I were going to stay here for ever.'

While Osborne was open to selected guests, Buckingham Palace still remained closed to royal visitors. The Queen declared that she was utterly incapable of entertaining great personages and refused to have the Tsar on a visit proposed by the Earl of Derby in June 1867. The Tsar had been invited to Paris with other sovereigns to attend the international exhibition organized by Napoleon III. Vicky and Fritz went to the exhibition but the former gave offence by suddenly packing up and leaving before the festivities were over. She was suffering from an 'isolation crisis' similar to the almost permanent one of the Queen's, following upon the death of her dearly loved little son Sigismund. 'Dear Vicky was so low the last days,' Alice wrote from Paris, 'and dislikes going to parties so much just now that she was longing to get home. The King of Prussia wished them both [Vicky and Fritz] to stop but only Fritz remained. She was in such good looks . . . everybody here is charmed with her.'

The sudden departure, her absence from the grand ball at the Hôtel de Ville and other *fêtes* caused offence to her hosts. Nearly all of Victoria's daughters, with the possible exception of Alice, suffered from a similar social defect, which they inherited from both their parents. They were unable to control their personal impulses and at official receptions and palace gatherings inclined, after an initial display of charm and courtesy, to withdraw suddenly, leaving their guests perplexed and irritated. They were at their best at small selective parties of liked and admired friends. Their attitude was not due, as many people believed, to arrogance, but to what can only be described as a pathological withdrawal trait.

Vicky was indeed far from arrogant; for instance, she sent a carriage to the station to meet Sir Ronald Gower and his wife when they visited Berlin, which was an unheard-of step to take for a non-royal person. Fritz tended to be more Prussian and formal. The Gowers described the life led by Fritz and Vicky in their palace: the children breakfasted with their parents and dined with them only when no visitors were present. Lord Ronald observed that the Princess was a strict mother, that Willy 'pored over the treasures of the Holy Roman Empire and appeared to be a romantic dreamer' who never confided in his mother. Fritz took him and Willy to the crypt of Berlin Cathedral to see the tombs of the old kings and they visited the mausoleum of Frederick the Great in the woods near Potsdam. Vicky had had a gardener sent over from Windsor and she herself never walked through the garden without taking secateurs to snip and dead-head on the way. Fritz, too, helped to clear branches and hedges and often carried garden scissors, even on horseback.

The Crown Prince and Princess also had a farm at Bornstadt close to the New Palace; here there was a dairy modelled on the one at Windsor, which provided butter and milk for the family's consumption. The children played with the dachshunds bred on the farm and helped to organize the June fête for the children of the neighbourhood. Tables were put out on the lawn behind the rose garden, where they served coffee and cakes they had baked themselves. There were sack races and Fritz joined in the fun with his children. They went swimming in the pretty little River Havel that skirted the palace grounds at Potsdam, rode on two Shetland ponies sent by Queen Victoria and listened to their mother's pleasant soprano voice singing *lieder* by Schubert and Schumann, or taking lessons from Sir Michael Costa of London. As all the daughters of Victoria had done, and continued to do before them, the children were taught to kiss their parents' hands on bidding them good morning and good night. Alice could still write to the Queen: 'I long so very much to see you, my own precious Mama, this summer. After a year's absence, I wish so intensely to behold your dear, sweet, loving face again and to press my lips on your dear hands . . .'

Alice was indeed often lonely, especially in the winter months when Louis was away on manoeuvres four times a week, from six in the morning until six in the evening, and when he returned from his shooting, he had work to do. She was accustomed to a house full of people, brothers and sisters, 'and the chance of being near you', she wrote nostalgically to her mother. Over and over again in her letters she referred to 'those happy, happy days at Osborne'.

> . . . It touches me to tears when I think of them. What a joyous childhood we had, and how greatly it was enhanced by dear, sweet Papa and by all your great kindness to us . . . I try to copy as much as is in my powers all those things for my children that they may have an idea when I speak to them of it of what a happy home ours was. I do feel so much for dear Beatrice and the other younger ones who had so much less of it than we had.

This could have been interpreted as a reproach for the sad life they led after Papa's death.

The Queen replied by lecturing Alice on the upbringing of *her* daughters, to which Alice retorted:

> What you say about the education of our girls I entirely agree with and I strive to bring them up totally free from pride of their position, which is nothing save what their personal worth can

make it. I read it to the governess, thinking how good it would be for her to hear your opinion. I feel so entirely as you do on the difference of rank and how important it is for Princes and Princesses to know that they are nothing better or above others save through their own merit and that they have only the double duty of living for others and of being an example: good and modest. This I hope my children will grow up to.

In that year 1868 Alice gave birth to a son, christened Ernest in honour of the Duke of Saxe-Coburg, his uncle. He had, according to Princess Marie of Battenberg

> . . . a small red face, pretty features and a little mouth which has already the shape of the mouth of all Queen Victoria's children. He looked round a little with half-opened eyes during the ceremony, then sneezed three times, yawned, and fell asleep again. He was carried by his nurse, Mrs. Clarke, in a white silk robe. Little Irene exclaimed in English, with some alarm: 'These people have done something to baby!'

Political circumstances had meanwhile prevented Vicky from going to England for three years. When she did so in 1868 Lady Augusta Stanley used her influence to persuade the Queen and the Princesses to visit the Deanery to meet Browning and Carlyle and the scientists Tyndall and Owen. She also took Longfellow to see the Queen. Vicky was delighted. This was the kind of company she enjoyed. After initial stiffness, the men of letters were put at their ease by the Queen. Carlyle found twenty-year-old Princess Louise lively and intelligent: 'A very pretty young lady, and clever too, as I found out in talking to her afterwards.'

When Vicky went back to Berlin the Queen wrote pathetically to King William: 'I have no doubt that you will allow me to see our dear daughter more often, if only for a comparatively short time; for you, dear brother, see your own daughter not only every year but several times a year. Your loving paternal heart will surely understand that I should not like to be parted from Vicky again for three whole years.' There had evidently been some friction, for the Queen went on: 'She will of course do her best to comply with your wishes as regards social life, only you and dear Augusta will certainly show consideration for her, for she does not really stand very hot rooms and late hours well.'

Vicky in fact saw more of Alice, with whom she spent a holiday on the Riviera in 1869. The contrast in the Princesses' respective retinues was an indication of the difference in their positions. Vicky brought twenty-five people in her train, while Alice had only one lady-in-waiting, a secretary, a steward, and Mrs Orchard, the English nurse for baby Ernest who had been recommended by the Queen. Their lives and homes were different down to the smallest detail: Alice's curtains were in chintz and Vicky's bedroom walls were covered with pale blue silk and golden fringes. Alice's few dreary holidays were usually spent in cheap hotels at Blankensee, Vicky's long ones with the children in luxurious villas in the Tyrol, by the Swiss and Italian lakes. At Portofino, Venice, where Lord Carnarvon offered her a villa for the season, the King and Queen of Italy put their private gondolas at her disposal and she enjoyed luncheons and teas in the house of Sir Henry Layard, the explorer of ancient Nineveh.

In the sun of the Riviera, where they stayed at the Grand Hotel in Cannes, Alice's rheumatism and neuralgia 'faded' and her spirits revived. Besides, it was always so stimulating to be in Vicky's company. They discussed the works of Dr David Strauss, a theologian and critic of the historical foundations of Christianity; he lived in Darmstadt and Alice had invited him to her house to give a series of lectures on Voltaire. These had pleased her so much that when they were subsequently published she asked the author to dedicate the volume to her; but Dr Strauss's name was anathema in orthodox Germany and Alice was taken to be an atheist. She may have lost her faith temporarily – although there was no mention of this in her letters to her mother. Vicky was the only person close enough to her to be able to discuss her feelings on such an intimate subject as religion. There were some things which could not be discussed with Mama, although Mama herself had once written to Augusta, in the early days of their close friendship soon after

Vicky's marriage: 'One can tell Alice *all* – very different from another quarter.' This was presumably a not very loyal dig at Vicky, or had the Queen intended to imply that she was aware of her daughter's difficult character and could therefore understand and foresee tensions between her and Augusta?

Another taboo subject, which the two sisters could freely discuss but which appalled Mama, was anatomy. Alice and Vicky had been learning a little about it to help them with their nurse-training work and hospitals. Alice did mention this to the Queen, who replied that she found such a study 'disgusting'. Alice replied quietly but firmly that she did not find it so, that such knowledge filled her with admiration and wonder at the ingenious structure and offices of the bodily functions. It was so useful, in the case of sudden illness, to know what to do before the doctor arrived. When, like her mother, one was surrounded by eminent doctors, such knowledge was unnecessary 'but for others it is most desirable'. The Queen, who, as we have seen, had written in one of her frequent sentimental moods that she sometimes longed to be able to devote herself to the poor and sick, was put out.

Alice had every reason to be envious of Vicky's grander life, but, oddly enough, it was the other way round as far as their personal relationships to the Queen were concerned. 'I know that you prefer to have Alice with you,' Vicky wrote, and her mother chided her for her fit of jealousy. As in all human relationships, they went through their ups and downs. The Queen thought that Vicky was acquiring a Prussian pomposity, nor could she keep up with the learned books she read. They were beyond her. Alice was intellectually simpler, but she too could be trying at times – particularly when she endeavoured, obliquely, to wheedle something out of Mama.

In the late 1860s, Helena was deeply involved in domesticity, Beatrice was growing to be a thoughtful child, her spontaneous childish reactions stifled by her adult environment, while Louise, according to the Queen, needed watching. Vicky had persuaded her to take an interest in women's emancipation and this word made the Queen purse her lips with distaste. Louise had even gone to the length of corresponding with Miss Josephine Butler, the champion of women's rights. 'I do take great interest in the happiness and well-being of women,' Louise wrote to her in November 1869, when she was twenty-one, 'and long to do everything that I can to promote all efforts in that direction. My dear sister the Crown Princess mentioned this in her letter to you. I feel pleasure in thinking you will let me know whenever any question arises in which my assistance and sympathy could be of any use to you.' There had been talk of founding an International Women's Review. Louise wisely believed that it would be better 'not to put anything about women in the title, as I think all appearance of exclusiveness should be avoided as it is after all only with the cooperation of the cleverest men that we can hope to succeed'. She concluded, from personal experience, 'I know the subject of women's rights, interests, etc. has become so tedious to the eyes of so many whose support it would be an advantage to gain.'

The Queen, realizing that she could no longer count upon her elder daughters as before, owing to their domestic involvements, turned her attention to her grandchildren. She told Alice that she would like to be able to count upon having a grandchild with her whenever she wished – There were now so many that 'it didn't make any difference. To have no children in the house is most dreary.' Children were charming pets, their sayings were so droll. Nothing could move the Queen to instant laughter more quickly than a story about a child. Of course, they were also a source of anxiety, as she wrote to Alice: 'The constant anxiety about the children is dreadful, and it is not physical ill one dreads for them, it is moral. The responsibility for these little lent souls is great and indeed none can take it lightly who feel how great and important a parent's duty is.' Yet almost at the same time she wrote to Vicky on the subject of Willy: 'Too much constant watching leads to the very dangers hereafter which one wishes to avoid.'

During the years 1869 and 1870, three of Victoria's daughters oscillated between the excitements of love and war: Louise fell in love and became engaged to the Marquis of Lorne, heir to the 8th Duke of Argyll, Vicky and Alice pursued their hospital work and were in a constant state of anguish over their respective husbands fighting in the Franco-Prussian War.

The apparent cause of the war was French fears of German influence in Spain, where the throne had become vacant. Napoleon III demanded that the Hohenzollern candidate should be withdrawn and then went further and asked the Germans to promise never to propose one again. An awkwardly worded despatch provided Bismark with his chance. Napoleon III overestimated his chances of victory, and he was being pushed by his Cabinet and by his Empress. Germany became united as never before, and by the end of the war King William I, prodded by Bismarck, became the first German Emperor. The Emperor who had led Vicky in a waltz through the Galerie des Glaces at Versailles in 1855 now invaded her husband's country, but disaster after disaster overtook the French; in August 1870 they were defeated at Weissenberg and Worth, and in September at Sedan, where Napolcon surrendered. In October Marshal Bazaine's army of seventy thousand men capitulated at Metz.

Queen Augusta organized hospital services in Berlin and Vicky left for Homburg in the Taunus Mountains near the French border, where barracks were put at her disposal for a military hospital. She added a Victoria Barrack of her own with two wards of twenty-four beds for special cases, provided with everything from the latest medical equipment to vases of flowers. She visited the hospital every day and many of the wounded wrote to her for years afterwards. But her 'English methods' and excessive love of fresh air for the sick irritated the Germans and finally the King ordered her back to Berlin to be near Queen Augusta. Vicky thought that the Germans were utterly callous about the fate of those who had lost the capacity to fight.

Meanwhile, in Darmstadt, Alice set up a medical depot in the grand ducal palace. 'What would beloved papa have thought of this war?' she wrote to her mother. 'The unity of Germany which it has brought about would please him, but never the shocking means. I hope I shall not live to see another war. We have over 500 wounded; as soon as they are better they will be sent north and worse ones will fill the beds.' Every day Alice heard the muffled drums for some soldier or officer being taken past her windows to his last resting place. 'How deeply I do feel for the poor parents and widows! The barrack at the foot of our garden contains 120 French prisoners, many of them ill. I feel for the Emperor Napoleon and Empress Eugénie so much . . .' 'Unfortunate Emperor and Empress – what a fate!' echoed the Queen.

> She, having been twice my guest and we hers, I could not be so unfeeling as not to say one word to her, so I have designed the following message to be conveyed to her 'that I was not insensible to the heavy blow which had fallen nor was unforgetful of former days'. I wish Fritz to know this. Oh, could not Paris be spared? How is that to be managed? It is a terrible anxious time for all and I stand much alone.

The Queen also wrote one of her unheeded letters to King William: 'Would it not be possible for you to stop now and make peace?' She wrote a similar letter to Fritz.

Bertie meanwhile dined with the French ambassador in London and announced loudly that he hoped the Prussians would be defeated and that the Austrians would join the French. Vicky wrote post-haste to say: 'The King and everyone is horrified at Bertie's speech which is quoted everywhere.' Bertie stoutly denied the accusation. Vicky then wrote sneeringly: 'Bertie must envy Fritz who has such a trying but useful life.' 'These divided family interests are fearful and almost unbearable,' the Queen replied sadly.

Helena wrote to the Duchess of Sutherland: 'My dear husband is so distressed about this war. He was so anxious to go and join in defending his country, but the Ministers thought he had better not go. I need not tell you my *gratitude* not to see him go, tho' I should have encouraged him to go had it been possible and if he could have thereby served his country. He feels it so much.' She badgered the Duchess for 'any old linen on behalf of the London Committee for Aid to the Sick and Wounded – their object being to relieve equally both French and Germans'. Eleven surgeons were sent out and five nurses. Referring to 'these glorious victories of my dear brother-in-law [Fritz] which have filled me with joy and thanksgiving,' she added: 'But oh! the other side of the picture is so terrible: the fearful loss of life, the misery and sufferings of so many thousands. It is a terrible time of anxiety we are all living in!'

The bombardment of Paris began on New Year's Day 1871. 'Every shot fired into the town wrung my heart,' Fritz wrote to Augusta, and Vicky said that she 'felt the deepest pity for our unfortunate enemy'. The Empress Eugénie was smuggled out of France and crossed over to England, where she was joined by the Emperor after the signing of the armistice. Queen Victoria, who had once again called upon King – now Emperor – William to be merciful to France in his terms, hurried to pay the exiled Empress a private visit and found that she was 'bearing her tragic fate with dignity'.

In between the anxieties caused by the Franco-Prussian war, and the divisions it produced in the family, the Queen found time to deal with the romance of pretty, artistic Princess Louise, who was engaged to the Marquis of Lorne.

But . . . a Princess to marry a Duke's son? Such a *mésalliance* had not occurred to a female member of a British dynasty since the times of the Plantagenets! It caused astonishment both within and outside the family circle. Bertie was one of the first to react angrily.

The Argylls, head of Clan Campbell, whose seat at Inverary Castle had been visited by Victoria and Albert when the Marquis of Lorne was a fair, fat little two-year-old, had been closely connected with the court for years. The Marquis, during his term at Eton, had been invited to Windsor Castle to play with Bertie. He was not, however, Bertie's type, being of a poetic, literary and even visionary bent, endowed with Highland 'second sight'.

(This was not strong enough, though, to warn him that his marriage to Louise would not be a success.)

For the Argylls the marriage was a great *coup*. Louise, whom they did not know intimately, was beautiful and talented, (though she was still undeveloped owing to her upbringing in the gloomy atmosphere of the Queen's widowhood). To the impressionable young Marquis of Lorne she must have looked like a fairy-tale princess. They shared literary, artistic and sporting interests. Both liked walking in the mountains and it was among those of Balmoral, the scene of her sister's betrothals, that the proposal was finally made and the engagement announced.

Louise had intimated from the age of twenty-one (in 1869) that she would prefer to make a British marriage and spend her life in England. Vicky had suggested a Prussian Prince, but the Queen would not hear of it and told her candidly that the 'matter must be considered at an end'. Bertie sided with Vicky and expressed his thorough disapproval. His main objection to the marriage with Lorne, he said, was political. Lorne was a Gladstonian Liberal and the situation would give rise to the innuendo that the crown was exposed to political influence. He also thought – being a stickler for etiquette – that there would be constant difficulties in assigning the correct official rank to husband and wife. The Queen sent him an eminently sensible letter in which the mother merged with the diplomat-stateswoman:

> Times have much changed; great foreign alliances are looked on as causes of trouble and anxiety and are of no good. What could be more painful than the position in which our family were placed during the wars with Denmark and between Prussia and Austria? Every family feeling was rent asunder and we were powerless. Nothing is more unpopular here or more uncomfortable for *me* and everyone than the long residence of our married daughters from abroad in my house with the quantities of foreigners they bring with them, the foreign view they entertain on all subjects. In beloved Papa's lifetime this was totally different and besides Prussia had not swallowed everything up. You may

not be aware, as I am, with what dislike the marriages of Princesses of the Royal Family with small German Princes ('German beggars' as they most insultingly were called) were looked on, and how in former days many of our statesmen like Mr. Fox, Lord Melbourne and Lord Holland abused those marriages and said how wrong it was that alliances with noblemen of high rank and fortune, which had always existed formerly and which are perfectly legal, were no longer allowed by the sovereign.

Now that the Royal Family is so large (you have already 5 and *what* will these be when your brothers marry?) in these days when you ask Parliament to give money to all the Princesses to be *spent abroad*, when they could perfectly well marry here and the children succeed just as much as if they were the children of a Prince or Princess, we could not maintain this exclusive principle.

As to position, I see *no* difficulty whatever. Louise remains what she is, and her husband keeps his rank (like the Mendorffs and Victor Hohenlowe) only being treated in the family as a relation when we are together. It will strengthen the *hold* of the Royal Family, besides infusing new and healthy blood into it, whereas all the Princes abroad are related to one another; and while I could continue these foreign alliances with several members of the family, I feel sure that new blood will strengthen the throne *morally* as well as *physically*.

Times had changed indeed and so had the Queen. It was not so long since she had chided Vicky for showing partiality to the country and people of her birth, and requesting her to keep up the German influence in the family. She had also been cross with Bertie for writing to Alix in English, recalling that she had always written to Albert in German during *their* engagement, even though she must have made many grammatical errors. 'That unbounded love for everything English I cannot share,' she had written to Vicky seven years before, 'loving and admiring my country as I do, I have seen too much of the cold, harsh cheerlessness of my countrymen and have seen with such grief the very bad effect it has had on your two elder brothers in so many ways that I cannot admire it as much as you do.' Vicky retorted: 'One never knows the value of a thing until one has lost it – With so few to whom I can think aloud, I cling to all that is English.'

Since then, the Queen's married daughters had become, both consciously and unconsciously, more foreign, while she herself had become more English. Albert's ghost was still at her elbow, but it had somehow become less Teutonic, partaking more of the neutrality of the celestial spheres.

Louise's engagement took place early in October 1870 during a walk from the Glassalt Shiel (a kind of Scottish anchorite's retreat which the Queen had built about two miles from Balmoral Castle and to which she repaired with one attendant and Beatrice when she 'wanted to get away from it all'). Despatch boxes, however, were sent up with the supplies of tea, scones and cakes.

Louise had gone to the Dhu Loch with Lady Ely, Lord Hatherley (the Lord Chancellor) and Lorne. The Queen had driven with Beatrice and the Hon. Mrs Ponsonby to Panmarich Wells, two miles from Ballater on the south side of the Dee, where she observed with regret that almost all the trees which once covered the hills had been cut down. The Queen's party returned home at seven. Louise arrived some time after and told her 'that Lorne had spoken of his devotion to her and proposed to her and that she had accepted him, knowing that I would approve. Though I was not unprepared for this result, I felt painfully the thought of losing her. But I naturally gave my consent and could only pray that she might be happy.' This being the fourth of the Queen's experiences of a similar nature she was in a much less agitated frame of mind than on former occasions – indeed the entry in her journal sounds positively placid.

She wrote to Augusta more or less along the same lines as to Vicky, with little consideration for the effect that her words might have upon her once so dear friend. 'Princes of small German houses are very unpopular here, whereas Lord Lorne is a man of independent future and really no lower in rank than a minor German royalty. The Campbells, of whom Lord Lorne would be the chief, are a clan of finer position and traditions than many of the ducal and princely houses of Germany which have sought brides in England.'

Louise was looking forward to a life of freedom. Like her sisters before her, she had never been allowed to dine outside the palace. When she was twenty, Gladstone had asked the Queen's permission to ask Louise to dine at his house when the Prince and Princess of Wales were thus honouring him. 'The Princess never dines out except at her brother's house,' the Queen replied. Sir Henry Ponsonby, the Queen's private secretary, foresaw terrible difficulties because Louise seemed to have such little idea of what her position would be. She talked to him of her two footmen: '*Footmen*, mind. I don't want an absurd man in a kilt following me about everywhere and I want to choose the men at once or I shall have some others thrust upon me.'

The court ladies said that Louise was not in love, but when she was told that Lorne was to come to Balmoral for only three days in October 'she burst out crying and said it was *so* hard', wrote Sir Henry. 'I think she will love him. All of these Princesses have made devoted wives whatever their faults may be and if Lorne steers well all will be very well. He will make her part of his family and one of themselves.' Unfortunately, the young man was not of a 'steering' disposition. Three days later, Lorne arrived with his father, the Duke of Argyll. Sir Henry reported: 'He looked radiant with joy and kissed the Queen's hand on coming in and out like the other children. The Duke looks majestic and solemn.'

A little while before their departure for Windsor, Louise took to her room with a bad knee. (Nearly all the princesses, and the Queen, suffered from rheumatism.) According to Sir Henry, she 'didn't want to go to London near the Wales's, because they were against her marriage. Messages were exchanged all night between her and the Queen through the agency of poor Lady Ely on the subject of doctors. Finally Dr Lister was sent for by special train from Edinburgh.' He prescribed a fortnight's rest so the household – to their regret – had to stay on at Balmoral; nobody except the Queen really enjoyed being there for any length of time. Sir Henry added: 'There was unnecessary asperity between mother and daughter, Louise not wanting to be moved and the Queen saying she should be wheeled into another room for an hour.' The Queen continued to be as fussy as ever with her daughters, but Louise, being wilful, stuck to her guns – all the more so now that domestic freedom was in sight – or so she hoped and believed.

On 4 March 1871, the Queen, surrounded by her 'flock', opened Parliament for the customary golden begging bowl ceremony, this time in favour of Louise. So many adverse comments had been made on the monarchy recently, so much dissatisfaction had been expressed at the Queen's isolation and apparent hoarding, that it was feared there might be trouble, but all passed off surprisingly well, without a murmur, to Gladstone's relief. A pretty Princess provokes sympathy even in the most rationally democratic minds.

The wedding took place on 21 March 1871, the groom entering the royal chapel to the appropriate lively air of 'The Campbells are coming' and wearing the uniform of the Argyll and Bute Volunteer Artillery. His best man was Lord Ronald Leveson Gower, a great friend of the royal family. The Queen's permanent black was almost hidden under a blaze of diamonds and Orders; Helena wore cerise satin and Beatrice was in pink. The wedding cake, designed by Her Majesty's chief confectioner, Mr Ponder, had taken three months to build. It was five feet high, decorated with figures representing the Fine Arts, Science, Agriculture and Commerce, as well as roses, thistles, doves, Corinthian pillars supporting a temple surmounted by figures of the four seasons, the whole crowned by the figure of Hebe; it was almost a miniature Albert Memorial – minus Albert.

The bride's shower of presents included emeralds and diamonds from the Queen, a tiara of sapphires and pearls from the Argylls, pearls from Balmoral, a Bible and casket presented by '4,755 Maidens of the United Kingdom', who had each subscribed from one penny to a shilling. The boys of Eton presented the Marquis with a magnificent silver tankard in memory of his old school. Lockets for the bridesmaids were designed by Princess

Louise herself from a Holbein model; they were in rock crystal, wreathed in roses and forget-me-nots, with a royal scroll in the centre with 'Louise' in gold letters, surrounded by a border of blue and white enamel on gold tracery inlaid with pearls, hanging from a true lover's knot of turquoise enamel bordered with emeralds and rubies.

Gladstone's daughter Mary was present at the wedding dinner, seated between the Dean of Windsor and the Rev. Charles Kingsley (who had been appointed court chaplain in 1859). She observed the Queen talking a good deal to Princess Louise: 'They must have a keen sense of humour from the way they laughed,' she said later. But Louise had in fact never found much congenial company at home. Her art teacher, Edward Corbould, was one of the exceptions. She had written to him a few months before her marriage:

> You have been one of my *few true* friends that I have looked up to all my life and from whom I have always had encouragement and sympathy, and from whom I have learnt much besides art, tho' art was the foundation of all things. When I am married, as I have the great happiness of remaining in my beloved country and among my friends and acquaintances, I shall hope often to see you and that our interest in each other's work will not diminish but increase if possible.

Louise's honeymoon – as in Helena's case – was a continental one and took in Florence, where Lady Paget was living and gave several entertainments and receptions. She thought that Louise was a lovely young princess, gifted with many talents, who might have graced a throne. Louise was delighted and amused to be able to go out shopping alone with Lady Paget – such simple pleasures having until then been denied her – until Lady Paget had to remind her that Lord Lorne must be waiting for his wife. Louise was already beginning to prefer liberty to her husband. She appeared at dinner looking very beautiful, her *cendré* hair studded with diamonds, in a cerise dress covered with Valenciennes lace. Then, suddenly, in the middle of the festivities, she turned shy and insisted upon beating a retreat through Lady Paget's bedroom.

Alice went to Balmoral in the late summer of 1871. She thought that her mother looked very unwell and suggested that she should always have one of her married daughters with her in the winter. The Queen, who had once suggested this herself, sniffed and made no reply. Alice felt hurt. She wrote to the Duchess of Sutherland: 'I see no prospect of my being able to remain in England for the winter . . . It is unpleasant to feel one is not wished for.'

Victoria was probably going through the menopause – she was now fifty-two – and feeling particularly nervy. She complained of being lonely, yet would not let any of her daughters go to her room.

The Queen has no friends [Sir Henry Ponsonby wrote to his wife], won't have her children round her, has no lady she really likes; it seems to me she is terribly alone. She sends for Dr. Jenner several times in the night. Alice can never see the Queen comfortably. Bertie paid a visit and Alice quietly took him aside and cautioned him against gambling at Bordeaux and Hamburg—an article had appeared about it in Lloyd's paper and been read by the Queen. If spoken to by anyone else he might have turned nasty.

The Queen had lost a stone in two months. It improved her figure, but not her temper. Lady Ely whispered confidentially to Sir Henry that a struggle was going on between Alice, Louise and the other children, the general tenor of which seemed to be: '[They] want to do what *they*, not what the Queen likes, and want her to pay for doing what they like, while she is ready to pay if they will do what she likes. The first thing she likes is that Alice should go back to Darmstadt and Alice won't.'

In fact, the children had gone into a huddle and made up their minds to write a joint letter to the Queen respectfully and affectionately requesting her to come out of the seclusion which was being so adversely commented upon by the public. The throne was in danger, the Queen's health was in danger. . . . This was not a new idea. Alice had given the matter much thought and discussed it with her brothers and sisters the year before. The Queen had got wind of it and accused her of mounting a cabal, to get her out of her retirement. There had been some acrimonious correspondence (quickly destroyed) and Alice had been in disgrace for several months. Now she returned to the attack. She read the newspapers, she knew what was being said and felt. Helena supported her warmly. So did Bertie. Vicky was more doubtful. Dear Mama could be so obstinate and she abhorred anything which could be interpreted as coercion. Nevertheless, she agreed and took over the task of drafting the letter as the eldest and most literate daughter. Then the Queen fell ill, with a combination of gout, neuralgia and an abscess on her arm which had to be lanced by Dr Lister. The letter was torn up. The Queen insisted upon being alone with Beatrice and her attendant John Brown as the sole attendants admitted to her sanctuary. 'A faithful servant,' she wrote when one of the Duke of Cambridge's servants died, 'is so identified with all your feelings, wants, wishes and habits as really to be part of your existence and cannot be replaced.'

Three doctors were present at the lancing of the Queen's abscess. 'I felt dreadfully nervous, as I bear pain so badly,' she admitted. Dr Jenner gave her some whiffs of chloroform while Dr Lister froze the spot, Dr Marshall holding her arm. The abscess, the Queen reported, was six inches in diameter. It was very quickly cut and she hardly felt anything. Alice, who had insisted upon taking over the duties of a nurse, had now become acceptable. 'Dear Alice was in and out constantly, and very affectionate and kind, helping my maids in moving me.' The lancing of the abscess helped to rid the Queen of the accumulated toxins produced by a combination of her critical age, her deep anxieties over the Franco-Prussian War, and her concern over so many issues, foreign or domestic, which ranged from the cut of sailors' beards in the Navy to her protest against a proposal to put a tax on matches, which she said would make no difference to the rich and would annoy the poor – the project was dropped. Nobody in her immediate entourage could grasp all the details which she had to deal with alone. She was overworked and strained. She was fully aware of this, for she observed to Theodore Martin, who had been entrusted with the official biography of her beloved Albert: 'I wonder what my ladies think of my want of courtesy. Sometimes I drive out with them for a couple of hours and all the time do not exchange a word with them. I am so taken up thinking what answers to make to the despatches and letters of the day.'

Then at the end of 1871 an event occurred which took the Queen out of herself and acted as a catalyst, for – as she herself had once declared – she was at her best in a crisis.

Bertie had been celebrating his birthday at Sandringham, the shooting retreat where he and Princess Alix entertained on a lavish scale people of whom the Queen mostly disapproved; during the eight years they had occupied it she had never set foot there. Now Bertie, her eldest son and heir, fell dangerously ill with diphtheria, then far more of a killer than now. The end of the year was approaching, and the ever dreaded anniversary of Albert's death on 14 December.

The Queen made a supreme effort, packed up and went to Sandringham, where she took over like a military commander to the point of standing at the door of the sickroom and vetoeing visitors. The Prince of Wales improved on the 'fateful' day of his father's death, recognized his mother and thanked her for going to see him. He had been tenderly nursed by Alice and by Alix 'especially the latter', the Queen stressed to Mrs Gladstone in one of the strange jealous fits that occasionally swept over her where her children were concerned. It was as if, by some unconscious process, she wanted the limelight to be evenly distributed, never centred for too long on one and the same person. Alice's devotion had been publicly acknowledged after Albert's death. Now it was Alix's turn to get some credit for her devotion. Alice slipped quietly back to Darmstadt.

# Section IV

# The First to Die; The Last to Wed (1871-87)

FOR Vicky, the 1870s were chiefly memorable for her summer visits to Osborne with her children: Willy, Charlotte, Victoria (Moretta), Henry, Sophie, Waldemar and Margaret. (Her last child, Margaret, called 'Mossy' in the family circle, was born in 1872. The Queen went to Potsdam for the christening. 'Let this baby remain the baby for some years,' she advised Vicky.)

Willy and Henry fired the brass cannons with Aunt Beatrice (who relaxed in the company of her nephews and nieces) in the miniature fort outside Swiss Cottage. Willy both loved and was in awe of his grandmama. It was the same at home with Grandpapa, the Emperor William, with whom he often dined when his parents were away. He was jealous of the affection which his mother lavished upon Waldemar, ('The most English of my children,' she said), who brought over his pet crocodile and let it loose at Grandmama's feet, causing her to shriek with alarm. (Waldemar died in 1879 at the age of eleven, from diphtheria.)

Grandmama Augusta came over for a visit too and stayed at Buckingham Palace. Friendly relations were resumed. She had not left the shores of England before Victoria, in her impulsive way, was already writing to her: 'I cannot let the opportunity slip of writing these few lines to tell you how happy I am to have seen you and to have had you staying with me so quietly and comfortably. No visit has left me with such peaceful and pleasant memories as yours since my destitute life began.' (Another death which greatly affected the Queen was that of her half-sister Princess Feodora of Hohenlohe in 1872: 'She often held me in her arms and pressed me to her heart when I was in such despair. I feel just like a deserted child.')

Feelings of affection did not prevent the Queen from lecturing Augusta on the subject of their mutual grandchild. 'Vicky told me how much Willy loves you, but you must not spoil him with your kindness. I have so many grandchildren that I have already had a good deal of experience where this is concerned.' She firmly believed in keeping a child – particularly a royal one – *a child* as long as possible. Augusta was inclined to agree with Victoria's words: 'You will find, as the children grow up, they are as a rule a bitter disappointment, their greatest object being to do precisely what their parents do not wish and have anxiously tried to prevent, and they generally suffer for it. There are no doubt bright exceptions.' One of these was Beatrice. 'I shall take care she never marries . . . she is quite happy at home and contented and sweet-tempered and without jealousy. No married daughter is of any use.'

The reference to jealousy was no doubt prompted by Alice's occasional cutting remarks about the affluent Prince and Princess Christian, whose situation contrasted so sharply with her own. Prince Christian was a serious, self-improving German, but what could he do? His scope as Ranger of Windsor Park was limited. He put down the frogs of which there was a plague at the appropriately named Frogmore, seeking advice from the naturalist Frank Buckland (who suggested importing more ducks to eat the frogs). Helena founded the Royal School of Needlework in a small room in a house in Sloane Street in 1872; the prefix 'Royal' was not in fact given to it until 1875, when the Queen became its patron and it was moved to Exhibition Road (where it still flourishes). She led the uneventful life of a well-to-do *Hausfrau*, but it was she, with Princess Alexandra, who started the new profession of bazaar-opening for royal ladies.

Alice's sixth child was born in the summer of 1872. This was Alexandra Helena Louise Beatrice Victoria, or 'Alix', who grew up to be one of the most beautiful women in Europe, and the most tragic; she became Alexandra Feodorovna, the last

Empress of Russia. Alice's son Frittie suffered from haemophilia. Alice wrote in April 1872 that he again had endless bruises with lumps but he was taking iron, as Sir William Jenner had advised: 'I trust he may outgrow this.' Very little was then known about the disease.

When Frittie recovered, Alice and Louis went on a tour of Italy. Alice had never been so far south before and she was enchanted. In Rome she was entertained by Lady Paget, who wrote in her *Reminiscences*: 'She was very poor but she bore this with great courage and simplicity: She wanted a *lectrice* or secretary, but could afford only a small salary. Lady Paget suggested a likely candidate. 'I should be very grateful if you would sound the lady,' Alice wrote, adding pathetically: 'The salary is very small but of course the ladies are at home in everything in the house. Will you send me word and find out whether she would feel inclined to pay me, first, a visit to see whether she would like it before we settle?'

On their return home, the children hung out wreaths of welcome. Then Louis left Darmstadt to inspect troops in Upper Hesse. Alice, exhausted by so much unaccustomed sightseeing, took to her bed. Next day the two little Princes Ernest and Frittie came in to wish her good morning. They began to play, running in and out of the adjacent room and leaning out of the windows. Alice got up and followed Ernest, leaving Frittie in the bedroom. During her momentary absence Frittie scampered over to the open bow window to play at bo-peep with his brother, who appeared at the drawing-room window opposite. He slipped and fell on to the stone terrace twenty feet below, was picked up unconscious and bleeding, and died that same evening from an effusion of blood on the brain. He was only seven years old.

Alice never got over the shock and grief. Even Ernest cried despairingly: 'Why can't we all die together? I don't want to die alone, like Frittie.'

It wrung Alice's heart to look at the flowers by the wayside. 'Frittie loved flowers so much I can't see one without wishing to pick it for him . . . You ask if I can play yet?' she wrote to her mother three months later. 'I feel as if I could not and I have not yet done so. In my own house it seems to me as if I could never play again on that piano where little hands were nearly always thrust when I wanted to play . . . I had played so often lately that splendid, touching funeral march of Chopin's and I remember it is the last thing I played when the boys were running in the room.'

A seventh child, Marie, was born in 1874. Alice fed the baby girl herself much to the Queen's disgust, so she had to explain patiently: 'I have no cow or country house to keep one in. In the tremendous heat where one can't keep milk, dysentry carries off so many babies . . . It would not be fair to deprive the poor little thing of its natural and safest nourishment till the hot months are over. These, darling Mama, are my reasons.'

She would have liked to go to Schveningen for the sea air and bathing, but it was too expensive, so she went to Blankenberghe instead. It was as dreary as it sounded: 'Dreadful – without a tree or bush – nothing but a beach and sandbanks.' The rooms were small but clean. The sitting-room also served as a dining-room and her husband's dressing-room. The Queen, far from sympathizing, lectured Alice on the control of her nerves and the management of her children. Alice shouldn't have them *around* her so much – as if that were possible in a minute Blankenberghe boarding-house! But Alice insisted:

I do *not* fuss over the children but circumstances have forced me to be the mother in the real sense, as in a private family, and I had to school myself to it, I assure you, for many small self-denials have been necessary. Baby worship, or having the children indiscriminately about one is not at all the right thing and a perpetual talk about one's children makes some women intolerable. [The Queen had forgotten that *she* had been through a 'continual baby talk' phase herself after her first-born.] I hope I steer clear of these faults. Louis has often complained that I would not have the children enough in my room but, being of your opinion, where it was necessary, I thought it better not.

Perhaps Alice had been – still was too attached to the home and memories of her parents? 'I know what an absorbing feeling that of devotion to one's parents is. When I was at home it filled my whole soul. It does still in a great degree and homesickness does not cease after ever so long an absence.' She returned to the theme on another occasion: 'No home in the world can quite become what the home of one's parents and childhood was. You, who never left country, kindred or home, can scarely enter into this feeling.' Prince Alexander said that Alice was always dissatisfied when she returned from England and did not try to hide her feelings of boredom.

But the Darmstadt family visits to England had become less frequent. The Queen no longer demanded Alice's presence with the insistence of former years. Alice wrote sadly in 1875, after a brief visit, the first in four years: 'How I do love you, sweet Mama! There is no sacrifice I would not make for you, and as our meetings are of late years so fleeting and far between, when they are over I feel the separation very much.'

In England people found that she had become very German. Alice spoke German with her husband, whose English was defective; according to Sir Henry Ponsonby, he talked politics at table, which made the Queen cough nervously. 'Louis's English and whole conversation consists in. "You have in your country a-a-what you call – ah so! Like what you call Alice, Alice! *Was herst ein wohlengeblandersuhe?* Fog. Ah so, yes. A fog, which makes what you call-ah-Alice! Alice! *Was ist geblandesbend?* Dark. Yes, dark."' He could not be described as entertaining company. He was reported to be an efficient general and went to drill every morning at home for three hours from 6 a.m. During his visits to England he visited the Parkhurst Barracks, where he delighted the officers and men by trying their arms, pulling at their belts, examining their buttons and hats and putting his nose into their cartouche cases.

Alice saw more of her brother, Prince Alfred, 'Affie', who enjoyed his informal visits to Darmstadt. It was there that he met and fell in love with the Grand Duchess Marie, only daughter of the Emperor Alexander II of Russia. The Queen was not very pleased at the prospect of a Russian daughter-in-law and a Greek Orthodox chapel in Claremont House, but Affie had so set his heart on Marie that she felt she could not refuse. A genuine romance seldom failed to touch the Queen.

On the occasion of Beatrice's confirmation in 1875 her French teacher, Mlle Norèle, wrote some sentimental verses, comparing the Princess to a lily. The Queen forwarded them to Sir Theodore Martin, with whom she had become extremely friendly since his biography of Prince Albert with the remark: 'She did so look like a lily, so very young, so gentle and good. The Queen can only pray that this flower of the flock, which she really is (for the Queen may truly say she has never given the Queen one moment's cause of displeasure) may never leave her, but be the prop, comfort and companion of her widowed mother to old age. She is the Queen's Benjamin.'

At Balmoral, she took Beatrice and Miss Phipps with her to her retreat at Glassalt Shiel. 'Why the Queen should like to bury herself in the icy solitudes of the Glassalt Shiel is beyond everybody's comprehension,' wrote Sir Henry Ponsonby to his wife. The household pitied the young Princess, who was so deprived of the companionship of her own generation. The Queen persisted in treating her like a vestal virgin. Sir Henry received a message from the Queen through Lady Ely asking him 'not to bring up the subject of marriage at table in front of Princess Beatrice'. Politics had always been taboo at table, now romance was too! Dinners were becoming more and more tedious, with everybody racking their brains for suitable topics of conversation.

The quiet, permanent presence of Beatrice soothed the Queen's nerves. 'Beatrice is really an unusually dear, gentle child, very quiet, always contented and with the most remarkable even temper and good spirits I have ever seen in young girls,' she wrote. But she certainly did not treat her youngest daughter like the tender 'lily' that she had been described as on her confirmation day. When Beatrice suffered from a bad cold, the Queen insisted on making her go out in her open carriage, and when she walked into her bedroom and found the windows shut, she ordered them to be opened immediately; 'I do not want my mother to be smothered,' she said sternly.

It had been dinned into Beatrice so often and so emphatically that she must watch her conversation at dinner with the ladies and gentlemen of the household that the poor girl – like so many of the Queen's guests – was at a loss as to what to say. She had become her mother's confidante and secretary and she lived in mortal fear of betraying Mama's royal confidence. When Sir Henry Ponsonby returned from a visit to Paris, she could not resist asking him a few questions, but they were limited chiefly to what his daughter had bought there: 'She repressed any real conversation on the visit as if he had been going to tell her the story of the *boule* or the *demi-monde!*'

Surprisingly, for a person who encouraged the RSPCA, took an interest in homes for dogs and cats and criticized experiments on animals, the Queen was tolerant on the subject of bullfights described to her by Sir Henry Layard. She thought him very prejudiced 'to object to this sport which the Spaniards love more than we love our foxhunting here'. And she thought a lady of the court who had not been able to watch a bullfight to its gory close 'very squeamish indeed'. Beatrice listened and made no comment. She was far from guessing that one day *she* would be forced to attend a bullfight during the wedding festivities of her daughter Victoria Eugenia, Queen Ena of Spain . . .

Beatrice helped Mama, too, with all the telegrams about their ailing acquaintances of whom the Queen kept unfailing track. This trait irritated the members of her household. 'The Queen is always full of telegrams and enquiries after sick people,' Sir Henry Ponsonby complained. 'Sir William Jenner "thinks there is some improvement", etc. etc. I couldn't understand who all the sick ones were.'

In September 1875 the Queen and Beatrice paid a visit to Princess Louise and the Marquis of Lorne at Inverary. The young couple drove out to meet her five or six miles from the castle.

Louise had devised a *mise en scène* which she knew would please her mother. First, an arch with a Gaelic inscription which, translated, meant 'A hundred thousand welcomes to the Queen to Inverary'; here a child, held in the arms of a stout tenant's wife, a Mrs McArthur, presented the Queen with a nosegay. Along the tree-lined road, halberdiers had been posted at intervals, dressed in Campbell tartan kilts with brown coats edged in red, and bonnets bearing the Campbell badge of a black cock's tail and a sprig of bog myrtle. In front of the house pipers were arrayed in kilts and red jackets and there were also the Artillery Volunteers, of whom Lorne was the Colonel, in blue and silver. The Duke and Duchess of Argyll and their six daughters were at the door outside the steps, ('under glass, made into a sort of conservatory,' the Queen observed), waiting to greet the royal party and escort the Queen to her rooms, which were part of Louise's apartments. 'Not large, but very comfortable and cheerful, with a beautiful view of Loch Fyne.'

Luncheon was served at 2 p.m. in the Duchess's dining-room at the foot of the stairs for the Queen, Beatrice, Louise and Lorne, waited upon by John Brown and two or three of the Duke's servants. After lunch they went into the large drawing-room next door, where the Queen and Prince Albert had lunched in 1847, when Lorne was two years old. 'Now I return, alas, without my beloved husband, to find Lorne my son-in-law,' wrote the Queen.

She was pleased with the accommodation provided for her, no doubt at considerable inconvenience to her hosts, for she behaved during her stay more as if she were in her own home than as a guest of the Duke. 'Evidently the Queen considers herself as paying a visit to Princess Louise,' observed Sir Henry Ponsonby, 'the rest of the family being merely accidental. She only occasionally sees the Duke and Duchess and even Lorne. At dinner and in the evening, Princess Louise seems to undertake all the arrangements.' The Queen found it perfectly normal to breakfast strictly *en famille* in her sitting-room with Louise and Beatrice. The room had been specially arranged in Louise's bedroom; in a recess was a picture of Balmoral, and a passage beyond it led to a small apartment in which Annie the maid slept. The Queen could not sleep unless there was a human watchdog near her; this may have been a throwback to her childhood, when she slept in a bed placed in her mother's room. Her dresser had a room next door to the bedroom and Beatrice one next to hers.

As at Balmoral, the Queen went out for walks armed with a sketchbook, accompanied by Louise, Beatrice and servants carrying tea-making equipment. 'The Duchess admired the bag into which the cups fit,' she observed with satisfaction; had she lived in modern times she would undoubtedly have been very gadget-minded. She drove along the banks of the river to a small farm and attended a ball given for the tenants, sitting on a raised platform decorated with flags. Reels were played by a pipe, then a band played country dances. Louise danced a reel with Brown, and Beatrice a schottische with one of the Duke's foresters; the Queen left at nearly half-past twelve.

The Queen found Louise 'so kind and attentive, so anxious that I and all my people should be comfortable, thinking of everything'. She was pleased when an old lady tenant told her: 'We are all so fond of the Princess. She is a great pet.' One day the Queen walked a mile and a half to the top of a hill, 'a long pull, but I walked well', and sketched between showers at Douglas Water, along the seashore. Louise sketched a glen near the Dhu Loch. 'She has such talent, darling good child, and I felt so sad to leave her.'

The Queen's description made the visit sound idyllic but she carefully omitted to pencil in the shadows. In fact, as Sir Henry had gleaned: 'There seemed to have been various troubles arising out of Inverary, where Princess Louise took the opportunity of pouring out her grievances, such as that her rooms were not good enough, that she could not dine alone when she wished, and the ladies Campbell did not treat her with becoming respect.' All of these complaints seemed outrageous to sensible Sir Henry. As he told his wife: 'She has married into a Duke's family and must live with them as a relation; it is absurd talking of two dinners in a private house.'

> Then she complains that she hasn't got a separate country house. The Duke built one for them but in an uninhabited desert

and they 'can't abide it'. The odd thing is that Lorne seems to support her in all these complaints and thinks that the Duke should do more for her.
Another complaint is the company the Duke asks to Inverary: Professors and Presbyterian ministers. I confess it seems dull, but it is the Duke's house and he asks who pleases him best. I would be uncommonly short if I were the Duke'.

Several people in the inner circle of the royal family, including Sir Henry, said that Louise was a mischief-maker: 'Louise plays old Harry with every household or person she touches. The once happy home of the Argylls seems to be a perfect pandemonium now and the departure of the Lornes for the rest of the winter in the south has caused but little grief to the worthy parents. I presume that Lorne is overborne by her.'

In fact, all of Victoria's sons-in-law were 'overborne' by their wives, who never forgot that they were princesses, or lost their authoritarian manner. In addition, there were sisterly bickerings and petty jealousies. Beatrice, who led such a dull, cloistered life, discovered that Helena and Louise were quite indignant at the appointment of a Miss Cadogan to be her lady-in-waiting, saying that *they* never had one when they were single. 'Certainly,' observed Sir Henry, 'whenever the Queen does do a good thing, her children pitch into her for it, so it is not to be surprised at that she hesitates.'

Beatrice had an odd way of not appearing to listen to anything said by the ladies and gentlemen of the household, or she talked to someone else while they were speaking; but: 'It is not lost – your story is reproduced afterwards correctly,' said Sir Henry, who was becoming devoted to Beatrice. He wrote to his wife:

If only she could marry now, at once, a good strong man who would make her do what he wished, I really think she would turn out well. I think she would want a Prince tho' for her sake I should like an Englishman. But it must be soon. That manner you dislike is crystallizing and her want of interest, which I believe comes from fearing to care for anything the Queen hesitates about, will become natural to her unless a good husband stirs her up. But, poor girl, what chance has she?

There were times, for instance, when they were out driving, when the Princess would have liked to get out and walk up a hill by herself, but this was not allowed – the carriage would turn and go home without stopping. This occurred many times in later years during the Queen's foreign travels with her daughter on the Riviera or in Italy.

'The Queen's affection for her children does not appear in her manner when they are grown up,' noted Sir Henry. (But her grandchildren were in full favour. She would chat with them at Osborne as they trotted at her side and called her 'Gangan'.) 'And she clearly don't love her sons-in-law. She dislikes Fritz, is bored with Christian ("Why won't he *do* something"? she often asks) and now I'm told she hates Lorne. I can't conceive why except he has sharp passages about "not allowing Louise to stay here or anywhere without him", which is natural enough.' (This appears to have been a temporary fit of sulks. Lorne told Lord Ronald Gower, after the Queen's death, that 'she had always been like a mother to him; for thirty years he had received nothing but kindness and affection from her'.)

As for the Queen's sons, they were 'all in terror of her', according to Sir Henry.

At Osborne in July it was noticed that Louise was not so bright and lively as she used to be. It looked as if she was getting a little bored with her tall, fair Highlander. It was rumoured that Louise had never had a menstrual period and was unable to have children.

Meanwhile, the Queen's attitude to Prince Christian became positively irritable. One morning at Osborne she looked out of the window, saw him pottering about aimlessly in the garden and immediately sent him a message that he must occupy himself with something, or ride somewhere. 'The Queen is terribly bored with Christian,' wrote Sir Henry, 'and cannot understand why Helena likes him. Besides, he is bald and fat and it's nonsense their being so affectionate with each other.'

Gossip spread. Someone – presumably Vicky – told the Queen that somebody who heard it from Prince Christian repeated to Gladstone that the Queen had said she hated him. 'Her Majesty is indignant, although her allusions to him are not overflowing with love, but what she did say was in confidence. Prince Christian had no right to repeat it.'

No wonder Beatrice weighed her words so carefully! A neighbour at dinner remarked sourly: 'Sitting next to a beautiful Princess is a reward for bravery in fairy stories, but if the gallant man were popped down every night next to Princess Beatrice, he would soon cease to be brave. Not that she has nothing to say, for when the subject moves her, she has a torrent, but what with subjects tabooed, the subjects she knows nothing about, and the subjects she turns to the Queen upon, there is nothing left but the weather and silence.'

Alice came over to England in September 1876 for a short visit from Antwerp and asked whether she could stay for two nights at Buckingham Palace. She was attended only by a colonel and a Miss Macbean, who lived at Darmstadt and whom she had probably secured with some promise of lodgings at the Palace. But the Queen would not hear of it and wired a stiff refusal. Alice insisted, saying that she could not put her two companion-attendants to the expense of going to an hotel. Sir Thomas Biddulph suggested that the Queen could pay the hotel bill. How long would it be for? 'Dear me – a couple of days – but she hasn't said. . . .' More telegrams were exchanged. In the end, Alice travelled from London to Perth alone. 'Royalty is a bore when they travel in a hugger-mugger way, half like commoners, half like royalty, in special steamers,' sighed Sir Henry. When Alice did arrive at Balmoral, she seemed to prefer to dine with her brother Leopold rather than with the Queen. Leopold, weak though he was, and coddled because of his tendency to bruising and bleeding, was her children's favourite uncle.

In the following year, 1877, Prince Charles of Hesse died, followed three months later by the Grand Duke, so Louis of Hesse succeeded his uncle and Alice became Grand Duchess. Her position was now a little 'finer', but she was overwhelmed by public functions and her health was unequal to the task. She took the children for a short holiday to a small house at Houlgate, near Trouville, from where she commented to her mother on the outbreak of the Russo-Turkish War: 'Russians can never be redressers of wrong or promoters of civilization and Christianity.' She feared that the declaration of independence of Bulgaria would

> ... make that country to them in the future what Roumania has been for Russia now, and therefore in twenty years hence they will get all they want unless the other powers prevent it at this late hour and bring about a change. It is bad for England, for Austria, for Germany if this Russian slav-element should preponderate in Europe and the other countries must sooner or later act against this in self-preservation.

In June 1878 Alice and Louis brought their children over to Eastbourne for the bathing and good air. Alice wished to stay at Buckingham Palace for a night on her way, but the Queen, 'fearing that this one night might be a precious long one,' wrote Sir Henry Ponsonby, suggested that the party should proceed to Eastbourne at once. They stayed for the summer at a house on Grand Parade, went about freely in the town and attended various festivities.

On 21 August Alice went to Devonshire Park for the opening of a bazaar for the building fund of All Saints' Church. G. F. Chambers, in his *Eastbourne Memories*, recalls being introduced to the Princess by Lady Fanny Howard. The thing which specially struck him in a conversation with her was how completely she had lost her pronunciation of English. The royal visit was 'a great lift for the bazaar, which yielded £720'. Princess Alice also gave away the prizes at the College and inspected the Christ Church schools. Eastbourne was not as fashionable as Brighton and was therefore cheaper and better suited to the Hesses' limited means. Princess Alice was so loved by the local population – there was a great deal of poverty in Eastbourne in the 1870s, and she visited many of the humbler homes – that subsequently a hospital was erected in her name. Princess Christian (Lenchen) laid the foundation stone in 1882, and the hospital was opened on 30 June 1883.

Although her Eastbourne holiday had somewhat restored her nerves and strained physique, Alice still felt so exhausted before she went to Balmoral in September that she wrote to the Queen:

Darling Mama, I don't think you quite know how far from well I am, and how absurdly wanting in strength. I only mention it that you should know that until the good air has set me up. I am good for next to nothing and I fear I shan't be able to come to dinner the first evenings. I hope you won't mind. I have never in my life been like this before. I live on my sofa and see no one and yet go on losing ...

Tragedy struck the Darmstadt household in November. On the eighth a telegram from Alice was delivered at Windsor: 'Victoria has diphtheria The fever is high I am so anxious. Alice.' This was followed four days later by another telegram: 'To-night my precious Alicky has been taken ill.' The Queen, in great alarm, despatched Sir William Jenner to Darmstadt on 13 November. The next day little May was taken ill, then the Grand Duke and Ernest. On 16 November a message came that May had died, but that Victoria and Alicky were out of danger. The Grand Duke recovered, too, and began to go out in a closed carriage. Vicky sent Professor Bertell of Munich to look after the patients.

Little Ernest, who had not been told of May's death, and was still ill himself, anxiously enquired after his sister because he wanted to send her some flowers. In an outburst of emotion, Alice bent down and kissed him on the forehead. She caught the illness, and in her weak state of health, increasingly fatigued from her tireless nursing of so many invalids, sank rapidly.

Jenner telegraphed the Queen on 8 December to say that the position was dangerous. On the fourteenth, the Queen walked into the Blue Room as usual to pray on the anniversary of Albert's death. When she returned to her sitting-room two telegrams awaited her: one from Jenner, saying that Alice had become suddenly worse at midnight; the second from her son-in-law Louis, informing her that Alice had died at 7.35 that morning. She was only thirty-five. 'That this dear, talented, distinguished, tenderhearted, nobleminded, sweet child, who behaved so admirably during her dear father's illness, and afterwards, in supporting me and helping me in every possible way, should be called back to her father on this very anniversary of his death, seems almost incredible and most mysterious,' the Queen wrote in her journal.

Helena, who had always admired her sister and tried to emulate her interest in charitable works, was heart-broken. A few years afterwards she made a selection from Alice's letters to her mother which formed the basis of a *Memoir* published in 1889. Bertie sobbed: 'She was my favourite sister . . . so good, so kind, so clever.' He, Uncle Leopold and Prince Christian went to Darmstadt for the funeral. Vicky and Fritz had been forbidden to go by order of the Emperor, who feared infection. A Union Jack was draped over the coffin, for Alice had always said: 'I want to go with the old English colours above me.' A deputation from the court theatre in which Alice had always taken so much interest sent a large wreath, a peasant woman sent a garland of rosemary and two little orphan girls whom she had once befriended sent a crumpled bunch of violets. At Windsor, on her funeral day, Alice's favourite hymn, 'Thy will be Done', was played at the Queen's request.

'She had a warm heart for all necessity,' conceded Princess Marie of Battenberg. 'She knew how to initiate schemes for the general welfare in the most practical fashion.' But she went on to hint that the Princess, like her sisters, had an authoritarian streak: 'To use a forcible expression, everyone had to put hand and foot into whatever she organised.' Her brother-in-law, Prince Alexander, whose favourite Alice had never been now referred to her as 'that remarkable and forceful woman'.

Vicky was grief-stricken: 'Sweet, darling Alice, she was my particular sister, the nearest in age, the only one living in the same country with me. It often tormented me to see her so frail, so white, though it only added additional charm, seemed to envelop her with something sad and touching that always drew me to her all the more.' The Queen began to think of a suitable tomb and addressed herself to the fashionable sculptor, Boehm, who presented a design of the reclining figure of the Princess. At the Queen's suggestion, the tiny figure of May was added, reposing in her mother's arms, and the inscription, composed by the Queen, read: 'To the memory of my much loved and lamented daughter Alice, Grand Duchess of Hesse, who survived but a few days the fever-stricken child beside whom she had watched "not counting her life dear to herself".'

The Queen invited Louis to Osborne with the children as soon as the doctors considered that it was safe for them to travel. Bertie was sent to escort them from Flushing in the royal yacht on 20 January 1879, and the sad, motherless little family stayed at Windsor for two months. The Queen 'organized' them all, especially her granddaughters, and on their departure ordered their English governess, Miss Jackson (supplemented later by Miss Pryde), to send her detailed reports upon their education and general progress. Aunt Helena, Princess Christian, was to go to Darmstadt every year to pay them visits and the children were to spend holidays with the Christians and their four children. Louise was unavailable – she had sailed to Canada in November; anyway, the Lornes had no children and were not suitable company for the little Darmstadt princesses, who would soon have to be prepared for their confirmation, a ceremony which would be attended by the Queen. (For a while, it seemed that she had actually contemplated a marriage between Louis and Beatrice so that the children would be adequately looked after. Such a relationship was in fact against the law. A Bill permitting marriage with a deceased wife's sister, rejected by the bishops of the Church of England, was finally passed several years later. It was strongly supported by the Queen and Bertie.)

It was clever Disraeli's idea to have the Marquis of Lorne appointed Governor General of Canada, the fourth representative of the Crown at Ottawa since the Confederation. It would flatter the Canadians, he believed, to have the Queen's son-in-law and daughter despatched to their snowy wastes. The Marquis of Lorne (with his Highland second sight) had had a premonitory vision of his interview with Disraeli six months before it actually took place. It would have been more useful if the Marquis had possessed more powers of leadership and less of the occult.

Lady Dufferin, the wife of the ex-Governor of Canada, confided to Sir Henry Ponsonby that in her opinion 'Lorne was very vague in his conception of the duties of his office but the real difficulty was how Louise would treat people in Canada – if as royalty, there will be trouble, but if in the same way as Lady Dufferin did, they will be flattered. But Lorne's administrative capabilities have still to be developed.' Lorne had been an MP for his native Argyllshire at the age of twenty-three and then secretary to the Duke his father, who was Secretary of State for India. He was said to fulfil his duties gracefully rather than actively.

Canadian newspapers were full of the Marquis's glamorous background: heir to the Campbells, the most powerful of the Highland clans of Scotland, whose blood was mingled with that of the leading families of the country, whose territories covered great areas of the west of Scotland, whose father was a statesman of the greatest ability, etc. etc. Princess Louise's beauty and artistic talents were stressed. The *Toronto Globe* wrote apologetically:

> We have few attractions for the rich and great in this country. Those who find enjoyment in the show and glitter of life are not apt to think well of Canada. It so happens, however, that both the Marquis of Lorne and his consort are possessed of qualities which render them independent of many sources of amusement. The Marquis is of literary tastes, with a disposition to engage in public business . . . The Princess has artistic tastes which can be indulged almost as well at Ottawa as at London and, like all the daughters of the Queen, she is clever and industrious. It remains to be seen whether this intelligent pair can find in Canada

sufficient of interest to induce them to remain during the duration of the Governor General's term.

Other papers were more guarded, pointing out that the majority of Canadian people were not wealthy and that 'it would be a cause for regret if the presence of the Marquis and his wife was to encourage extravagance in equipage or dress'.

November was not the best month for a long voyage from Liverpool to Halifax in the SS *Sarmatian* of the Allen Line, although it had been equipped, the *Brighton Herald* reported, 'with a patent berth which will reduce the incidental discomforts of the voyage to a minimum, if it does not obviate them altogether'. This it certainly did not. Staggering through surging seas, the *Sarmatian* had to be towed into Halifax with its foresail and mainsail torn away. The man-of-war promised by the Admiralty to pilot it into the harbour had not appeared. Everyone had been seasick except Lorne, who paced the deck with a captured seagull which he wished to sketch.

The usual salutes and receptions took place before the long rail journey to Ottawa. Louise remarked on the striking appearance of the French peasants headed by their priests who drove up to see them in old-fashioned carrioles. Lorne spoke to them in French. The English Canadians cried: 'Welcome to the Rose of England and the Chief of the Clan Campbell!'

Louise was pleasantly surprised by their residence, Rideau Hall, overlooking the St Lawrence River. It had been greatly improved by the Dufferins, their predecessors, and contained a ballroom for fifteen hundred guests, tennis courts, skating rinks, a movable stage and a large crimson and white tent for garden-party style suppers in the summer. At first all went smoothly. Louise was an attractive hostess and she was stimulated by the novelty of the scenery and the sports: curling and tobogganing in the park. The ladies admired her grace at receptions and employed self-appointed dancing masters to teach them the proper backward walk and courtly graces. The *Toronto Telegram* was indignant that the 'usages of St James's were being introduced, as well as social distinctions that had no place in

Canada, which was becoming a nation of flunkeys'. Yet although the severe moral code of the French Canadians prevented them from wearing low evening dresses at Government House – the Catholic clergy frowned upon them – Louise exclaimed with a hoot of laughter: 'I should not care if they came in blankets!' At drawing-room receptions, Louise wrote home 'there is no hand-shaking, no kissing and no feathers'. On New Year's Day there was cake and champagne and a State ball, but too much wine was drunk and the gentlemen's behaviour tended to be uproarious. It was noticed that the English members of the royal suite behaved with less reserve if there were no Canadians present.

During the Lornes' stay the Canadian national hymn was first sung, to music composed by Sir Arthur Sullivan, who was visiting Canada at the time. Louise was delighted to see him. (In the happy days at home, her mother had sung airs from his operas, including 'Dear little buttercup'.). The Canadian national hymn she described as a 'rumtitum, glory and gunpowder affair, but it may take with the people.' It ran:

> O bless our wide Dominion,
> True freedom's fairest scene,
> Defend our people's union,
> God save our empire's Queen . . .

To pass the time, Louise wrote an operetta herself: a modern version of Enoch Arden based on a Gaspèsie fishermen plot with ballads written in the *patois* of that region. She also redecorated the interior of Rideau Hall: her drawing-room was painted in blues and greys and adorned with costly bric-à-brac. Her boudoir door was white, relieved by a blossoming apple branch which she painted herself. She sketched and illustrated an article on Canada for the English magazine *Good Words*. She went fishing on the Restigouche River, which divides New Brunswick from Quebec; it was an angler's paradise, and she 'roughed it', enjoying the camp life and the magnificent scenery. But in the end everything palled and, on the pretext of her fragile health and the 'impossible Canadian winters', she returned home for a long respite. She was reported to have complained that there was 'no refined society or aesthetic enjoyments' to be found in Canada. The *Globe* therefore suggested that the Princess should acquaint herself with the legends and songs of the people, and the *Christian Guardian* ventured to point out that she was not the only intelligent and cultured person in Canada.

It was observed at receptions that Louise would monopolize a person in conversation, one who had caught her fancy or had something interesting to say, and neglect the other guests. The same, incidentally, had been said about Vicky and the late Princess Alice. The American press, quick to seize a juicy piece of domestic royal gossip, reported that the Marquis of Lorne was a hen-pecked husband. This may have been true in private life, but the couple knew how to keep up appearances in public. Marie von Bunsen (the granddaughter of the Prussian ambassador who had been so popular at the English court) paid a visit to Canada during the Lornes' term of office and remarked:

> All honours were paid to Lorne as the Governor General. Louise played second fiddle on every occasion. She walked on his left, entered the room behind him, rose with all the rest of us when he came in and, like all the rest, remained standing until he was seated. In England, only on rare occasions he was commanded to join the family at table—the daughter took meals with her mother and he as a general rule with the household at the Lord Chamberlain's table.

Marie described Louise at that time as 'a tall, slight, handsome figure, who wore black velvet with diamonds and emeralds in the evenings. She was clever and had artistic tastes but was even shyer than most of the Queen's daughters and, although most likeable, without our Crown Princess's charm of manner.'

After Louise's holiday in England, she rejoined Lorne for a tour of the 'wild, woolly west'. Lorne wanted to see something of Canada's resources and especially to know about the conditions that awaited emigrants to the newly-opened north-west territories. The trip covered 8,054 miles, from Halifax to Fort MacLeod in Alberta, via Montreal, Toronto and Winnipeg. At the Hudson Bay Fort, Sioux Indians from Jumping Deer Creek gave a buffalo dance and at Red Deer a buffalo hunt was held in honour of the Marquis – it was the last but one to be held in Canada. Everywhere the Indians turned out in all their barbaric finery. Lorne thought that one of the chiefs looked remarkably like Gladstone.

The railway had not yet been extended to British Columbia, so the journey between Winnipeg and the Rocky Mountains was made across prairie trails in waggons with relays of horses, and nights were spent under canvas. Louise was impressed by all she saw, and so was Lorne. He was inspired to write a long poem entitled 'Westward Ho', which included the following lines:

> The West for you boys, where God has made room
> For field and for city, for the plough and for loom.
> The West for you girls, for our Canada dreams
> Love's home better luck than a gold-seeker's dream.
> Away and your children shall bless you, for they
> Shall rule o'er a land fairer far than Cathay.

Louise wrote home enthusiastically about Canada's future possibilities and asked her brother Leopold to go out and visit them. He did so, and from Canada the Lornes and Leopold paid a visit to Chicago, freshly rebuilt since the great fire of 1878, where several wealthy residents had designed houses inspired by Osborne and Balmoral.

The *Chicago Tribune* of 9 June 1880 reported:

> The royal party drove on the boulevards and through the south park, and the striking resemblance to the environments of Paris was mentioned by the Princess. Later they spent an hour and a half looking through the stock of jewelry and silver ware of N. Matson and Co, corner of State and Monroe streets, and made several important purchases. They were much surprised to find such a fine stock of goods in the western country and the Princess was particularly pleased with the unique styles of American jewelry and the exquisite manner in which the rare gems were mounted. The large and elaborate display of solid silver and plated ware amazed the Prince and Princess, as they did not expect

that people in the wilds of Illinois had use for such massive services. The superbly cut cameos and elegant designs in pins, rings, and ornaments were a revelation to our Canadian cousins and they marveled greatly at the richness of the exhibits. The bronze busts and statuettes of which the firm keep a large line, were very much admired. The Prince and Princess, on leaving the store, expressed themselves as being very much pleased with their visit and Messrs. Matson & Co will hereafter be regarded as 'jewelers to their Royal Highnesses'.

Under the heading 'Politeness of the Royal Guests', the *Chicago Tribune* added: 'H.R.H. Prince Leopold called in person upon one of our citizens, Joseph Ward, 210 South Clark, to thank him on behalf of Princess Louise for a beautiful bottle of his Toilet Foam, which he made up for her especial use and presented to her when at the Palmer House.' Other papers reported Louise and Leopold's movements in minute detail, occasionally referring to them as 'Queen Vic's chicks'.

Louise and Lorne encouraged the arts and sciences in Canada. A Royal Canadian Academy of Art was opened in 1880 and Lorne nominated the Academicians, each of whom was to donate a painting so as to form the nucleus of a Dominion Gallery. 'The merely money-getting days are over,' it was said a little prematurely. When they were in the west, Lorne's tracks crossed those of an expedition from the Smithsonian Institute which was collecting Indian relics on Canadian soil; this prompted Lorne and Louise to convene a meeting of scholars and scientists upon their return to Ottawa to organize a Canadian Royal Society. Lorne also popularized the idea of the Canadian engineer Sandford Fleming to have a common meridian and divide the world into twenty-four time zones, to bring about a world regularity; he wrote letters to the learned societies of Austria, Prussia, Switzerland, France and Russia until the idea of a universal or cosmic time was generally accepted.

In the winter, Louise had an accident. The sleigh in which she was driving to a reception overturned; she was thrown against a tree and suffered severe concussion and laceration of the left ear. She was so badly shaken that she travelled away soon after to convalesce: to Bermuda, England and the Continent. Was this an excuse to get away from Canada and, more particularly, from her husband? That is what was rumoured at Balmoral the following summer. 'Boyle's opinion,' wrote Sir Henry Ponsonby, 'is that Louise don't care for Lorne. He did for her, but kept a strong hand over her which she submitted to while with him but struggled to be free. The cure at the German baths was an excuse. True, she was shaken by her fall, but Canada was quite as restoring as Germany.'

But Louise continued to wander happily on the shores of Lake Constance until everyone began to doubt whether she would ever go back to Canada. 'Lorne seems not to press it – he is apparently happy without her. Princess Louise is away so much from Canada that she hasn't been a success there,' Sir Henry Ponsonby observed.

In 1883 for the first time in her life, Beatrice was separated from her mother when she went to Aix-les-Bains for a three-week cure for her rheumatism, upon urgent medical advice; she was twenty-six. The Queen missed her sorely and poured out her feelings in a letter to Augusta:

> Beatrice's absence is very grievous and unpleasant and increases my depression and the horrible ever growing feeling of emptiness and bereavement which nothing can ever really remove. But recently she had been suffering a great deal from neuritis, especially in the hand and right arm, which was a great inconvenience to her in writing and especially in playing the piano, and before that she had it in the knee and foot too. So we thought it would be advisable to try a thorough cure for three weeks.

The Queen was none too well herself. In May 1883 she complained: 'Many things unite in rendering the Queen's remaining years terribly hard and destitute. Her lameness does not improve much. She can walk very little indeed (and that is great labour) out of doors, and never without two sticks indoors, and is carried . . .'

Beatrice returned from Aix much improved and fortified, to console her mother during her next two tragic trials: first, the death of faithful, outspoken John Brown, which was minutely described to Augusta and accompanied by a photograph. The Queen also lamented her loss to Alfred Tennyson:

> Lately I have lost one who, humble though he was, had no thought but for me, my welfare, my comfort, my safety, my happiness. Discreet, speaking the truth fearlessly and telling me what he thought and considered to be just and right, without flattery. He was part of my life and quite invaluable . . . I have a dear, devoted child who has always been a dear, unselfish companion to me, but she is young and I can't darken her young life by my trials and sorrows. My other children, though all loving, have all their own interests and homes. And a large family is a great anxiety . . . My dear Beatrice returned well this morning [from Aix-les-Bains] to my great comfort . . .

Beatrice was 'dear' and necessary, but she was not a man, and the Queen badly needed the presence of a man about the palace, preferably a young and vital one. If he could carry her, so much the better. Albert had carried her to and from her sofa when she was pregnant; John Brown had carried her in and out of her carriage when she was old and infirm. Now, there was nobody.

Another domestic tragedy occurred in March 1884 when Prince Leopold, who had been married for little over a year to Princess Helen of Waldeck-Pyrmont, died from the results of haemophilia after a fall in Cannes. 'This awful disease – the worst I know of – it seems to persecute our poor family,' the Queen had moaned when her grandson Frittie died. (Leopold left two children: Charles, born posthumously, who married Victoria of Schleswig-Holstein, and Alice, who married the Count of Athlone.)

The Empress Eugénie drove over from Chislehurst to Windsor to present her condolences through Beatrice (she was always rather terrified of the Queen). She did not wish to upset Victoria, who groaned: 'I am a poor, desolate old woman and my cup of sorrow overflows. Oh, God in His mercy spare my other dear children!'

In April, however, mourning was momentarily put aside for the wedding of Princess Victoria, Alice's eldest daughter, to her

Balmoral in 1880.

*left* Beatrice, Mama's 'Benjamin', a rather solemn sixteen, and *right* Louise, a beautiful, sharp-tongued twenty-five, in 1873.

*top* Alice and Louis with their family (Victoria, Ella, Irene, Alix, Mazie and Ernest) in 1875.
*bottom* Beatrice and Prince Henry of Battenberg on their wedding day in July, 1885.

The Queen's private sitting-room, Windsor Castle, 1890.

*left* Princess Helena in 1911. A formidable Lady Bountiful, wrapped up in domesticity.
*right* Vicky, ex-Empress of Germany, a sadly mellowed widow, in 1900.

*top* Princess Beatrice in the early 1920s. She never left the Queen's side and saw little of her children.
*bottom* Princess Louise, Duchess of Argyll, in the late 1920s. She disliked being photographed in her old age although she was still attractive.

first cousin Louis of Battenberg. The royal family converged upon Darmstadt in force for ten days of excitement, romance and high comedy. Sir Henry Ponsonby described the bride, Victoria, as 'bright, lively but full of strange ideas. She locks herself up with her mother's books and papers and has imbibed Kant. Some say that she has shown her condemnation of princely titles by insisting on marrying a semi-Prince, going as low as she could in the scale of Princes without hurting susceptibilities. They will have no money from Hessian Parliament as she's not marrying a real Prince.'

The Battenbergs, fresh arrivals on the stage, were reputed to be the handsomest noble family in Europe. Prince Alexander of Hesse, uncle of the reigning Grand Duke Louis (Alice's widower), had married, morganatically, a Polish countess, Julie Theresa von Hauke (whose grandfather had been a pastry-cook). Alexander had in fact accompanied his sister Marie to Russia when she married the Tsar but was banished for making advances to the Grand Duchess Olga. After a hectic wandering life with Alexander, the Polish Countess had been created Princess of Battenberg, a small Hessian district, by the Grand Duke.

Of their four sons the eldest, Prince Louis, influenced by Alfred, Duke of Edinburgh, and his love of the sea – they had often met at the palace in Darmstadt – had become a British subject, and entered the Royal Navy as a midshipman in 1863.

Louis was described by his sister Marie as 'the most German of us all', although he had become a naturalized British subject. He was of a sunny nature and drew well; he had illustrated Bertie's travels in India for the *Illustrated London News* when their own artist fell ill and he was accompanying the Prince of Wales as a fifteen-year-old midshipman. He was musical and had an adventurous spirit.

His second brother, Alexander, was more adventurous from a political point of view, and even more handsome. He had been elected Prince of the allegedly independent, but in fact Russian, satellite state of Bulgaria in 1879. He was a favourite at the Crown Princess's court at Berlin, and her daughter Victoria [known as Moretta] had fallen in love with him and he with her; (a German gossip said that she had taken the initiative by kissing him in the palace library). Moretta was described by Mary Ponsonby as 'a kind of wild, Scandinavian woman, with much of her mother's impetuosity and a streak of her brother Willy's eccentricity'.

Moretta and Alexander ('Sandro' to the family) had become secretly engaged the year before the Darmstadt wedding. This romance caused a rift in the family, endless scenes and very nearly an international incident. Bismarck and the Emperor William, seeing the eagerness with which Vicky encouraged the love match, were convinced that it was part of a scheme – supported by Queen Victoria – to alienate Germany from Russia. (England had taken an anti-Russian stand in 1878, when Vicky had advocated putting Prince Leopold on the throne of Turkey to stop Russian encroachments.) The Crown Prince hesitated – he too foresaw difficulties. Nor did he think that a dethroned Prince – be he ever so handsome – was a good enough match for Moretta. Willy sided with Bismarck and his grandfather. Sandro had been invited to Windsor, where his looks captivated the impressionable Queen; she felt very sorry for him, was inclined to be influenced by Vicky's enthusiasm, but she also reserved her judgment.

The third Battenberg brother, Henry, was in the Hessian Army and possessed a fair share of the Battenberg looks and charm. When he and Princess Beatrice first set eyes on each other at Darmstadt in 1884 it was a case of 'love at first sight'. For once, the usually observant Queen noticed nothing. There were other matters to occupy her mind.

Also present at Darmstadt, and helping to fill the Lilliputian princely establishments to bursting point, were the two Romanovs: firstly the Grand Duke Serge, whose sister Marie was unhappily married to Prince Alfred, Duke of Edinburgh; Serge was an Anglophobe, cold, reserved, with grey-green eyes, unpopular even at home; and secondly Nicholas, who eventually succeeded to the throne of Russia. The two Romanovs fell respectively for the bride's sisters: Serge for Ella, Nicholas –

later – for little Alix. Ella, wrote Sir Henry Ponsonby, 'has got her fine, bold Russian. He isn't handsome, but she likes him and prefers him to the gentle but rather dull Baden prince who was told off for her.'

Finally, and very much in the limelight, there was the bride's father, Grand Duke Louis, whom the Queen believed to be still broken-hearted and sorrowing for his late wife, Alice. But – he was not. He had found consolation and probably more affinity, in the attractive person of thirty-year-old Countess Alexandrine von Kolomine, a Pole divorced from a flighty Russian diplomat; she had been introduced to the lonely Grand Duke by Prince Isenberg and his wife. Grand Duke Louis had become so infatuated with this lady, whom his daughters liked and approved of, that he was determined to marry her there and then. He could hardly have chosen a more inappropriate moment. How to break the awkward news to Queen Victoria? And to whom should a mission, which was bound to produce royal fireworks, be entrusted?

The wedding guests and their retinues were being entertained by drives and boar hunts. The Grand Duke went off to Frankfurt to shoot capercaillie and put off the awful confrontation and its consequences.

While whispered consultations took place between the various worried members of the family, the Queen wandered through the cold palace rooms in which her daughter had lived and died. No fires had been lit in them for a year. The country was 'looking brilliant and lovely in its spring attire of most vivid green; the birch woods are quite beautiful. It seemed almost an irony to see nature so bright and beautiful when the heart was so sad and could feel no pleasure . . .'

All at Darmstadt [reported Sir Henry,] is the inspiration of Princess Alice, on whom the worthy but stupid Grand Duke entirely relied. Many customs borrowed from England go on here and even our rooms in the old Schloss, though badly furnished and cold, are provided with excellent washing arrangements. Princess Alice's rooms in her palace are very comfortable, decorated in Morris style, much by Henry of the Tapestry Works. In her bedroom, preserved untouched, are several crosses and some texts which belie the stories of her being surrounded by positivist sayings. One window is a memorial window; it is that out of which her child, Frittie, fell. 'Suffer little children' is the text on the window. There are several beautiful little pictures round the room with views of Windsor, and royal portraits adorn the walls. We went to the mausoleum, which is nothing remarkable, except being neatly kept, and then to the Alice hospital which she began and is now completed by the memorial subscription. All speak of her with respect, but I imagine this is all. She was too stirring for them, she was proud of England, and they don't care for that and I don't think they are altogether sorry in the town that she has gone and they are relapsing fast into their dull German ways.

But the atmosphere during the royal visit was certainly very far from dull. It positively sizzled.

The Hessian Princesses had confided their troubles to their English governess, Miss Jackson, ' a worthy but not very wise woman', according to Sir Henry, 'who advises that the Tsar should be asked to order Kolomine back to Russia. But if she won't go? "Ah, but she must." '

Then Vicky arrived, full of Bulgaria and dear Sandro. From the way she spoke about him one would have thought she was a little in love with him herself: 'If only England would support Sandro!' Sir Henry assured her that the government did, as far as it could, but the English could only give moral support and only lately, as Gladstone and others had objected to Prince 'Sandro' upsetting the Constitution. 'Under all this is the "secret" that her daughter Victoria [Moretta] loves Sandro; he reciprocates, but once or twice is a little oblivious. Bismarck is against the whole thing. Sandro arrives next week. The Princess of Battenberg [Sandro's mother] is ambitious to push her children into princely marriages.'

On 21 April Lady Ely was informed about the scandalous Kolomine – Grand Duke Louis *affaire* by the Crown Princess, who had also broken the news to Bertie. Poor Lady Ely was in a terrible state because they wanted her to tell the Queen about Grand Duke Louis's proposed marriage. His daughter Princess

Victoria insisted that no one else could do so. 'The Grand Duke,' wrote Sir Henry, 'is in a horrible fright. I must say he has behaved very badly in not telling Her Majesty before she came here, for it places her in a most awkward position. If she goes away, it will look as if she approved. The lady [Mme Kolomine] is pretty and pleasant. Princess Victoria [of Hesse, his daughter] is always with her and the Grand Duke. She is in a terror that it may get out and so thinks it should be announced beforehand.'

The 'lady', Alexandrine Kolomine, had arrived on 23 April in radiant spirits, and on the twenty-fifth the Queen was finally 'told' – delicately – by Vicky. She was carefully led to believe that it was a temporary passion and that she would be able to persuade the Duke to give it up, that nobody else could possibly deal with the difficult situation. On the twenty-sixth Grand Duke Louis arrived back from his capercaillie shoot in Frankfurt. He too was radiant. 'None of the party can shy stones at the Grand Duke,' observed Sir Henry, 'his uncle Alexander married a lady-in-waiting and a daughter was born before the marriage . . .' A whisper spread like wildfire round the palaces and ducal establishments, where everyone had heard about the scandal. 'The Grand Duke's intended marriage *must* be broken off. There will be lively work at the New Palace.'

On the twenty-ninth, Vicky – who had been enlivening dinner conversations by discussing every topic from China to Peru – told the Queen more about 'la Kolomine', and informed her that most people knew about the affair. Her entourage suspected that Vicky was writing to the Emperor of Germany for further instructions. On the thirtieth Vicky announced that Bertie was to 'work' the breaking-off and was said to have secured a postponement.

Fritz, who did not favour the Moretta – Sandro romance, was sent away to amuse himself for the day in the woods round Darmstadt 'so as not to interfere with the billing and cooing'. The Russians disliked Sandro, who was said to be up to his ears in debts. Princess Moretta was alleged to have 'a facility for falling in love with anyone who devotes himself to her'. Nor were the 'upper Darmstadtians' in favour of the Louis –

Victoria wedding, saying that it was due to the ambitious Princess of Battenberg and that there would always be difficulty about rank for the couple.

The wedding did, however, take place on 1 May. Sir Henry considered that it was 'very well managed'. The civil marriage took place at 5 p.m., then a procession formed, headed by the Queen, her son, her five granddaughters, the two Hessians and the three Waleses. 'Her Majesty walked off at a splendid pace.' A banquet was held between 6 and 9 p.m.; in the course of it it was whispered that Princess Battenberg would continue to be the head lady of Hesse, because 'la Kolomine' wouldn't live in the palace. Maybe she had even encouragd the affair . . . Bertie was reported to be angry that the Queen should have been told anything at all.

Almost immediately after his daughter's wedding, Grand Duke Louis proceeded with his own in the privacy of his apartments. The service was read by Minister Storck, and the witnesses were Prince Isenberg and the bride's brother. The bride stayed with friends and the marriage, according to one source, was not consummated. According to another, a son was born and later adopted as a brother by Alix, Empress of Russia. 'We quite liked the lady, who was full of attentions for us,' Victoria of Hesse wrote in her *Memoirs*, 'and I hoped my father would feel less lonely when married to a woman he was much in love with.'

When the news of the secret marriage leaked out, the storm broke over Darmstadt. A royal family conclave was held on 2 May to discuss a joint protest against the Grand Duke's marriage. As the Prince of Wales was heard to state: 'We are a very strong family when we all agree.' On the other hand, Fritz declined to have anything to do with the scandal and was of the opinion – shared by the Queen – that the Emperor should not be bothered with it.

Grand Duke Louis then announced that Ella and the Grand Duke Serge of Russia had become engaged. This news displeased the Empress Augusta, who was already ruffled by the Sandro-Victoria romance. When she heard about Grand Duke Louis's own marriage she was beside herself, and ordered Fritz and Vicky to return to Berlin at once. So off went all the Prussians and their suite, leaving the Prince of Wales to cope with Grand Duke Louis and the lawyers appointed to discuss the annulment of his hasty marriage.

Grand Duke Louis was no match for this concerted attack; he meekly gave in and was eventually convinced by the Queen that he had acted rashly. The annulment, she insisted, would have to be settled in time for Ella's marriage to Serge in St Petersburg, in June, so as to avoid more scandal. Grand Duke Louis was reduced to tears of gratitude and sobbed as the Queen was taking her majestic leave from Darmstadt: 'You have saved me from myself.' She gave a satisfied nod, nearly patted him on the head.

But Her Majesty's complacency was of short duration. Soon after her return home her darling Beatrice, timidly but in tones of unusual firmness, informed her that she and Henry Battenberg had fallen in love. This was too much for Mama to stomach after the stirring events of Darmstadt. What? Her precious, innocent flower – her Benjamin ... how could she betray her mother by contemplating marriage, the word which had been taboo for so many years at the royal table? The Queen was incensed. Had Beatrice gone temporarily out of her mind? Could it have been deranged by those *dreadful* scenes at Darmstadt, although the worst details had been kept from her innocent ears? Oh yes, she agreed privately, young Henry of Battenberg was *very* handsome ... like a fairy-tale Prince. But no, it could not, *must* not be. She prayed fervently that this last, much-loved child would be spared to her virginal and unsullied.

Beatrice remained obdurate. The Queen had never known her like that. That dear child was developing a will of her own! Verbal relations between mother and daughter were severed; for eight weeks the Queen sent orders to her by way of written notes from one end of the breakfast table to the other at Windsor and at Osborne. Beatrice had been sent to Coventry like a naughty child.

In England, Prince Louis of Battenberg was settling down cosily with his new bride at Sennicotts, a country house near Chichester. Here, with the help of the penitent Grand Duke of Hesse (now fully restored to royal favour) urging the Queen from Darmstadt, Bertie *sur place* and Vicky in her letters, gentle pressure was put on the Queen to give her blessing to Beatrice's romance. Vicky brought the greatest weight to bear by reminding the Queen of beloved Papa's love for Beatrice, how he had always wanted his children to be happy, how she herself had told her, Vicky, when she married Fritz, how lonely she had been before her marriage to Papa and lacking in companions of her age; now that poor dear Leopold was dead there was nobody near Beatrice's age – she was now twenty-seven – round her . . . All this was tactfully expressed, and little by little the Queen relented. Very well, she agreed, at last. She would allow the marriage to take place, but on the express condition that Henry of Battenberg would live in England and at court. Beatrice would have to continue to be her secretary and confidante; on those terms alone would she give her consent.

The enamoured twenty-five-year-old Henry, in the first flush of young love, joyfully agreed. Prince Christian could perhaps have warned him that it would be a hard bargain, but he wisely preferred not to interfere. He never interfered. Life at Cumberland Lodge was a little dull at times, but it was pleasant. He enjoyed family life; he allowed Helena to have her way, busy herself with charitable works and organize dinner parties; he supervised the menus for he was a gourmet. Good food, good wine, good cigars, good hunting; the children to tell German fairy stories to of an evening; a few light duties in his capacity as Ranger of Windsor Park . . . he asked no more from life.

Prince Henry was invited to Osborne, during the Christmas holidays; he had been staying near Chichester with his brother Prince Louis and his sister-in-law Victoria, from where he had written to the Queen after a preliminary approving reception at Windsor. The 'terms' having been made plain to both parties, 'Liko', as Henry was called *en famille*, was asked to a dinner party on 23 December. The Queen noted in her diary that he had asked for her consent to speak to Beatrice; 'for whom, since they met at Darmstadt eight months ago, he had felt the greatest affection. I had known for some time that she had had the same feelings towards him. They seem sincerely attached to each other, of that there can be no doubt. I let Liko know to come up after tea and I saw him in dear Albert's room. Then I called the dear child and gave them my blessing.'

Now it was the family's turn to pronounce themselves displeased by the proposed marriage. Victoria, who could not bear to be contradicted, defended her youngest daughter as vehemently as she had hitherto opposed her. The Empress Augusta wrote 'a most unamiable letter'; even 'dear Fritz' considered Liko's background too low. Willy and his wife Dona were 'insolent, impertinent and unkind'. Fancy Dona, that foolish, poor little insignificant Princess . . . (Willy had married Princess Augusta Victoria, daughter of Duke Frederick of Augustenberg, one of the claimants to the Duchy of Holstein, in 1881.) And Willy, that unfeeling, undutiful boy! He deserved a 'good skelping, as the Scotch would have said'! The Queen was indignant with them all.

Augusta, in particular, had no right to address Victoria in such a tone. Who did she think she was? The Queen turned vindictive and bitchy, opened princely cupboards and jubilantly dragged out skeletons. Did people believe that she had not known of their existence? Of course she had! Few family trees were unscathed. Augusta's son-in-law and his brothers and sisters were 'the children of a Fräulein von Geyersberg, a very bad woman'. And fancy dear Fritz being such a snob! 'He speaks of Liko as not being *geblüt* stock – a little like about animals.' If one were to look closely enough, said the Queen, there were black spots to be found in the background of most of the royal families of Europe.

The wedding took place at last on 22 July 1885 at Whippingham Church on the Isle of Wight; it was the first time that this little church, befriended by the royal family, had ever been used for such an important occasion.

Canon Prothero of Whippingham had written to Sir Ponsonby Fane at St James's Palace on 29 June: 'I had already settled to dress up the stump of the pulpit with ivy and ferns, but your idea of the corresponding one the other side is brilliant. Will you give orders for it? If you would order a light iron rail round each stump the gardeners can make a pyramid of flowers in pots, which would look well. I only hope they will send me plenty of flowers, and in good time!'

Relatives came from the continent after a stormy sixteen-hour crossing in the royal yacht *Victoria and Albert*. The Hessians and their suite arrived 'all green and yellow' from seasickness. What a contrast, they agreed privately, with Ella's grand wedding in St Petersburg the year before! They were accommodated all over the island: at Osborne Cottage, Kent House, Norris Castle, Park Villa, Cowes Castle; some were rocked at night at sea in the royal yachts.

The ladies wanted to know what they should wear at the wedding – the previous ones of the princesses had been so private. The Queen was vague on the subject but, when pressed, stated that '*demie-toilette*' would be in order. What did this mean? Nobody knew what she meant and nobody dared to ask for clarification until the Duchess of Buccleuch took the matter up with her and then on 6 July issued the following proclamation:

> Ladies staying in the Isle of Wight are to wear long dresses with demie-toilette bodies cut down on the back and with sleeves to the elbow. Jewels to be worn on the dress and in the hair as for full dress evening party. Only those ladies who travel down to Osborne for the day are to wear bonnets and smart morning dresses. In case it may be of any help to you, I will desire my dressmaker, Miss Metcalfe, 111, New Bond Street, to make my 'body' at once, so that anyone who cares to see it can do so by calling there.

The wedding service was performed by the Archbishop of Canterbury, assisted by the Bishop of Winchester, the Very Rev. The Dean of Windsor and the Rev. Canon Prothero of

Whippingham. Parrat, the organist of St George's chapel, Windsor, played the organ.

The choir imported from Windsor for the service was meanly treated. Sir John Cowell, Master of the Household, telegraphed: 'We cannot provide in any way for choristers coming from London. They should make their own arrangements for refreshments, I suppose at East Cowes.'

Princess Louise's Argyll and Sutherland Highlanders mounted a guard of honour in front of the little church, together with the Isle of Wight Volunteers of the Queen's at Osborne. Owing to previous wrangles over precedence on similar occasions, the order of signing the royal register was drawn up and signed by the Queen beforehand.

Beatrice was of 'stately build', with the large bosom common to all the Queen's daughters; nor was she a débutante, so she wisely preferred heavy but simple materials and was averse to pastel shades. Her wedding dress was in heavy white satin trimmed with orange blossoms and a Honiton lace overskirt which had been worn by the Queen at her own wedding; Beatrice was the only one of her five daughters to be allowed to wear it at hers. It was looped with bouquets of entwined orange blossom and white heather. She was given away by her mother who, after the ceremony, 'tenderly embraced her darling Baby. . . . A happier-looking couple could seldom be seen kneeling at the altar together; it was very touching.' It was the ninth time the Queen had stood near a child at the altar and the fifth and last time near a daughter, but she had never felt more deeply than on this occasion, she wrote.

The Queen took in every detail, as usual, through her tear-filled eyes: 'The simple, pretty little village church, all decorated with flowers, the sweet young bride, the handsome young husband, the ten bridesmaids [all nieces of the bride] six of whom quite children with flowing fair hair, the brilliant sunshine and the blue sea all made up pictures not to be forgotten,' she wrote to Lord Tennyson on 7 August. The Queen wore black even for this festive occasion, but a very special material described as 'a black grenadine mixture, double *broché* and double wire silk, woven on a special loom at Lyons and destroyed afterwards so that the pattern could never be copied'.

The bride went off for her honeymoon in a real period-piece going-away outfit: a dress and mantle of ivory French *broché crêpe de chine* with a pattern of leaves, the mantle trimmed with lace and ivory ribbon, and a small bonnet of white velvet caught with silver thread, trimmed with small white ostrich feathers and tied under the chin with velvet strings. To complete the pretty museum picture, she carried a little white lace parasol.

After her wedding, the Empress Eugénie took Beatrice in her arms and said: 'I have always looked on you a little as my daughter-in-law. So that the bonds between us are not completely broken, please promise me that your first daughter will be my godchild.' And so it was that this first daughter was eventually given the name of Victoria Eugénie, whose destiny was to spend most of her life in her godmother's native land: Spain. The Queen wrote prophetically to Lord Tennyson from Osborne: 'I could not but feel sad in thinking that their [Beatrice's and Henry's] hour of trial might come, and earnestly prayed God would spare my sweet Beatrice and the husband she so truly loves and confides in, for long, long to each other.' It was destined to be for only ten years. And the 'trial' would be brought about slowly, irrevocably and unwittingly by the erosive influence of Prince Henry's imperial and imperious mother-in-law herself.

Meanwhile, the young couple were allocated a suite of rooms at Windsor in the south turret between the Victoria and York towers, and adjacent rooms overlooking the Long Walk. Handsome Liko began to adapt himself to the royal household, bringing to it a refreshing sense of fun and a lively humour. Since his childhood, as his sister recalled in her *Memoirs*, he had been 'fond of merry pranks'. In the summer he went to Balmoral and wore a kilt. Fritz and Vicky came over. 'The Crown Princess enjoys being here,' Sir Henry Ponsonby observed, 'and the Prince of Wales delights in going about with her. She's up at 6 a.m. and away over the hills.' He found the Crown Prince pleasant to talk to and 'proud of being a soldier, but he does not push it forward'. (This was not the view of Sir Robert Morier, the British ambassador in Berlin, who thought that the Crown Prince was 'a visionary, without energy or fixed purpose, allowing his wife to commit follies while he himself thinks he is going to put on the Crown of Charlemagne'.)

Louise arrived to liven up the party with 'a real story of second sight'. A Mrs Symons had told her that she had dreamed that her brother died, and he did die. 'Mrs Symons saying so now is no proof, but Louise declares she told Lorne before the event. Princess Louise,' wrote Sir Henry, 'makes our evening parties particularly pleasant . . . Whatever people say of her I must say she is charming and I don't know what I should do at these long dreary evening parties if it were not for her. With such a sweet smile and soft language she says such bitter things!'

Vicky took Liko aside at Balmoral and asked him to act as a messenger between Victoria and Sandro, for fear that letters might be intercepted between Berlin and Sofia if they were sent from the New Palace. There were spies everywhere, she told Liko, even in her own household, placed by Bismarck and the Emperor. Liko reluctantly complied. The Sandro affair was brought to a head in 1886, when the Russians paid a band of Bulgarian malcontents to break into the palace at Sofia and drag Sandro to the station, from where he was packed off to the Austrian frontier. After various adventures he finally reached his native Darmstadt, 'broken in body and spirit,' he wrote to his brother. The Queen invited him to Windsor and found him sadly changed. The thought must have crossed her alert mind that the poor boy was hardly a suitable match for her granddaughter. In his present state, however, he did not constitute a political menace. The Queen was furious with the Russians and convinced that they intended to take over Constantinople. Vicky protested against the Russian coup in Bulgaria and wrote to her friend Lady Paget: 'All temporizing with anarchy is criminal weakness, abandoning the keep to the wolves and damaging in every way the cause of true liberty.'

A far graver problem confronted Vicky at the beginning of the new year. In January 1887 her husband Fritz caught a bad cold and a persistent hoarseness developed which would not yield to treatment. The household physician Dr Wegner summoned the throat specialist Professor Gerhardt, from the University of Berlin, for consultation. On 6 March a small growth was found on the Prince's left vocal cord. This was treated by galvano-cautery but there was no improvement. The Crown Prince was sent to Ems for a cure until early May, but by that time the growth had become enlarged. Another Professor was called in: Professor Bergmann, considered to be one of the greatest authorities in Europe and a personal friend of the Prince's. He was of the opinion that the growth should be removed immediately, but he would not say whether or not it was malignant.

Vicky wrote in despair:

> I own I was more dead than alive with horror and distress when I heard this. The idea of a knife touching his dear throat is terrible to me. Of course Fritz is as yet not to know a word about this. He is at times so very depressed that he now thinks his father will survive him . . . my fear and dread is that a swelling of this kind, if not removed by some means or other, might in time develop into a growth of malignant and dangerous character.

Both the Emperor and Bismarck insisted that no operation should be performed without the Crown Prince's consent. Bismarck arranged for a consultation and confrontation of six German doctors, who unanimously agreed that cancer existed and that the operation should take place. Bismarck was not satisfied and asked for another opinion from an international expert. From three names put forward, Dr Morell Mackenzie was finally chosen by the German doctors. Vicky had never heard of him, although she was later accused – when he too had failed – of having sent for him to replace the German doctors, since this move tallied with public opinion about her known partiality to everything and everybody British. Queen Victoria asked Sir William Jenner for an opinion on Mackenzie. He reported that he was an expert on throat diseases, but greedy and grasping about money.

The long drawn-out drama slowly gathered momentum and, tragically, instead of binding the members of the German royal family closer together, drove them still further apart. Mackenzie arrived in Berlin on 28 May and examined the Crown Prince the next day. He was not sure of the necessity of an operation, preferring first to remove a fragment of the infected larynx and send it to Professor Rudolph Virchov, the famous pathologist, for a microscopic examination. The Professor declared that he could not detect any sign of cancer in the tissue.

Mackenzie now took over. Perhaps, if he had confided in the German doctors, his critics would have been silenced. Vicky, in her fear and anxiety, clung to the British doctor who had given her a ray of hope. All her prejudices against German doctors rose to the surface: the doctor who had brought Willy into the world and deformed his arm and his personality for ever; the doctors and surgeons with whom she had battled for better hospital conditions during the Schleswig-Holstein and Franco-Prussian Wars. 'I wouldn't have a German doctor near me if I could help it,' she had written to her mother years before. Mackenzie then said that he would like to treat the patient in England; Vicky agreed to this suggestion with alacrity, for she badly wanted to attend the Queen's Golden Jubilee in July 1887. Fritz *must* take part in the triumphal procession!

A storm of protest broke out in Berlin when it was known that the Crown Prince was going to England with his wife to represent Germany at the Golden Jubilee. Willy wanted to take his father's place and worked hard behind the scenes to achieve his object. Bismarck had decided that Mackenzie was a quack and Vicky was accused of endangering her husband's life to satisfy her personal ambitions. The old Emperor, torn between so many divided opinions, wisely declared that his son should be allowed to make up his own mind.

On 12 June, Fritz and Vicky set out for London, where they had rented a house in Upper Norwood, in the belief that the air there would be purer for the invalid. Mackenzie was in constant attendance on his illustrious patient, who visited the

Throat Hospital in Golden Square during his stay, before proceeding to Osborne and Balmoral after the official celebrations.

In that year 1887, the old Emperor William I celebrated his ninetieth birthday, Queen Victoria the fiftieth anniversary of her accession to the throne, and their grandchildren Irene of Hesse and Prince Henry of Prussia became engaged.

It was 'Queen's weather' for the Jubilee, hot and sunny. London had never presented a more brilliant aspect, nor a more exotic one, for there were Indian princes in their magnificent jewels, and maharanees to whom the Queen presented Beatrice in the Hindustani she had learned from the turbaned Indian servants who had replaced kilted John Brown. They hovered behind the sixty-eight-year-old Queen-Empress, a constant reminder of the distant empire on which she had never set eyes.

The Queen was excited and elated. She hurried over dressing, so as to breakfast early with Beatrice and Liko at Frogmore. They accompanied her to the station through a beautifully decorated Windsor Town. From Paddington she drove in an open landau to Buckingham palace, where all the royalties were assembled; they made an enormous and diverse party, including the Queen of Hawaii, the Japanese Prince Kamatsu, a Siamese and a Persian prince. There was tea in the garden, with Beatrice at the Queen's side to help, a 'family' dinner of royalties, eaten off gold plate. It was all very fatiguing, however, and the Queen slipped away, 'after talking to as many people as I could'.

Early next morning she woke to the sounds of cheering and passing troops and bands playing, and breakfasted in the Chinese room with Beatrice and Liko, Helena and Arthur. At 11.30 she left the Palace, wearing a bonnet trimmed with white Alençon lace and studded with diamonds, and drove to Westminster Abbey in a gilt landau drawn by six creams with 'dear Vicky and Alix'. There were thirty-two princes in the procession. 'Dear Liko wore English uniform for the first time,' while 'Fritz looked so handsome and well'; onlookers observed that he resembled Lohengrin; they did not know that he could hardly speak above a hoarse whisper.

At the door of the Abbey, the Archbishop, in the cope of rich velvet and gold that had been worn at the Coronation, was waiting to receive her like St Peter at the gates of Paradise. Once inside, the Queen sat alone, 'in the old coronation chair, with the old stone brought from Scotland, and listened to the *Te Deum* composed by my darling . . . for whom this would have been such a grand day. It sounded beautiful . . .' Less so the 'God Save the Queen' intoned by three thousand poor school-children assembled in Hyde Park later in the afternoon. The Queen remarked that they sang 'somewhat out of tune'.

In the Palace, she sat on a sofa to open telegrams. There were more receptions afterwards, again with the assistance of Beatrice and Liko, Helena, Vicky and Louise, who had been chosen as the sculptor for the statue of the Queen to be placed in the Broad Walk in front of Kensington Palace, to which the principal contributors were the lady residents of Kensington. Always dilatory, Louise did not complete the statue until 1893, when it was unveiled by the Queen, who 'felt very proud of her'.

Everybody had been so kind. The family appeared to be united. Even Willy and Dona had been affectionate. Serge and Ella, too, although they wrote so seldom now. Ella assured her: 'Words cannot express all that I feel when I have the joy of seeing you. It is quite as if you were my own mother. Do not think that because I write seldom my thoughts are less often with you. My background is peopled by men and women whom you are unlikely ever to meet . . . All I can repeat is that I am perfectly happy.'

But when the splendid day was over, the cheers had subsided, the jewels, copes and gold plate put away and her daughters departed for their respective homes and families, the Queen sat down and confided to her journal: 'How painfully do I miss the dear ones I have lost!' To her married children she felt that she was now 'only Number Two or Three in their affections'.

# *Section V*

# *Era of Shadows (1887-1901)*

VICKY was happy to be back in her native land, where Fritz appeared to be improving. She played tennis at Osborne with her daughter Victoria, her Comptroller Count Seckendorff and Canon Prothero's son Rowland. Fritz watched them from his wicker chair under a cedar tree, where he drank tea and fed Bijou, his blue-grey Italian greyhound, with brown bread and butter. Vicky played tennis, according to Rowland Prothero, 'partly from love of the game, partly because it might, she thought, be a useful agent for raising the position of German women'. This missionary aspect of the game strongly appealed to her. She hoped that an amusement which women could share with men would help her sex to escape from the domestic slavery in which they lived in German middle-class society.

Meanwhile Bismarck, although he did not agree with the Crown Prince's liberal views, was genuinely concerned about his illness. The old and ailing Emperor could not last much longer. As for Willy, Bismarck had shrewdly summed him up, anticipating his eventual dismissal: 'He is like a balloon; if you don't keep fast hold of the string, you never know where he will be off to'; he rightly feared that he could plunge Germany into war at the wrong moment. (Bismarck was all for war at the right one, as he had proved in 1866 and in 1870.) At that moment, however, Bismarck, the Emperor and the German people fulminated against Vicky for keeping the Crown Prince so long out of his country.

Vicky and Fritz had left in June 1887 and did not return to Berlin until September, after a stay in the Tyrol, in the hope that the air would do Fritz good. The doctors thought that Berlin was too cold for him. Then they moved south, to Venice, to Baveno on Lake Maggiore, to San Remo, where a sudden deterioration took place and Mackenzie was summoned by telegram from London. He found that a new growth had formed. Fritz asked him bluntly: was it cancer: Mackenzie replied that it looked very much like it but he was not certain. He called in other specialists and Willy, despatched by the weakening Emperor to find out the true position, had a stormy scene with Vicky, who wished to prevent him from upsetting his father. She thought that Willy was behaving as though he were about to take over the imperial crown. He was furious with her for preventing him from seeing his father.

Five doctors now unanimously agreed on the diagnosis. It was cancer. The patient was left to decide between the drastic treatment of an immediate excision of the larynx or a more conservative treatment involving the opening of the windpipe. Whichever method was chosen, it was only a matter of gaining a little time in the race with death. The Crown Prince heard the verdict with heroic stoicism: 'I suppose I must set my house in order,' he replied quietly. Vicky was broken-hearted. All that she had planned and worked for during thirty hard years was crumbling like a sandcastle. To add to the drama, the Villa Zirio at San Remo was constantly besieged by a none-too-friendly press and emissaries from Berlin. There was no refuge from them, no retreat; her eldest children had turned against her too. Moretta, Sophie and Margaret supported her, but there was little that they could do.

At 11 a.m. on 9 March 1888 a telegram arrived in San Remo from Berlin announcing the death of the ninety-one-year-old Emperor. Fritz rose from his sickbed; slowly and painfully he donned his uniform, put on the ribbon and star of the Order of the Black Eagle, the highest order of the House of Hohenzollern, and walked into the drawing-room, where the little court had assembled to pay their respects to the new Emperor Frederick William III, whose short reign was to last only ninety-nine days.

Unable to speak, he wrote out the proclamation of his succession, removed the Star of the Order from his tunic, and pinned it on his wife's dress. Overcome by emotion, Vicky fell sobbing into his arms. 'I thank you for having made me live long enough to recompense the valiant courage of my wife,' Fritz wrote to Sir Morell Mackenzie (who had been knighted by the Queen.) Then he despatched a telegram to his mother-in-law confirming his 'sincere and earnest desire for a close and lasting friendship between our two nations'.

It was freezing in Berlin, but duty obliged the new Emperor to present himself in his capital. He and his suite left San Remo, in deep mourning, on 10 March. He then issued a proclamation to be published throughout Germany in which he referred to the principle of religious tolerance – there had been an anti-Semitic movement in Germany for some time. Behind his back people called him mockingly 'King of the Jews'.

The royal family took up residence at Charlottensberg, outside the city. Vicky had no illusions: 'I think people consider us a mere passing shadow to be replaced by reality in the shape of William . . .' She made her sad entry into hostile Berlin with a heavy heart. It was as cold as the day on which she had made her first triumphant appearance as a happy young bride thirty years before. How the people had cheered her as she drove through the streets in her little ermine-trimmed cloak! Now they hated her. There were even rumours that she was only waiting for the chance to marry Count Seckendorff. This gossip reached England: 'I really think they are most outrageous in their abuse of her,' exclaimed Sir Henry. Sir Robert Morier had already hinted that Vicky had given malicious tongues the opportunity to wag by going off to Switzerland with the Count for weeks. Seckendorff was a cultured man with a profound knowledge of antiques and, moreover, he was an excellent bargain-hunter. This appealed to Vicky's parsimony. 'Well,' observed Sir Henry, 'if she likes to retain a man about her who can choose old pots and pans for her at a cheap rate and ruin her fair name, she cannot do so without remonstrance and warning.' Apparently the Queen and Prince Christian had heard the rumours; the Queen was annoyed with the Count when he accompanied Vicky at Balmoral and sent him out stalking with Fritz.

There was no more truth in this gossip-mongering than in the story of Queen Victoria's alleged romance, or secret marriage, with John Brown. In any case the Count, after so many years in her service, knew Vicky too well to be sentimental about her. He warned Marie von Bunsen in later years, when she had been asked to read the newspapers to Vicky: 'Don't let yourself be put into harness; the Empress is the most exacting woman in the world. If you don't hold out against her you will become her slave.' How very much like her Mama!

The Queen sent Bertie to represent her at the late Emperor's funeral. He found Fritz thinner but didn't think he looked ill. Vicky shook her head sadly. 'We are our own masters now, but shall we not have to leave all the work undone which we have so long and so carefully been preparing? Will there be any chance of doing the right thing, any time to carry out useful measures? It is hard . . . it is cruel.'

One of the private 'measures' she had set her heart on was to settle Moretta's romance with Sandro, and she cajoled Fritz into writing a consent to their marriage. Queen Victoria, when informed, wrote guardedly that she could understand that Vicky wanted to settle everything that was of importance, owing to dear Fritz's uncertain state of health, but she was opposed to anything that went against the late Emperor's wishes; 'above all, do not even contemplate such a step without the perfect acquiescence of Willy. You must reckon with him – as he is Crown Prince and it would never do to contract a marriage which he would not agree to. It would simply bring misery on your daughter and Sandro, besides placing her in an impossibly humiliating position.'

Vicky ignored these words of wisdom and advised Fritz to call Sandro to Berlin so as to reinstate him in a military appointment and pave the way for the marriage. The reluctant lover was placed in an inextricably difficult position, for his affections had now been transferred to a Darmstadt opera singer, Fräulein Johanna Loisinger.

Queen Victoria, accompanied by Beatrice and Liko, set out for Florence on 23 March for a month's holiday, planning to return through Berlin to visit her dying son-in-law and pour oil on the seething waters. Both Lord Salisbury and Sir Edward Malet, the British ambassador in Berlin, warned the Queen that in view of Bismarck's raging mood and hold on the press, her visit was not desirable: there might be demonstrations; the visit would be misconstrued.

They were right on the last point only. Bismarck firmly believed that 'the old lady was capable of bringing the fiancé and the parson with her in her carpetbag', but they were wrong about the demonstrations. Victoria disarmed Bismarck by agreeing that the Moretta–Sandro marriage was out of the question. The German press immediately swung sharply round in fulsome praise and the Queen was greeted with loud cheers and public applause. Flowers were thrown into her carriage as she drove to the British Embassy.

Beatrice admitted to Sir Henry Ponsonby that five years before the Queen, influenced by Vicky, had been in favour of the marriage. But Liko had always been against it: 'The young people liked each other, that was all, but they had been pushed on by the Crown Princess. Sandro had proposed and been accepted and considered himself bound in honour to proceed whenever the Empress desired it – and no doubt Princess Victoria [Moretta] and her mother were most eager for it. But Prince Henry [Liko] and his father knew he had nothing to live upon. He would be driven out of Germany if such an unpolitical marriage took place and he would be ruined. Princess Moretta would never like love in a cottage and their life would be miserable.' 'But my dear sister is determined on it,' Beatrice told Sir Henry, 'and the immediate question is: can we get hold of Sandro to prevent his being sent for to Berlin?' Sir Henry suggested that he might be sent to Malta to see his brothers Henry and Louis, who were there at the time. But Beatrice wanted nothing to be done without her husband's advice: 'The Queen doesn't want to put herself forward to get involved in controversies with the Empress Victoria'; and, as Lady Paget and others had observed on various occasions, the Empress was very determined when she had once taken up a plan.

A few days later Sir Henry discovered:

> [Sandro] was not particularly keen on the marriage, his love having somewhat cooled and his prospect of a poor marriage and the general dislike shown to it making him still more opposed to it. But he feels himself bound to it, so he packed up his things but suddenly got a telegram 'Don't come', so he did not. Two days later he received a letter from Willy saying 'if you marry my sister I shall consider you the enemy of my family and country'. It is rumoured that Herbert Bismarck [Bismarck's son] is in love with Princess Victoria and that Herbert stirred up Willy and dragged in the Russian scare and met the Empress's moves by telling the newspapers that his father will resign if the marriage takes place.

Sir Henry helped Beatrice to draft a letter to Sandro

> ... which she really made very good, advising him to answer Willy that he cannot discuss his marriage with a brother while the whole question is in the hands of William's father and mother, and has also advised him that he, Sandro, cannot give up Princess Victoria himself but if—as the Princess Beatrice hopes—he does so to avoid unhappiness to both, the breaking off should be done by his father, old Prince Alexander of Hesse.

Meanwhile, the Queen asked Vicky pertinently: 'Have you ever thought or wondered what Sandro's own feelings would be?' And the harassed Prince wrote a carefully worded letter to Moretta to prepare her for the end of their ill-starred (and indeed rather pallid) romance.

During her visit to Berlin, the Queen called on her one-time dear friend, the Dowager Empress Augusta; she found her in deep mourning, shaking with palsy, crumpled up in a wheelchair and looking, as the Queen remarked with her usual candour, 'rather ghastly'. Then she sat beside poor Fritz, who now spent most of his time in bed and was deeply distressed at Vicky's 'terrible despair'. When she waved her mother off on the station platform, Vicky broke down and the tears rolled down her cheeks: 'It was terrible to see her standing there in tears while the train moved slowly off, and to think of all she was suffering and might have to go through.'

Vicky went back to Fritz. She hardly ever left his room. His throat was such a painful and shocking sight that she could often hardly bear to look at it and when it was dressed she had to rush away to hide her tears. She felt, she said, as if she were bleeding from a thousand wounds.

On 24 May, the Queen's birthday, Prince Henry of Prussia married his cousin Princess Irene of Hesse in the private chapel of Charlottensberg palace. Ella and Serge came from Russia and Bertie from England. The Emperor made the supreme effort of rising from his bed to meet Irene at the station, and he attended the wedding in general's uniform, standing beside his mother's wheelchair. Herbert Bismarck observed to the Prince of Wales that a sovereign who could not enter into debates should not be allowed to reign. The Prince said later that he felt like throwing him out of the room.

During his last moments on earth, Fritz joined Vicky's hands and those of Bismarck's in a vain last-minute silent supplication to them to bury the hatchet. On 14 June he murmured to Vicky: 'You . . . I . . . the children . . .' and a few moments later expired in her arms. Guards surrounded the castle upon Willy's instructions, allowing nobody to leave, so as to prevent any documents, particularly copies of his mother's letters, from being carried away. Vicky sat down to write to her mother, recalling how she, after her own terrible grief in 1861, had found time and strength to write her daughter a few lines: 'Oh, my husband, my darling, my Fritz! I am his widow, no more his wife. How am I to bear it? You did and I will. Now all struggles are over. I must stumble on my way alone.'

'Poor, dear Vicky! God help her,' exclaimed the Queen. 'The tragedy for my poor child is too ghastly – much worse than mine in 1861.' She sent a telegram to Willy, urging him to help his mother in this time of trial, and followed it up with a letter which, she stressed, 'mama does not know I am writing to you' Tactfully, she asked Willy to bear with his mama if she was somewhat irritated and excited. She did not mean it – she had been through months of agony, suspense, and sleepless nights. 'I am so anxious that all should go smoothly that I write this openly in the interests of both. There are many rumours of your going and paying visits to sovereigns . . . I hope that at least you will let some months pass before anything of this kind takes place.'

Willy ignored the Queen's request. He was now the Emperor (or the Kaiser, as he liked to be called); and as such, he told her, he had a duty to show himself and assert his powers. Grandmama must realize that they were now writing to each other as equal to equal. Willy was no longer a little boy to be scolded and told what he must do. As for his mother. 'We have the same characters. I have inherited her good, stubborn English blood which will not give way.'

Vicky, who was only forty-seven, wrote to the Queen: 'My voice will be silent forever. We were Papa's and your children, we were faithful to what we believed and knew to be right. We loved Germany. We wished to see her strong and great, not only with the sword but in all that was righteous in culture, in progress and in liberty.'

In his speech to Parliament, Willy promised to 'follow the same path by which my deceased grandfather won the confidence of his allies'. He did not even mention his father's name. Lord Salisbury warned Bertie, who had spoken a little tactlessly in public about 'William the Great needing to learn that he is living at the end of the nineteenth century and not in the Middle Ages', that the Kaiser appeared to be 'a little off his head'. The Queen, too, wondered at times whether Willy's head was 'quite right'. After he had declared that he wished to be addressed in private as well as in public as 'His Imperial Majesty', she declared: 'If he has such notions, he had better not come to England.'

Prince Christian was sent to Berlin to try to bring about a family reconciliation, but there was nothing that anyone could do. Bertie, snubbed by Willy, rejoined: 'I have also my own dignity to uphold.' It was an insoluble impasse. Christian wisely suggested that it might help if Vicky were to take Willy into her confidence by consulting him about trifles; that would flatter him and enable her to gain more influence than she had at the present – but Vicky could not swallow her pride or alter her ways.

Then the Queen ostentatiously invited Vicky to spend three months in England with her three daughters, sending the royal yacht *Victoria and Albert* to meet her at Flushing and welcoming her personally when she landed; this was an unprecedented step, for Her Majesty had never gone farther than her front entrance to meet her most exalted guests. Vicky arrived draped in crêpe, her face invisible, trembling with grief. Two days later there was a family gathering in honour of her birthday and a 'present table' laid out as in her childhood, covered with gifts.

Willy was allowed to pay a 'penitential visit' during Cowes Week in August, a week which he ultimately spoiled for everybody, particularly his Uncle Bertie, who was obliged to give up yachting because of Willy's overbearing and unsportsmanlike behaviour.

There was also poor Moretta to soothe after the break-up of her romance. Sandro had asked leave to give up his family name after he married Fräulein Loisinger and was now known as Count Hartenau. 'Perhaps they loved each other,' murmured the Queen who had recently been absorbed in the novels of Marie Corelli. When the name of the popular authoress was brought up at dinner in Balmoral, Vicky sniffed: 'She writes rubbish for the semi-educated!' The subject was hastily dropped.

Vicky was now desperately looking round for another suitor for Moretta. The Queen rebuked her; she thought it dreadful to press Moretta into marrying for marrying's sake, and besides it was hardly dignified to go matchmaking so openly.

The latest candidate to be put forward was the Grand Duke Alexander Michaelovitch, who spoke English perfectly, had been to India and Australia, was very good-looking and had charming manners – but nothing came of it. Vicky was in dread of her daughter's becoming attached to a person she might meet casually who was not of her rank, since then there would be more trouble with Willy, which might cause a lasting unpleasantness. Vicky's fears were only too well founded, but fortunately she did not live to see Moretta's ultimate fate, which brought her a second marriage at the age of sixty to a Russian adventurer, Alexander Zoubkov, who ran through her money and left her destitute and abandoned by most of her family.

A year later Moretta was invited to England by the Queen. Vicky wrote asking her mother to try to dissuade her daughter from her current slimming craze – she would only eat a little meat and apples, in small quantities. Moretta went to bed too late and took too much exercise – she was far too thin. At Balmoral, however, she soon shot up to 10 stone 10½ lb helped by 'elevenses' of whisky and lemon squash sent to her on the Queen's orders. In Victoria's opinion there was nothing better to cheer people up than theatricals; she herself laughed till she was red in the face at Alec Yorke's sketches produced for palace performances. So Moretta, scared and stage-struck, was made to take part in them. Another pastime much in vogue then at Balmoral was the 'willing' or telepathy game. The Queen was much impressed and slightly mystified when lady-in-waiting Marie Mallet 'flew over to Lord Knutsford and unpinned his jubilee medal as she had been "willed" to do by the other participants'.

Moretta was finally married off to Prince Adolf of Schaumberg-Lippe and lived uneventfully between the Palais Schaumberg in Bonn and the old castle of Detmold near Bückeburg, with its green shutters, grey roof and English chimney pots, which she furnished in English style. The Prince eventually had to relinquish most of his properties as the result of a rival family's claims and he died leaving Moretta a lively widow, still fond of tennis, riding and dancing – and terribly bored. A local antique dealer eventually introduced her to Zoubkov who amused and interested her by hair-raising fantasies of his escapades (leaving out the more unsavoury details of his many love affairs). It was as a consequence of her disastrous remarriage that Moretta was obliged to sell the heirlooms bequeathed to her by her mother; so wedding presents taken to Germany from England had to be sent back to a London auction room.

Beatrice and her husband were beginning to assist the Queen and take over some of her minor engagements. Poor Beatrice was still so shy and easily flustered that when she was asked to open the new wing of the Hospital for Chest Diseases, make a speech and receive purses of donations from various distinguished ladies, she was so relieved at the conclusion of her speech that she promptly sat down and forgot all about the purses, which had to be laid down by the donors on their seats before they left. Nevertheless, the press, especially the women's magazines, 'took her up' and extolled her housewifely virtues. They gave the recipe for a 'Beatrice cake'; there was a 'Beatrice waltz', and a 'Beatrice bridal march'. The Battenberg nursery above the Queen's private rooms in Buckingham Palace filled with four children: (Alexander, Marquess of Carisbrooke, Leopold, Maurice and Ena). The Princess was now becoming too matronly to continue to be called 'the royal British Rosebud'!

In March 1889 Beatrice and Liko accompanied the Queen to Biarritz and San Sebastian. It was the first time that the Queen and Princess had set foot in Spain. The party was entertained with Basque dances and music before taking their departure at Irun. Later in the year they listened to a very different kind of music: the songs of Welsh choirs during a visit to Sir Theodore Martin's residence near Llangollen. The Queen was much impressed by the Welsh singers, who 'were composed merely of shopkeepers and flannelweavers'. She asked Sir Henry Ponsonby to write to the Prince of Wales about their excellent reception, and to Sir Fred Knollys to tell him

> ... how much this naturally sensitive and warm-hearted people feel the neglect shown them by the Prince of Wales and his family and how wrong of him it was not to come here—it is only five hours from London and as the Prince takes his title from this country, which is so beautiful, it does seem very wrong that neither he nor his children have come here often and indeed the Princess and the children not at all.

Alix and Ernest of Hesse, Alice's children, were now invited to Balmoral for the 'season'. The Queen had been toying with the idea of marrying 'sunny' Alix to her grandson Eddy, the Duke of Clarence, Bertie's son. She had no misgivings about the marriage of first cousins. But Alix was in love with the Tsarevitch Nicholas. The only drawback was Alix's reluctance to give up the Lutheran religion, which she would have to do before she could marry the Prince next in succession to the Russian throne. The romance was being kept a dark secret from Grandmama, whose prejudices against the Romanovs and Russians generally were well known.

Ella wrote to her brother Ernest from St Petersburg: 'I find the idea of Eddy's marrying Alix quite dreadful – first cousins it is best to avoid – but the chief objection is that he does not look overstrong [She was right. He died in 1892.] and is too stupid. England with such a husband is not at all a place for Alix. I long to know her as happy as we three are.' (She was referring to Victoria with Louis of Battenberg, Irene with Henry of Prussia and herself with the Grand Duke Serge.) Ella anxiously followed events at Balmoral from Moscow and sent further advice to her brother:

> Give Alix courage – be yourself very careful what you say in your conversation with grandmama; it would be much better not to speak about Pelly [Nicholas] or, if she does, tell her there has been nothing whatever between Alix and Pelly, that you have of course no voice in the question. If she wishes to know frankly your opinion about Pelly, say what a perfect creature he is – adored by all, and that Alix deserves this loving being in every way. Give an idea of the happy family life [of Alexander III] so that grandmama's prejudices may be lessened. That will be a great step and help when the deciding moment arrives. Through all the idiotic trash in the newspapers she gets impossibly untrue views and founds all her arguments on facts which probably never existed. God grant this marriage may come true!

Ella was converted and joined the Greek Orthodox Church in the following year. She explained to her family abroad that she adored her husband and her new country and so had learned to love their religion. Oddly enough, the younger generation was the most horrified, especially Irene, Alix and Willy, who spread the story that Ella had been coerced by her husband. Queen Victoria showed more understanding; Ella was touched and surprised: 'I was so afraid you would not understand the step and the comforting your dear lines gave me I shall never forget; to have the same religion as one's husband is such a happiness; the only thing which made me wait so long was that I knew so many would be pained and not understand.'

In fact another of Victoria's granddaughters had entered a Greek Orthodox family: Vicky's daughter Sophie, whose marriage to Crown Prince Constantine of Greece (his brother Nicolas became the father of Princess Marina, the late Duchess of Kent) took place in Athens on 27 October 1889. The 'royal mob', as Queen Victoria described her family and its ramifications, descended upon the Greek capital in force, with Willy, rather surprisingly, in the uniform of a British Admiral. He believed, much to his Uncle Bertie's annoyance, that this entitled him to criticize the British Mediterranean Fleet. The heat was so great during the wedding service that the candles melted in the cathedral and bent over, wax fell on the ladies' bare shoulders and the gentlemen behind them were kept gallantly busy picking it off.

Sophie was now Crown Princess of a beautiful but undeveloped country which ignored the first principles of hygiene. This was a challenge which Vicky promptly took up. It helped to restore her flagging spirits. She began to pester her daughter with letters as she herself had been pestered by Queen Victoria when she was a newly-wedded bride. She tried not to meddle, but she made endless 'suggestions', which came to the same thing. She even advised Sophie's 'dear, kind mama-in-law', Queen Olga, sending her batches of reports on the charitable institutions she had founded in Germany and upon which she considered herself an authority. Vicky believed, for instance, that a sanitary engineer ought to check the drains and pipes at

Tatoi Palace ('What trouble they have had with them at dear old Windsor!') while Sophie should appoint a private secretary and a man of business to manage money affairs; she should form a circle of friends, distinguished university people, wealthy men who had done much for the town, and young rising people; she should improve and reform the prisons (the one she had seen at Nauplia had given her the creeps). In Germany, Vicky belonged to a society for the employment of prisoners. She was also doing all she could to found a Ladies' College along the lines of Newnham or Girton, in Cambridge. Willy thought that women's education was unnecessary, but Vicky firmly believed that 'if women remain a sort of upper servant the whole of the nation must suffer'.

Soon a baby was on the way in Athens. Vicky now began to fuss, as Queen Victoria had fussed over her at her first confinement. Sophie *must* have an English doctor, an English baby nurse, and a first-rate English-trained nurse to help her in case she fell ill. Queen Olga, her mother-in-law, had other views on the subject, but Vicky had cunningly planned in advance. She had provided Sophie at the time of her wedding with a 'housekeeper', who was in fact a London-trained midwife, just in case: 'Of course, I could not tell you her real profession when you were a young girl, so I had to invent the name and function of housekeeper.' When the baby finally came, Vicky implored her son-in-law '*not* to tumble and shake and lift baby about *too much*. It is rather dangerous with little children as any jerk or slight wrench may give them an injury for life.' Then she went on to explain how he should be held.

There was another family rumpus with Willy when Sophie, following upon Ella's footsteps, announced that she too had decided to adopt the Greek Orthodox faith. Willy believed that his mother was behind it all, though it is difficult to imagine why. Both he and his wife Dona were so violent and disagreeable that Vicky took herself off to stay with her son Henry and his wife Irene of Hesse at their *Schloss* Kiel where the atmosphere, away from Berlin mischief-making, was happy and harmonious.

Willy now went so far as to ban Sophie from visiting Germany. Queen Victoria, grieved and distressed, waited patiently for the fuss to blow over. She herself, she said, could not understand such narrow-mindedness: 'If people change their religion willingly, out of conviction and without compulsion, I could not blame them or be angry with them for it.' Willy then shortened the ban to three years. Sophie pleaded with him to lift it altogether, but in vain. She received a reply which she reported to her mother by telegram: 'Keeps to what he said in Berlin. Fixes it to three years. Mad. Never mind. Sophie.'

Vicky occupied herself with her new palace and gardens of Friedrichshof near Kronberg in the Taunus Mountains; in one of his infrequent gracious moods Willy had given his mother the old *Burg* adjoining the estate as a Christmas present. Vicky gathered wild flowers, picked blackberries and mushrooms and wrote to Sophie: 'Your mama is still like a baby over these things.' She invited neighbours' children to tea and games under the chestnut trees. She gave land and paid for a little hospital at Kronberg. And she saw Bertie when he went to take the waters at the spas of Homberg and Wiesbaden, sometimes accompanied by Louise (who frequently travelled on the continent incognito as 'Mrs Campbell'). Vicky enjoyed seeing them, but the grief of Fritz's death hung over her like a pall. She missed him physically, as Victoria had missed Albert, and she confided to Sophie: 'I try to be brave and not to think of myself, but oh, the longing for one squeeze of papa's big hand, for a kiss, for the sound of his voice or his step . . . To face life and struggle on without him seems too hard, too incomprehensible . . . I miss darling Papa so cruelly and in the morning on waking his empty pillow, his silent and empty rooms, make me so wretched.' Was she in danger of withdrawing and of neglecting the younger generation, as Queen Victoria had done after her loss?

Sophie now hinted that her young unmarried sister Margaret ('Mossy'), who was attracted to Prince Max of Baden and liked Berlin society, was leading a rather unexciting life. Vicky flared up. So Mama was dull and a bore? It wasn't her fault if she was not at the centre of a brilliant court. In the end, Mossy married shy Prince Frederick of Hesse, a close friend of Max's; the latter's feeling for Mossy had been only fraternal, while Frederick was deeply in love with her. 'It is something to be so much loved in this world,' Vicky remarked, 'many a woman and especially a Princess passes through life without ever knowing what it is to be truly loved.'

Early in 1890, Vicky's mother-in-law, the old Empress Augusta, died and was laid out with the pomp and circumstance which she had so much loved in her lifetime.

Vicky described the scene for her mother in minute detail. She had become more matter-of-fact and capable of giving the circumstantial details which the Queen had begged her to send them when she was newly married. Vicky told her exactly how 'dear Augusta' looked in death:

> ... with her false hair in ringlets on her brow, her eyebrows carefully painted as in life, a golden myrtle wreath on her head and an ample tulle veil, well arranged, flowing and curling about her head, neck and shoulders, hiding her chin, her hands folded, her bracelets on and her wedding ring. She was dressed in an ermine-trimmed and lined gold robe and train which she had worn for her golden wedding, and looked wonderfully well and young. I felt that if she could have seen herself, she would have been pleased. She was "the Empress", even in death.

For the fiftieth anniversary of their mother's wedding on 10 February 1890 (the wedding anniversary was never forgotten in the royal family), Beatrice wrote to Lord Tennyson that all the children were going to give Mama a prayer-book in an antique cover; they were anxious that a few appropriate words in verse should be placed at the beginning: 'Mama being such a great admirer of all you write, words of yours on this momentous anniversary would greatly enhance the value of the book . . . my only fear is you may think we are asking too much of you.' But the Poet Laureate complied with the following:

> Remembering Him who waits thee far away,
> And with thee, Mother, taught us first to pray,

Accept on this your golden bridal-day
The Book of Prayer.

The Queen sent the poet a message of thanks and photographs of the *tableaux vivants*, to which his son, Hallam Tennyson, had been invited.

All these anniversaries, with their accompanying gifts, verses, visits and amateur performances, brought the members of the family momentarily together in their efforts to please one another, the Queen being the immovable sun round which the satellites revolved. Immovable? The ageing little lady would have bristled. She was feeling brighter and lighter than she had been for many years. She even danced a quadrille with Bertie's son Prince Eddy, Duke of Clarence, at Osborne in 1890; after dinner, the furniture was pushed back in the drawing-room and the band was so *entraînant* that: 'We had a nice little impromptu dance . . . I did quite well.' Waltzes and polkas followed the quadrille.

One day Louise, Lorne and Helena listened with her to 'such an interesting lecture by that wonderful traveller and explorer, Mr Stanley'. Then Beatrice and Liko went to the station to receive Queen Isabella of Spain on her first visit; she was the lively grandmother of the little King of Spain and lunched with them all at Windsor. Beatrice and Liko also met the Queen of Roumania, the novelist Carmen Sylva, who wore her beautiful national dress to dinner and read an ancient Greek story – 'very tragic – with an inspired look . . .'.

In 1891, Beatrice, Liko and Helena joined in the laughter at a programme of Sir Arthur Sullivan *The Gondoliers* at Windsor; and the Queen beat time as they sang: 'Then one of us will be Queen and sit upon a golden throne.' Beatrice, usually so placid, became irritated by the Queen's habit of talking and offering suggestions during amateur performances. On one occasion the Princess was actually bold enough to bid her mother sternly to 'be quiet'. The Queen took the admonition in good part, hid her face in her hands like a little girl, and cried: 'I will be good, I will be good!' Mama could be terrifying, but she had her endearing moments. She also took a hand in censoring and rewriting plays, either to prolong her daughters' roles (Louise and Beatrice were the principal stars)' or to strike out exchanges such as the one in a French play where a daughter was called upon to say: 'I have nothing to offer as dowry but my virtue,' and the male *replique* was: 'Ah, little enough!'

Willy and Dona went to Balmoral in July 1891 and were met by Beatrice and Louise. The French fleet called at Osborne in August, and Beatrice and Louise stood beside the Queen during the playing of the *Marseillaise*, which greatly gratified the French admiral and officers, although the Queen admitted afterwards that she had not 'particularly liked doing it'. Then in November, Louise and Lorne, Beatrice and Liko and Helena listened to *Cavalleria Rusticana* in the Waterloo Gallery at Windsor, the first Italian opera that the Queen had heard for thirty-one years. She found the story pathetic and touching beyond words and loved the 'melodious, characteristically Italian music'. Sarasate played Spanish dances on his violin. They too were new to the Queen.

Two or three times a year, Beatrice accompanied her mother to lunch with the Empress Eugénie at Farnborough.

After this brief respite, tragedy struck again and then again: Prince Eddy, the Duke of Clarence, Bertie's son, died in January 1892 on the eve of his marriage to Princess Mary of Teck; and in March, the Grand Duke Louis of Hesse, Alice's widower, died. In both instances, the telegrams announcing the news were brought to the Queen by Beatrice. The Queen felt quite crushed. But, in her old age, she recovered from shocks more rapidly. After the news of Grand Duke Louis's death, Sir Henry Ponsonby wrote to his wife: 'The Queen is by way of being plunged in grief and did not go to church in consequence, but little messages here and there show she is not prevented from giving orders on sublunary matters.'

Meanwhile dear Louise – one never knew what she would be up to next or where or with whom – continued to behave at times in such an extraordinary way. The Queen was astonished, during one of her drives near Cimiez on the Riviera in 1893 to see Louise standing surrounded by *twelve* young priests on the opposite side of the road. Louise whooped with laughter when she saw the surprise on her mother's face. She had been out shopping informally, as she liked to do, and when she caught sight of the Queen's carriage had run across the road to hide herself in a shop but, as she tried to enter the door, twelve young priests came out and she couldn't get in. At Balmoral, Louise would suddenly get into her little pony cart and drive off – where to, no one knew. The royal household liked her; she made herself so agreeable and pleasant whenever she took Beatrice's place, because she was 'capital at entertaining strangers'.

In the autumn of 1893 the new Grand Duke of Hesse, Ernest, became engaged to his first cousin Princess Victoria Melita of Saxe-Coburg, daughter of Alfred, Duke of Edinburgh; she was a restless young woman who alternated between high spirits and bouts of brooding, and disliked official duties. The marriage had been arranged by Queen Victoria. It was not a success – she admitted it herself years afterwards and declared that she would 'never try to marry anyone again'. (When the Queen died, Victoria Melita known as 'Ducky' married her childhood sweetheart, the Grand Duke Cyril of Russia, and Ernest found happiness with Princess Eleanor of Solms Hohensolm, who kept up the schools and hospitals inaugurated by Alice.)

The Queen travelled to Coburg in April 1894 to attend the wedding of Ernest of Hesse and 'Ducky' where the Tsarevitch Nicholas finally overcame Alix's religious scruples and they announced their engagement to the 'thunderstruck' Queen. The Queen invited Alix to Windsor and arranged for her to talk with the bishop of Ripon, Dr Boyd Carpenter, who showed her 'the points in common between the Orthodox church and the Church of England'. Then, after Alix had taken a cure at Harrogate the Queen asked the Tsar's new confessor Father Yanisheff, to Windsor to instruct Alix in her new faith. She was very impressed that 'sweet, simple little Alicky is to become the Empress of Russia'. Indeed, after the sudden death of

Alexander III, Nicholas found himself on the throne of Russia one week after his wedding.

Vicky commented tersely: 'It is another world – there is something so squalid and sad, suggesting poverty and loneliness, about the landscape and population, so much in contrast with the wealth of the imperial court, the money and jewels and the almost reckless extravagance with which some things are carried out and presents lavished on people.' She also deplored the persecution of the Jews and the oppression of the Protestants in Russia.

Princess Beatrice had little time to spare for her children, but this did not distress her unduly. Of the five daughters of Queen Victoria, she appears to have been the most lacking in maternal instinct. She was too much taken up with her filial-secretarial duties, which had become an integral part of her way of life. She read aloud to the Queen, transcribed and sent messages, accompanied her on her daily drives and followed her daily and dutifully into the dining-room. Lady Ribblesdale described the scene which was re-enacted almost every night at Windsor Castle.

We and the guests invited for dinner waited in the corridor for the loud call of 'The Queen!' and then I saw a little old black and white lady, full of dignity though so round, leaning on a beautiful Indian servant's arm, dressed in scarlet with a striped turban and sash—such a picturesque couple, I longed for an artist to paint them. She stopped for a second on her way to the dining-room and Lady Carrington and I hurried towards her and curtsied low and kissed her little hands, and she passed on. Then came Princess Beatrice, her husband and the Duchess of Albany [Prince Leopold's widow]. Then followed the ladies alone and then the gentlemen. The Queen always has her own family next to her. It must be very dull. Everybody has to talk very low to their next door neighbour, no general conversation is allowed, so it makes the dinner not very lively. The Queen had a quite low black dress on well off her shoulders, and a diamond and sapphire necklace. She has an excellent appetite . . . After partaking of a stodgy trifle of jam and sponge cake, she topped up with a finger biscuit also of a sponge cake nature. [In private, she liked to soak cake in her coffee.] After dinner she sits in the corridor and sends for people to come and talk to her . . . I hear she retires at eleven but does not go to bed till about two in the morning, particularly at present when she is tremendously interested in the elections. She is a wonderful woman.

For those who could not, or were not allowed to, take a close interest in politics, life was dull indeed and active Prince 'Liko' of Battenberg was becoming increasingly frustrated. He had gained a reputation for charm, humour and confidence in his official capacities as Governor of the Isle of Wight and Hon. Colonel of the Isle of Wight Rifles, although he was the first to admit that 'the duties and responsibilities of my office do not present much scope for activity'. He was gay and enjoyed appearing in tableaux such as 'King Richard among the Saracens', in which the Queen's Indian servants appeared as Saracens and Liko as Saladin, but he was too young, vital and intelligent to be content with such a futile existence. The womenfolk made his life even more unbearable. Sir Henry Ponsonby found him 'moping and miserable . . . If he is not allowed to hunt (this is thought dangerous for him after Lord Guildford's recent death at hunting) he will have positively nothing to do.'

When Liko tried to escape for a few days' fun in Corsica in 1894 with his brother Prince Louis, during a royal visit to Cannes, Beatrice had him quickly fetched back from Ajaccio on the man-of-war *Surprise*. She kept on asking Sir Henry: ' "Have you ordered *Surprise*? Has *Surprise* gone? Have you made it clear to Tillard [the Captain] that he is to bring His Royal Highness back?" It was suggested that it would be better to wait for Prince Henry's answer to the summons, but Beatrice could not. Why the hurry? It was whispered that the Princes were "keeping low company" in Ajaccio where the carnival was in full swing. This not being in Princess Beatrice's line, she thought it well to bring him home soon.'

Liko was delighted to be able to join the regiment of the Volunteer battalion for a week at their barracks in Hampshire. 'Altogether I feel quite in my element again among soldiers,' he wrote to Beatrice, 'and I am glad, even for so short a time, to take up once more my old profession. I feel like a fish in water. Everyone seems to have confidence in me.'

It was now rumoured that a lady of the court was paying too much attention to Liko; that in fact she was pursuing him so actively that the poor man did not know what to do to escape from her clutches. Putting two and two together – Louise's propensity to fall in love and her subsequent remarks about Prince Henry's 'always having been her confidant' – it may be presumed that she was the ardent lady in question. But the main reason for Prince Henry's joining the Ashanti expedition in 1895 was his desire to be active and to prove himself useful.

The kingdom of Ashanti, north of the Gold Coast Protectorate, also known as the Land of the Golden Stool (an eighteenth-century local prince's invention to link the various tribes under a pretended 'soul' of the country represented by the said stool) had pretensions to independence which displeased the British Government. King Prempeh, who had been enstooled in 1888, declined the British offer of protection; if he didn't accept, this would result in the 'withdrawing of Her Majesty's friendship'. To this veiled threat Prempeh replied courteously that after due consideration he believed that 'Ashanti must remain independent as of old, at the same time to remain friendly with all white men'; Ashanti was progressing; he thanked Her Majesty's Government for its good wishes. But the Government, aware of the commercial possibilities of the Gold Coast and the Northern Territories, wanted to make Ashanti part of the Protectorate. Invoking the 1874 Treaty and on the pretext of the stipulated indemnity not having been paid up, an expedition was organized under the leadership of Sir Francis Scott, which Prince Liko persuaded his wife and mother-in-law to allow him to join. The sight of the Queen's son-in-law, appointed Military Secretary to Sir Francis Scott, riding a donkey and carrying a white parasol to shield his face from the glaring sun, caused a stir on the Gold Coast.

Liko wrote enthusiastically to Beatrice, describing the tropical scenery: the gigantic cotton trees and bamboos, the houses of reddish clay, the curious barking of the sloth ... 'The whole thing is like a dream ... I am really happy and pleased to have received permission to see all that is going on.' At Prasu, Liko organized shooting parties from the camp. So far it was all very exotic and rather fun. But when they penetrated into the interior the heat became unbearable. Soldiers of the West Yorkshire regiment on their way back from Aden, who had already spent several years in India and Burma, and were now diverted to Africa, 'fell like rotten sheep' on the first day's march.

Meanwhile, unknown to the advancing British party (reinforced by members of the West African constabulary) the senior Chiefs of Kumasi held a meeting and decided that it would be wiser not to wage war but to submit to British 'protection'; so they sat down and waited in the shade, drinking and fanning themselves – or being fanned – by their slaves, for the British to arrive. Completely unaware of this, the British troops shadow-boxed through the jungle, making their way through the undergrowth, ambushing phantom enemies. On 17 January a weary Hausa band played Sir Francis Scott and his disgruntled men into an almost empty Kumasi to the highly inappropriate tune of 'Home, Sweet Home'.

But Prince Henry never reached this final stage of the farce. Stricken down by fever, he had been carried back to the coast. Telegram after telegram was despatched to Windsor Castle; the final, fatal one came soon after the cruiser *Blonde* had left for Madeira with the Prince's corpse preserved in Navy rum.

Princess Radziwill recalled in her memoirs that when Prince Liko was an officer in the Garde-du-Corps in Berlin, where he was a favourite in society, a fortune-teller at a party had told him: 'Whatever you do, beware of a blonde, because evil shall come to you through her.' It was not 'through', but 'on' the cruiser so-named. His last message for Princess Beatrice was: 'In case I die, tell the Princess from me that I came here not to win glory, but from a sense of duty.'

Prince Henry, 'dear Liko', died on Monday evening, 20 January 1896, the same day that King Prempeh made his submission to the Governor of Cape Coast.

'The life has gone out of me,' Beatrice exclaimed when she heard the tragic news. She would not hear of its being said that Liko ought not to have gone. 'She talks so heart-renderingly of her vanished happiness. They were so absolutely devoted to one another. God bless and help my poor child,' the Queen wrote in her diary for 22 January.

The Empress Eugénie now urged Beatrice to go to the South of France for a break and offered her her villa at Cap Saint-Martin. Her offer was gratefully accepted, all the more so since a discordant note had been sounded by Louise, who declared that *she* had been Liko's confidante, that Beatrice meant nothing to him. Helena was grieved and Beatrice distressed beyond words. The Queen gladly assented to her daughter's departure. Beatrice told her before she left that she hoped to have more courage to go on when she came back and she thanked the Queen for 'all her kindness during this terrible time'. The Queen was 'most upset'.

From Osborne, the Queen sent Beatrice cuttings from the *Illustrated London News*, whose artist-reporter in Ashanti, H. C. Skeppings-Wright, sent laudatory accounts of her late husband.

> Everybody liked Prince Henry [wrote Skeppings-Wright], he was one of the best. He was was very merry on the night he dined with the press gang before the start of the expedition. He made himself and others completely at home; he had a fine voice and sang an Italian air. 'We're all in the same billet', he was heard to say; he felt one of us. He practised with a four-barrelled revolver which he never had a chance of using in earnest. During a riot among the Africans, he rolled up his sleeves and rushed to the rescue of a wounded native. On the march into the interior, the Prince's party passed a soldier being carried back on a stretcher. 'You look fit, Sir', the soldier said with a wan smile. The Prince rejoined: 'Well, a man never knows'. The next day he went down with fever.

Liko's sister, Princess Marie of Battenberg, went to Osborne for the funeral and sat for a long time with the Queen in her private room. She wrote in her *Reminiscences* that the Queen reproached herself bitterly for having let Liko go to Ashanti. She did not seem to realize that she had forced him into it by the 'terms' laid down in the tacit marriage contract imposed upon him.

Beatrice returned from France and took up residence in Osborne Cottage, which had been occupied by the late Sir Henry Ponsonby before he died in 1895. This was to break with the old routine, but in other respects she continued to be as symbolically wedded to the Queen as she had been before her widowhood. The Queen, and her children, were all she had to live for. The Queen had to come first. The children were lonelier than ever without their gay father to play with them. Beatrice, like her mother, was not given to 'romping' with her offspring.

The Queen lost no time in planning a memorial for Liko, and Louise, too, worked upon a monument for his tomb at Osborne: a Crucifixion with an angel of Resurrection supporting the head of the Saviour, which was unveiled in 1898. (She had become more amiable and visited Beatrice during her 'retreat' at Cap Saint Martin.)

Vicky wrote sympathetically: 'Broken hearts can be found in palaces just as well as in hovels.' She went to Osborne at the end of January 1896, from where she wrote to Sophie: 'How I missed Liko and how saddened the house is without him! Auntie Beatrice seems in very low spirits indeed, but between times when the tears do not flow, she is cheerful and her old self. Dearest grandmama is looking very well only, alas, more infirm. I have not seen her walk at all and her sight is very bad.' Plans were being made for her Diamond Jubilee in 1897. This time Victoria wanted no 'royal mob', no foreign royalties, just a family party, with all her grandchildren round her. It would be her 'swan song', she said.

At Buckingham Palace, Louise graciously took a Drawing-room for the Queen in May 1896. She looked splendid, in a rich cream satin dress trimmed with lace, a corsage studded with emeralds and diamonds, a train of black velvet trimmed with pink satin and roses of various shades, black feathers and a veil. An elderly gentleman who had known the three younger Princesses informed the present writer that 'Louise was the most royal of them all'. (But Vicky, as ex-Empress, was treated royally even at home in England. To her embarrassment, Queen Victoria always made her precede her in and out of rooms; she nearly always did so crabwise in her confusion.) Louise was warm-hearted too. For instance, in that same year – 1896 – she invited Lord Ronald Gower to accompany her on a visit to her eighty-three-year-old nurse, Mrs Thurston, who was living in a snug little house close to Kensington Palace, as he recalled in his *Reminiscences*. Yet there was definitely somthing a little odd about Louise. Princess Moretta of Prussia, on a visit to Windsor, remarked: 'Auntie Louise is not right at all; she complains of everything, but is charming as usual to look at.'

In June the little parish church of Craithie opposite Balmoral was dedicated for the use of the royal family and the tenants. The Queen presented a stained glass window in three panels in commemoration of the Duchess of Kent, Princess Alice and her husband Louis; Beatrice presented a peal of four bells, and the royal household a granite pulpit inlaid with pebbles collected by Louise during her wanderings on the island of Iona. At Balmoral, too, the Queen erected a massive monolith in red granite 'to the dear memory of her beloved and lamented son-in-law Henry' which was added to the many other memorials.

Alix and her husband Nicky went to Balmoral that year but the visit was not a success. It went badly from the start. Nicky – now the Tsar Nicholas II – wearing the bearskin of the Scots Greys, heartily disliked his drive through the streets of Edinburgh in pouring rain and the special train to Balmoral rocked so violently that Alix was nearly sick. Grandmama met them at the door of the castle, which the young couple found colder than the wastes of Siberia. ('The only place where one is warm is in bed', Mary Ponsonby wrote when she was a lady-in-waiting). Then Bertie insisted on taking Nicky out deerstalking all day in torrents of rain and gales of cold wind. He never got a stag and hardly ever saw his beloved wife, from whom he could not bear to be separated for even a few hours, for the crowds of aunts, uncles and cousins that surrounded her. The Queen on her side found that 'the children' had changed. Alix was distant and aloof – she did not feel at all at home; she had grown away from her English relatives, and Nicky evaded the political issues that the Queen would liked to have discussed with him. Trees were planted to commemorate the visit and a picture was taken by the new process to show the family strolling on the terrace with the Queen in her wheelchair: '1,200 photographs were taken in 10 seconds by the animatograph process,' the press reported.

The Tsar and Tsarina returned home via Paris, which they found much more congenial. The old Darmstadt – England era was over. The 'sunny' little girl of former days had become a neurotic and superstitious Empress, while her husband went about with a piece of dried garlic in his pocket to protect him against Nihilists, though this talisman did not prevent his eventual assassination by the Bolsheviks. The marriage between Alix and Nicky had not helped – as the Queen had hoped – to restore friendly relations between England and Russia, any more than the marriage between Vicky and Fritz had helped to improve relations between England and Germany.

The Queen's 'at home' daughters continued to assist her to receive the constant stream of visitors from overseas as the Empire grew larger. At Government House in Ottawa Earl Minto received a letter stamped with the new Canadian imperial stamp. It bore a map of the world with the British Empire marked in red. An American Senator, asked for his opinion on the new stamp remarked: 'Very pretty, but a great deal too much red about it.' This 'red' gave the Queen more anxiety than pleasure. 'I dare not look forward,' she said. She was now seventy-seven and beginning to feel very tired. Beatrice read her telegrams, as her sight was so bad and she 'couldn't find spectacles to suit'. The Princess had no grasp of politics or world affairs, for she did not possess the lively intelligence of her sister Vicky. This, at a time when the Queen's sight was failing, was unfortunate, especially when they were abroad. As Sir Frederic Ponsonby (Sir Henry's son) wrote in a letter to his mother from Nice: 'The most absurd mistakes occur . . . Imagine Princess Beatrice trying to explain our policy in the East. Biggs or I may write out long precis, but they are often not read to Her Majesty as Princess Beatrice is in a hurry to develop a photograph or wants to paint a flower for a bazaar . . . When her sole means of reading despatches, precis, debates, etc. lies in Princess Beatrice, it is simply hopeless.'

The 1897 Diamond Jubilee was the last grand official 'occasion' on which the Queen's four remaining daughters appeared with her, and surrounded her with all their affection. As on all these important family anniversaries, there were inevitable family frictions. In this instance, Willy's declared intention of crossing over for the celebrations in honour of his 'unparalleled Grandmama' caused a panic. Bertie and Vicky were unanimous in their fear that Willy would bring an enormous suite and want to run the show.

The Queen had decreed that no reigning sovereigns were to be invited, since she was too old – she was now seventy-eight – and weary to entertain. But her spirits rose as 21 June approached and details of the preparations were submitted to her. Bertie insisted that she should wear 'something smart' and so her new black dress was embroidered down the front in gold specially worked in India; she wore diamonds in her cap and a diamond necklace given to her by her younger children. But she set out from Windsor for Buckingham Palace in her 'second-best mantle'. All her 'mantles' were made for her locally. 'It has always been clear to the female subjects of the Queen,' observed Lady Monkswell, 'that her mantles were made in the year one. I was immensely amused but not at all surprised, to hear that Victoria, by the Grace of God Queen of Great Britain and Ireland, Empress of India, gets these garments in *Windsor*. Mrs Cayley, the wife of the chief Windsor haberdasher exclaimed: "Oh, Ma'am, I could have cried to see Her Majesty start for the Jubilee in her second-best mantle after all the beautiful things I had sent her." ' She was relieved to be informed later that the Queen had taken her 'best' mantle with her to Buckingham Palace in a box.

The State dinner was followed by a ball at the Palace; the Queen remarked that it was 'dreadfully hot' and retired to her room a little after 11 p.m. The streets were noisy, for many people were sleeping out in the park. Her Majesty spent a restless night. Deep down, she was still the shy little woman who simultaneously wanted to be seen and applauded and yet withdrew from the limelight.

Next morning she breakfasted with Vicky (who had come over with her three daughters), Helena and Beatrice in the Chinese Luncheon Room, and watched the procession. Then at 11.15 a.m. she started from the State entrance in an open landau with eight creams – Alix (Princess Alexandra, Bertie's wife) and Helena opposite her – feeling 'so agitated in case anything went wrong'. Before leaving the Palace she had pressed an electric button which relayed a brief message by telegraph throughout the empire: 'From my heart, I thank my beloved people. May God bless them.'

Vicky was in the carriage next to hers, for her rank as Empress prevented her from sitting with her back to the horses, or else the Queen would have liked her to share her own carriage. There was such a shortage of carriages for the many guests that they had to double up, one of them bringing together such opposites as the special legate from the Vatican and the Chinese ambassador.

After the service at St Paul's, the Queen had a quiet luncheon with Vicky, Beatrice, Helena and Louise, and rested before tea in the gardens of Buckingham Palace and dinner in the large supper-room. The huge beehive moved in perfect order and concord and the Queen bee allowed herself a few moments of self-indulgent smugness. It had been a 'never to be forgotten day . . . no one, I believe, has met with such an ovation as was given to me passing through those six miles of streets.'

Vicky lingered on, always happy to be 'at home', whether at

Osborne, where the bright yellow damask was beginning to fade, or at Windsor, where Mama's apartments were stuffed to overflowing with family mementoes and gifts from children and grandchildren; all these were lovingly preserved, even to the vast collection of spotted china dogs, 'the like of which,' a visitor observed, 'for quaintness and hideousness could not be matched through the length and breadth of Her Majesty's kingdom'. Then there was the Queen's favourite dinner service made for her by Minton eighteen years ago, with blue borders and medallions enclosing a rose, shamrock and thistle. Vicky loved these heterogeneous objects for the warm aura that surrounded them. She came back later in the year to Balmoral, where she carried off six books at a time to read in her room, finished them in a couple of days and 'put as much energy as ever in her speech when talking about books and people and houses'. She suffered from neuralgia and toothache but the change of air did her good. Perhaps even better for her was the absence from Germany, where she saw little of Willy, who rarely went to see her, even when she was ill, and kept his children from her. This upset her very much, for she was passionately fond of children.

In April she had been to Bonn to visit her darling Moretta. The King of Saxony had just awarded the Schaumberg-Lippe succession to the Biestefelds, which meant that Princess Moretta and her husband Prince Adolf had had to give up 'their charming house at Bückeburg, lovely country, position, occupation, future . . . all gone'. Moretta had no children to console her, so Vicky went to a hotel in Bonn to supervise the furnishing of a little villa for her favourite daughter. Her eldest daughter Charlotte she disapproved of for smoking too much. 'It is not ladylike,' Vicky said, with an asperity reminiscent of her mother. Also like the Queen, Vicky forbade smoking in her own house. She was so house-proud that when the English ambassador, Sir Frank Lascelles, visited Friedrichshof he took his shoes off as soon as he reached his room and went about in socks, 'for even the softest slippers might have marked the parquet and "She" would have discovered it and even in the lightest of footgear my footfall would have disturbed "Her".' To her great friend Mary Ponsonby Vicky confided: 'My own personal friends have dropped into the background, are dead, or silent or have gone away and from those in other circles who think as I do, I am shut off, so that my loneliness is great. Of course I follow closely all that happens, but I am not in touch with the official world, though I meet them often.'

Vicky was still on occasion 'disrespectful' to Mama. Onlookers were highly amused at dinner to hear the Queen and the ex-Empress discussing the state of the Italian Army with much heat and contradicting each other vigorously. 'All shook with interior laughter to see two people who are never contradicted neither giving way. It ended by the Queen turning to Beatrice and the Empress to Sir Frank Lascelles when they continued their pet arguments in undertones.'

At Osborne in July the officers who had been on board the *Blonde* at the time of Liko's death came on shore to be presented. Beatrice's eyes were red, but she 'took photos and talked cheerfully . . . she must have no imagination – that is the only explanation I can offer,' Mary Mallet wrote rather unkindly. Every year in February there was a 'gloomy little funeral service' in honour of Liko's burial day. The royal household found these reiterated memorial services very trying, 'but I really think the Queen enjoys them,' Sir Henry Ponsonby had once observed, adding: 'There is nothing that the Queen likes better than to arrange a funeral service.'

The services, the drives, the meals, had fallen into such a set pattern that ladies-in-waiting, returning after a long absence, found that scarcely anything had changed. The same chairs were in the same places, the same plum cakes were served at tea, even the number of biscuits on the plate and their variety, the same things were said and done, only some of the old faces had gone and there was a selection of new dogs. There were no more balls. The Queen was horrified to be told that no one now learned quadrilles and that parents like Lady Lytton allowed their girls to visit without their mama. The Queen watched her daughters Beatrice and Helena at the Sunday services in the private chapel at Windsor to see whether they were doing their bit, then her own voice would be heard once she had approved of the efforts of others. Her once clear soprano had turned into a mellow contralto, like her character. But grandchildren and greatgrandchildren were still expected to kiss her hand and were slapped when – like four-year-old Alice (later Princess Andrew of Greece and Prince Philip's mother) – they refused to do so; Alice slapped her back, saying tartly 'naughty Grand-mama', and had to be hurriedly removed.

The Court still went into mourning on 14 December, and at Christmas the Queen and the Princesses continued to dress the Christmas trees; a baron of beef weighing 180 lbs, roasted at Windsor, was sent to Osborne, where it adorned the sideboard, garnished with the Queen's monogram in shredded horseradish. 'The Birthday Book', which some people took for a Bible, travelled with the Queen from Windsor to Osborne, the Riviera and Balmoral. The list of anniversaries grew longer every year.

Vicky paid her last visit to Balmoral in the summer of 1898. On her return to Friedrichshof she had a fall when out riding. Her horse had become restive at the approach of a traction engine; a bailiff tried to lead the horse past but in its terror it reared to such an extent that Vicky was thrown off. A small lump formed on her head; her right wrist was sprained and her hand was slightly injured by the horse stepping on it. She made light of the accident. She had ridden for fifty years, she said – she was then fifty-eight – and it was not surprising that accidents should sometimes occur. 'I would rather the accident occurred to me than to someone else – the day after tomorrow I shall ride again, and in spite of the sprain I shall try to paint a little and write a few more letters,' she told her secretary. The next day, however, she had to admit that she had passed a bad night. Her long, four-year period of suffering had begun. She slowly developed cancer of the spine. Letters to the Queen were carefully worded so as not to cause her anxiety. She sent the Queen three handsome silver candelabra for her eightieth birthday in May 1899.

Anniversaries, always anniversaries! Beatrice went in early to see her mother and present her with a nosegay, and in the afternoon accompanied the Queen in her pony chair to see Affie march past with the Scots Guards. The Queen then planted a tree and drove out at 5 p.m. with Beatrice and Princess Alexandra across the Long Walk to the mausoleum to place a bouquet at the foot of the 'dear tomb'. There was a family dinner at the castle, attended by Beatrice, Helena, Louise and Lorne, and Bertie's wife Princess Alexandra, followed by the first and last acts of *Lohengrin* sung by the de Reske brothers, who enchanted the Queen. They were 'beyond praise' and the music was 'so poetic, so dramatic, and one might almost say religious in feeling'.

This was a brief interlude of gaiety before the tragedies of the Boer War. On 1 January 1900, the Queen wrote in her diary: 'I begin today a new year and a new century full of anxiety and fear of what may be before us. May all near and dear ones be protected, above all darling Vicky, who is far from well . . . I hope and pray dear Christle [Helena's eldest son] will be spared . . . I pray that God may spare me yet a short while to my children, friends and dear country, leaving me all my faculties and to a certain extent my eyesight. May He bless our armies and give our men strength to fulfil their arduous task . . .'

From her bed of pain in Germany Vicky wrote:

> The first words this morning, and my motto for the century: God Save the Queen! Never was this prayer breathed more tenderly and devotedly, nor from a more faithful heart . . . My thoughts are so much with you all today and how I should love to talk over the many subjects of deep interest and anxiety which crowd in upon one . . . I am able to be up for a little in an armchair and on the sofa. The pain is still very acute.

To Sophie she added: 'The injections [of morphia] dull the pains a little for about a quarter of an hour, then they rage again with renewed intensity.'

The Queen drove to the cavalry barracks with Beatrice to inspect the composite household cavalry regiment of six hundred men before their departure for South Africa; she also inspected the 240 Canadian troops in the quadrangle at Windsor. On 31 July Helena and Beatrice broke the news of her son Affie's death from tuberculosis. Then on 28 August the Queen paused for a few moments to recall 'this ever dear day has returned again without my beloved Albert who, on this day eighty-one years ago, came into the world as a blessing to so many. How I remember the happy day it used to be and the preparation of presents for him which he would like!'

She was at Balmoral in October when the news came of the death of 'beloved Christle' Helena's favourite son, from malaria. The Queen broke down and drew her lady-in-waiting, Mary Mallet, close to her and let her 'stroke her dear hand. I quite forget she is far above me and only realize she is a sorrowing woman who clings to human sympathy and hungers for all that can be given on such occasions.' Beatrice was so self-controlled that she gave the impression of being unsympathetic. Mary Mallet wanted to shake her. Louise, on the contrary, was full of demonstrative affection. She was always at her best when people were in real trouble – 'she is a complex character'.

Louise, too, had taken an active interest in the war wounded and organized a set of rooms at the Savoy hotel, facing the river, for six officers and non-commissioned officers, to be looked after by two nurses and a ward nurse. She wrote to General Wolseley that she had been carefully over the rooms 'and they seem very suitable and comfortable, having two lifts to the kitchen and stillroom, two bathrooms and a storeroom'. She added that she would provide the two nurses, who had had three years thorough London training, and obtain the services of the best London medical men. In addition, Louise proposed to devote a wing at Rosneath, Dunbartonshire, where she and Lorne were living, to a hospital home for the Highland brigade. She described its situation to General Wolseley as being 'close to the pier, so the steamers can come up near, and the patients wheeled to the door of the building'. She enclosed a ground plan which she had gone into with medical men. There would be room for fifteen men and three officers, two nurses and a ward-woman. Rosneath was only one hour from Glasgow, so the best medical advice would be available.

In London, during one of Princess Louise's visits to the Chelsea Hospital, a woman had appealed to her on behalf of her son, who had been wounded at Ladysmith and was at the Hasler Hospital in Portsmouth, where she could not afford to visit him often. Louise wrote off to Lady Wolseley to find out what could be done for the woman. Were there not special half-price fares on the railways for such cases? She worked, too, for the Soldiers and Sailors Families Association and was anxious to 'get the work more uniform in the various districts'. All of Victoria's daughters were capable organizers and had a practical turn of mind in addition to their artistic talents.

There were wounded soldiers to be visited, with Beatrice and Helena, at Netley Hospital; at the Palace, everybody was busily engaged in making things for the troops. 'The Queen,' wrote Mary Mallet, 'turns out khaki comforters as if her bread depended upon it and says so sweetly: "I like to do something for my soldiers although it is so little". She had also "made things" during the Crimean War, "but they *would* give them to the officers, not at all what I intended". She expressed the fear that war will never cease as long as the world exists.' One day she opened a children's ward in the hospital at Ryde, Osborne, and enjoyed talking to the children and giving them toys.

Vicky bought a bronze bell for the English church in Venice, dedicated to the memory of the officers and men of the Army and Navy who had fallen in South Africa. It was a private gesture which went unreported in the press. (She had to dissuade Sophie, who was of a less practical nature than her mother, from sending Turkish Delight for the wounded war heroes.)

The old Queen was crushed and exhausted by grief, but she was able to appear at a garden party at Buckingham Palace in 1900 sporting white roses in her bonnet, white feathers, large pearls and fringed parasol. Looking at her, Lady Monkswell observed: 'When I thought of her immense age and of the way she had stood up against misfortune this terrible winter, I felt as if I ought to kneel as she passed. Lady Ripon, who had been with her a good deal in her early married life, felt none of the passion and admiration and worship we now feel. She did not stand out then as the heroic figure we all recognize now, particularly after this war.'

Vicky wrote her last letter to her mother on 5 October 1900: 'I shall be prevented for some days from leaving my bed, and the attacks of spasms that seize me in the back, limbs and bones are so frequent that it is difficult to find a pause long enough to write in.' Thereafter she dictated letters to her daughter Charlotte, with whom she was now on better terms. Beatrice went to see Vicky for a couple of days after a visit to Frankfurt. 'What a joy and comfort to me!' Vicky exclaimed as they carried her down from her bed to the terrace for a little while. Helena – 'dear Lenchen' – visited her too, read to her and 'was most kind', but the days dragged on interminably with little respite from suffering.

For Christmas, Vicky sent her mother a present of a special magnifying glass. The Queen dictated her thanks to Beatrice, for she too was incapable of writing in person: 'Darling Child, a thousand thanks for the most beautiful magnifying glass which I shall always use in thinking of you. I have not been very well; no cause for alarm. I have been able to get out a little most days.' That was the Queen's last letter to her eldest daughter. How typical that it should have been about a gift for that most cherished of anniversaries in the royal home: Christmas!

On Wednesday 16 January 1901 the Queen went for her usual donkey-chair ride in the grounds at Osborne House, but when it came to the door again in the afternoon it was sent away empty. Victoria was never to ride in it again.

She sank quickly and peacefully. Beatrice, Helena, Louise took turns by her bedside. The Duke of Connaught was recalled from his visit to Germany and Willy insisted upon accompanying him and driving the engine to Flushing himself. He guessed, rightly, that 'the petticoats who are fencing off poor grandmama from the world and I fear often from me, will kick up a row'. But when he arrived he behaved unexceptionably and took the family by surprise; he held the Queen in his arms ('she was so little and light,' he said) for two hours before her death on 22 January. Before she died, the Queen whispered her children's names and asked that Turi, her white pomeranian, be put on her bed.

The Queen, who 'had always liked to arrange a funeral', had laid down meticulous instructions for her own, including the music to be played during the service. There was to be no black upon her – not now. She was at last to be reunited with Albert and so it was appropriate that her face be covered with her wedding veil and her wedding dress placed over her, under the Union Jack.

When Vicky heard the news she cried: 'I wish I were dead too!' Bertie wrote to her describing the funeral and her son's exemplary conduct.

> Willy was kindness itself and touching in his devotion, without a shade of brusquerie or selfishness. I know full well how your thoughts will be with us and how, as my eldest sister, you will give me your blessing to fufil my arduous and onerous duties which I have now inherited from such a Sovereign and Mother. God bless you, dearest and beloved sister, and may He mitigate your sufferings now.

Helpless, prostrate with pain, Vicky had to read about the funeral from her bed: how the royal yacht *Alberta* had passed through eleven miles of battleships and cruisers bearing the white coffin with its crimson and gold pall to the mainland; how the hulls of the advance guard destroyers had been painted in black; how the coffin had lain all night in the Albert Memorial Chapel after the funeral service at St George's Chapel before being taken to Frogmore mausoleum, past the pond where Vicky and her brothers and sisters used to skate with beloved Papa.

Vicky dissolved into tears.

Oh, my beloved Mama, is she really gone? Gone from us all to whom she was such a comfort and support? To have lost her seems so impossible and I, far away, could not see her dear face or kiss her dear hand once more. It breaks my heart. What a Queen she was, and what a woman! What will life be to me without her, the wretched bit of life left to me, struggling with a cruel disease. How her affection and sympathy used to cheer and help and comfort me . . . My dear home in England, my home no longer . . .

That was the tragedy for the eldest and the youngest of Queen Victoria's daughters, Vicky and Beatrice. The centre of their existence – this applied particularly to Beatrice – had gone, swept away by Bertie's compulsive desire for change and renewal. It was natural that he should be impatient to make use of the little time he had left – he was sixty – to live as he had always wanted to and to bury the musty past with its mementoes of the Victorian Age. He was bursting to initiate the Edwardian Era, *his* era. He had had to wait so long! Now it was his turn to echo the comment made by his mother when she had visited Queen Louise of Prussia's apartments in the Berlin *Schloss* so many years before: 'All looked so sad and cheerless, for the colour is gone out of everything and the whole is oldfashioned.'

Louise, who had always appeared to be the least attached of the Queen's daughters, wrote to her friend Audrey, Hallam Tennyson's wife, when her mother died; 'I know the sorrow; it never wears off, at least with me it don't. And I can never realize that she is gone, only that for a bit I cannot see her. The desire to write to her, and feeling she expects news, is still on me. She was always wanting to hear and to know.'

Queen Alexandra was disturbed by her husband's haste. She wrote to Vicky in May 1901; 'Alas, after returning to Buckingham Palace from Copenhagen, during my absence Bertie has had all your beloved mother's rooms dismantled and all her precious things removed.' Osborne was even more of a 'museum' than the other royal domains. It housed a forty-year-old collection of anniversary gifts, curios and souvenirs, including

The Queen had bequeathed her two private residences, Balmoral and Osborne, to the sovereign, with certain proprietary rights held by other members of the family. These, plus Sandringham, were maintained out of the privy purse; Bertie considered that they were too great a burden for the royal exchequer. He was satisfied with Sandringham, which had been his home for years. The Queen had liked the idea of her children and grandchildren holidaying together at Osborne, keeping up the memories and anniversaries of the 'old days', but there was nothing they wanted less, now that the binding force had disappeared. Bertie cast a brief nostalgic glance at the children's gardens at Swiss Cottage, but he quickly repressed his emotions and convened his sisters to meet him at Osborne and agree upon its future. He had already decided what he wanted to do with it. The Admiralty had just scrapped the old training ship H.M.S. *Britannia* for naval cadets at Dartmouth, to establish a preparatory school on land. Lord Esher, who was then Secretary of the Office of Works, suggested that the grounds and stabling of Osborne House would provide a most suitable site. A convalescent home for Royal Navy and Army officers was also needed, and Osborne House would be ideal for the purpose. The King set out to mark off the grounds, adding to those occupied by Beatrice, who was living in Osborne Cottage, on the confines of the park. Louise was established at Kent House, a large villa outside the park (although she was more often than not away at Rosneath in Scotland, in London or on the Continent).

Beatrice was broken-hearted. She was the daughter who had the most to suffer from her mother's death – she who had been her constant shadow and companion all her life. Now all was changed: her position, once stupidly envied by so many, her support, even her house, which was to be surrounded by strangers! The Empress Eugénie, ever understanding, once again invited her to stay at her villa at Cap Saint-Martin. On her forty-fourth birthday in April 1901, Beatrice wrote to Mary Mallet:

...This first sad return of my birthday without my beloved mother! No one knows what the daily missing of that tender care and love is to me, coming as it does on the top of that other overwhelming loss, so that my heart is indeed left utterly desolate. If it were not for the dear children, for whom I have alone to live now, I do not know how I should have the courage of struggling on.

I felt sure it would be most awfully trying for you going to Windsor under such altered circumstances and do not wonder that you were always on the verge of breaking down. I am thankful to be well away from everything and to have still some time before me ere I see all the old places again.

In spite of her references to her children, Beatrice could be curiously callous about them, as Lady Mallet observed when she accompanied the Princess and her little family to Kissingen in Germany that June. Leopold, the Princess's haemophilic son, was ill and confined to his bed in the hotel where they were staying. Lady Mallet feared – only too accurately – that he would not be long-lived. 'The Princess,' she wrote to her husband, 'tries to cultivate the maternal instinct – she loses so much. Leopold is an angel child, so sweet and attractive. He pines for someone to cling to – he wants petting and spoiling...' Beatrice was not accustomed to nursing, she did not take after her sisters in this respect; she became impatient and prepared to visit Vicky at Friedrichshof, leaving Leopold behind in the hotel at Kissingen, Lady Mallet could not understand this unfeeling attitude in a woman whom she otherwise admired and respected. She thought that Beatrice had a 'wonderfully cheerful, contented nature [as the Queen had observed years before]; she is very German in the way she can concentrate her mind on a given line of thought or action. She delights in theology and all religious questions. Science is a dead letter – in politics she is conservative, but broadminded.' Lady Mallet added in another letter home that Beatrice was

... terribly unhappy, but she never grumbles or repines or regrets the luxurious advantages of the past...she only dreads returning to the familiar haunts where all is now so fearfully changed and is anxious about the future of the three boys, who must work their own way; they are handicapped rather than helped by rank. I am sure that Leopold and Maurice will give her serious anxiety . . . I am also sure Princess Beatrice would far rather live in Germany, but for the sake of her children that would not be wise.

The Princess became more communicative every day, though on some occasions she was capable of turning her back on Lady Mallet; this was a facet of her 'strange manner', which she herself deplored but did not appear to be able to control. Lady Mallet was embarrassed to be the depositor of 'family secrets and skeletons. Sometimes I feel quite alarmed lest I should let them out. The more I know of royalties the more I pity them – the race is a most extraordinary one and I'm glad my station in life is of a less exalted degree.' She did not believe that people would ever properly appreciate Princess Beatrice's 'great simplicity of mind and ignorance of the world, which goes against her; she is more fitted to be a clergyman's wife than a Princess, except of course in matters of finance.' In brief, Beatrice, in Lady Mallet's opinion, had been wrongly cast.

From Kissingen the party proceeded to Kronberg, where Vicky was enduring the last weeks of her martyrdom. Schloss Friedrichshof was a centre of disharmony. Lady Mallet wrote: 'Princess Victoria [Moretta] keeps visitors at arm's length. She is feared and detested here. The poor little Court is torn by petty intrigues and at this terribly solemn moment.' She caught a brief glimpse of Vicky coming back from a drive, 'a little crumpled figure lying in a carriage, Beatrice and Princess Victoria by her side and Dr von Wedel. She drives in the open air from 3 to 7 p.m.':

Beatrice's description of the Empress is ghastly: every feature and limb distorted and that charming countenance quite unrecognizable, her mouth drawn up, her teeth project, her nostrils are dilated by her terrible struggle for breath which makes her nose bleed constantly and the whole face yellow. This horror has been going on for four years; the iron constitution still keeps death at bay. The doctors think she will gradually get weaker for she eats nothing. It is difficult to understand what she says, but she is read aloud to seven or eight hours a day and loves English novels and travels. I fear religion is not much comfort to her, poor thing. She finds no help or consolation in prayer and this is a great distress to some of her children, but she is and has been such a good woman that one always hopes she may have more faith than she allows to appear on the surface.

Lady Mallet had probably guessed correctly, because, in a letter addressed to her friend Mary Ponsonby in 1886, Vicky had written on the subject of religion, apropos a pronouncement of Mrs Humphrey Ward's:

I see she says 'we have the task to believe and live'. What are we to believe, and who sets it as a task? I think we must shape our religion i.e. our minds and opinion, for ourselves, daily examining and adding to the store of what we think—improving it, deepening it, eliminating mistakes and shallowness, in short: trying to mould a philosophic soul in ourselves until our minds are in the best balance we can obtain. I say mind, I might say heart—they are all words and only approximately express what we mean. All this religious strife and discussion is useful as a process of elucidation and education. The world has always thought on these matters, and always will. Faith is a frame of mind and nothing else. I prefer not to stare at one point in the Heavens alone, but to look all round and take as much of it as I can. One feels the richer and the better and consequently the happier for it, but then I am not anybody else. It often gives me pleasure, however, to see the same feeling expressed in books by others and see how very natural it is.

Hers was the philosophy – and life – of a Stoic.

At the beginning of August 1901, King Edward invited his three sisters, Helena, Louise and Beatrice, to meet him to make the final decision about the fate of Osborne House. It was purely a matter of form. The King withdrew with his sisters to a secluded part of the grounds and a discussion took place between them in German, so that their respective suites could not understand what was being said. Sir Lionel Cust related: 'The King returned after some time flushed, but with a happy smile on his face. He had convinced – or coerced – his sisters, who could not have presented a united front.

Beatrice had the most to lose. Osborne meant more to her than to any other member of the family. There she had been brought up as a child, there she had been married, there her husband was buried, there she had made her home, next to dearest Mama. She had been made Governor of the Isle of Wight. It was all hers. Helena, good, benevolent, placid Lenchen, did not care much either way; she was contented with her life at Cumberland Lodge and was closer to Queen Alexandra than her other sisters. As for contrary Louise, she was only too happy to rid herself of irksome memories. Louise had never been 'one of the set'. Speaking on education when she was over eighty, she stated: 'Luckily the habit of moulding all children to the same pattern has gone out of fashion. It was deplorable. I know, because I suffered from it. Nowadays individuality and one's own capabilities are recognized.' She got on better with Bertie than with her sisters at the beginning of his reign. She was more decorative, more modern, more broad-minded, and a better conversationalist. She shone at his parties and she enjoyed being seen at them. She wanted to be able to work quietly in her studio in the gardens of Dornden near Tunbridge Wells, or at Kensington Palace, and spend the rest of the time travelling. She occasionally went to Sandringham – her sisters never did.

Bertie had only just won his little victory over his three sisters at Osborne when a telegram was handed to him. His smile of triumph was replaced by an expression of acute distress. Vicky was dead. Her sufferings had ended at last, on 5 August 1901. Hurriedly he made arrangements to attend the funeral. He was met by Willy, who had not left his mother's side for thirty-six hours. Had there been a last-minute reconciliation between mother and son? According to Marie von Bunsen, the Kaiser had hoped for a reconciliation but it was denied him. His mother neither could nor would forgive him the injury he had done to her beloved husband.

Bertie and Willy walked side by side by torchlight to the little church at Kronberg. The coffin was covered by the Union Jack and the Prussian Royal Standard, then the body was taken by train to Potsdam to be buried beside the late Emperor Frederick and little Waldemar. 'It is an irreparable loss,' Bertie exclaimed, 'hardly a week elapsed without our writing to each other.' Later he ordered in his will that their private correspondence should be destroyed.

Soon after her husband's death, Vicky had written: 'One day there must and there will come a reaction ... by then I shall rest next to the Emperor Frederick in my grave and people will hardly know what we wanted and how much we loved our fatherland for which we were permitted to do so little. Our tragic fate belongs to German history. . . .' Had she lived she would have witnessed more tragedies: her son Willy dying in exile after the holocaust of the First World War; Moretta dying in penury and grief; Sophie exiled to Switzerland; Mossy bravely living on in an army-occupied castle after the Second World War and the loss of two of her sons; Schloss Friedrichshof converted into an hotel (except for her private rooms). She would have seen three great dynasties, the Hohenzollerns, the Habsburgs and the Romanovs, disappear, the members of her family sink into obscurity. She would have seen Beatrice forced to drop her married name of Battenberg, suppressed by her grandson George v in 1917. She was more at peace in her grave.

Helena, Princess Christian, lived on unobtrusively until 1923, devoted to 'good works' and hospitals in Windsor. Lord Playfair once declared: 'Queen Victoria was the jolliest woman I ever knew, and Princess Christian was the best.'

Louise ended her life at Kensington Palace in 1939, at the age of ninety-one. She had led very much her own kind of life, not very close to Beatrice who, as her mother's literary trustee, found consolation – to the dismay of Bertie and George v – in 'editing' Queen Victoria's letters and papers, omitting and censoring as she thought fit. Many records of historical interest have been lost in the process, many of the 'family skeletons' once confided to Lady Mallet buried for ever. Beatrice's children and grandchildren were brought up according to the strict Victorian code which she adhered to until her death in October 1944: the last born of Queen Victoria's daughters, she was the last to die.

# *Epilogue*

THE daughters of Queen Victoria sound so remote that it seems unlikely that anyone alive today could have seen and known them, but the present writer had the privilege of discussing four of the royal Princesses, Vicky, Louise, Helena and Beatrice, with their surviving niece: Princess Alice, Countess of Athlone (daughter of Victoria's son Prince Leopold) in her drawing-room at Kensington Palace, in the quadrangle where Louise and Beatrice lived for so many years, next door to the rooms in which Queen Victoria herself was born and brought up. (They are now converted into the London Museum, which houses many relics of the Queen, including her dolls and some of her toys.)

I rang the bell and waited for what seemed a very long time. Did it function? Could it be out of order – as so many things had been in Victoria's time – or getting as old as the present occupier of the house, in her eighty-eighth year? Footsteps finally approached at a ritualistic pace and the door was opened by an impassive manservant who appeared to be well aware that no royalty was expected. 'You may leave your coat in the hall,' he instructed me, nodding towards an Aubusson-upholstered armchair. He then led me into a little study overlooking the quadrangle, occupied by a large desk and small tables dotted with family photographs. I sat in a small armchair by the window for the space of two or three minutes and then, in she came, lively as a squirrel, gracious and captivating, Princess Alice, Countess of Athlone who had actually *seen* Queen Victoria and four of the royal princesses.

After having read so many volumes of letters, memoirs and journals about or by the Queen and her daughters, after having lived with them in spirit for so long, until I had reached the stage when I actually felt their presence about me, I had at last reached the final stage of seeing and clasping the hand of an actual survivor of the Victorian age, a lady who, in her childhood and youth, had been admitted into that large circle of now remote and faded figures whose loves and quarrels and family tragedies I had shared from an immense distance. A dainty slender figure with laughing blue eyes, blue-tinted hair, discreet make-up, dressed in a sage green suit, wearing a diamond brooch, ear-rings and rings, high-heeled shoes, neat legs, elegant hands and feet. The Princess talked to me gaily and unaffectedly.

She did not ask me not to quote what she told me; she had graciously consented to receive me for the specific objective of talking about her aunts, so that I feel free to transcribe the candour of her comments. To my question: 'What were the Princesses like – how did they appear to *you*?' she smilingly replied: 'All the aunts were authoritarian, part of a conscious royal caste, telling people what to do and getting on each other's nerves, with the possible exception of Alice [whom the Princess had not known, since she was not born until 1883]. Helena, Princess Christian, was very kind and equable. She bore herself with great dignity, always walked with her head well back, but she too was authoritarian. She brooked no contradiction at the Committee meetings of the many benevolent institutions at which she presided. "So we all agree on that point, don't we? Therefore, let us pass on...," she would say determinedly, whether or not everybody present *had* in fact agreed with her views.'

Vicky was 'a little tiresome, and she irritated Queen Victoria by telling her what to do ... she liked to run things her own way. They all did ... Beatrice was kept very much in the background; her children obeyed grandma more than their mother. Beatrice could not understand her lively children. She was shy, always sidled into rooms, afraid of being noticed. She was quite lost when her mother died ...'

Louise? Princess Alice laughed at the recollection of the last of her Victorian aunts. 'Louise could be heard all over Kensington Palace yard whooping with laughter in her high, penetrating voice. She was very fond of her brother Leopold [Princess Alice's father] and jealous of his wife; she got on well with the Kaiser – indeed, with any man – she ran after anything in trousers. She was also on friendly terms with Bertie, who never invited any of his other sisters to stay with him. Louise liked Louis Battenberg too . . . oh, all the men. Lorne, her husband, was a dear . . . good-looking, kind, vague . . . too soft with her. She found him dull. He was a little odd in his behaviour; he would wear a Norfolk jacket for a formal occasion and at other times appear at breakfast wearing the Order of the Garter . . . All the aunts were a little eccentric – they had funny little ways – and we of the younger generation used to have great fun mimicking them. They would never stoop to pick up an object they accidentally dropped, even from an armchair; they always had an enormous retinue of servants, but then that was common to Victorian ladies of any standing . . . Yes,' mused Princess Alice with a twinkle in her eye, 'my aunts belonged to another world.'

As she led me out herself, she observed how pleasant it was for her to live 'so close to the family' (at Buckingham Palace).

The white door closed behind me. The delicate little porcelain figure had vanished, my first and last vision of Queen Victoria's granddaughter, the last link with the royal Princesses whose family life and relationships with the Queen I have attempted to relate, beginning my story out of a sense of historical curiosity and concluding it with that blend of affection, compassion and nostalgia which overcomes one after one has closed a fading family album.

When I stepped out of Kensington Palace I asked myself: if I had lived long enough to have known Victoria's daughters, which of them would I have preferred to see and talk to, had I been able, like the famous 'Boy Jones', to scale the palace walls?

Undoubtedly Vicky would have been the most stimulating and provoking conversationally; a hard taskmistress, though, who would immediately have enrolled me to work for one of her 'causes'. Alice too, although she was a more self-effacing do-gooder, inclined to be a little too earnest. All five sisters took an active interest in helping the sick and the maimed.

Vicky, Alice and Louise patronized the arts, particularly music and the theatre, in a conservative sort of way.

Louise would surely have been the most amusing travelling companion, inclined to be bitchy and make devastating remarks.

Helena I think I would have found dull, but sympathetic in a crisis. Beatrice, that admirable model of Victorian filial piety, must have been rather awesome but I may be prejudiced. Mr Hector Bolitho, who lunched with her and the Dean of Windsor many times in his younger days, told me: 'She was shy at first, but once we broke through her defences, she was full of information . . . all of warm and pleasant days, mostly at Windsor. Royal people usually recall royal occasions, but Princess Beatrice was naturally warm and personal.'

Had their position been different, would any of the Princesses have become a queen of their mother's stature? Vicky would not have listened to her ministers as her mother did or curbed her quick tongue; Alice did not possess the physical stamina for public life and international tensions; Helena and Beatrice did not have the brains; and Louise was too capricious and individualistic.

The Queen was a possessive mother; in this she was not unique nor particularly Victorian, but she was genuinely concerned with her daughters' happiness and did not drive them into marriages of convenience like other European royalties. Louise and Beatrice imposed their will on her in this respect. The Queen bowed to them, for she had experienced and valued love. Autocratic? In her position, Victoria could hardly help it, but she took a closer personal interest in her daughters' upbringing than the average affluent Victorian mother. She needed her daughters' affection. Vicky, Alice and Beatrice needed hers. Beatrice 'missed her mother's daily tender care' when she died, although, to the outsider, it would have appeared that it was Beatrice who administered 'daily tender care' to the Queen. Vicky, apparently the most self-contained and independent of Victoria's daughters, wailed: 'How can I live without her?' It was a genuine *cri de coeur*. It is only when emotional ties have been severed by death that one can truly assess their depth.

Queen Victoria, in spite of her dictatorial traits and meddlesomeness, was basically a wise, tactful and compassionate mother with her daughters. Time and time again she intervened to smooth their difficult relationships with in-laws or children. She vetted innumerable brides, delighted in and abetted true romances, endeavoured – in their own interest – to keep her family free from dangerous involvements. In times of stress she sent out doctors, nurses, governesses and personally looked after hosts of grandchildren. There were times, both at the beginning and at the end of her reign, when she pronounced children to be 'insufferable'. She preferred them in small doses. Nine children and thirty-six grandchildren were a little too much for her.

A nervous woman by temperament, the Queen needed a calm, loving presence constantly at her side. Beatrice fulfilled this role, for which the Queen was genuinely grateful, as she recorded so frequently in her journals and letters; but was Beatrice demonstrative enough? One is inclined to doubt it. The Queen probably loved Beatrice most of all her daughters, for she hardly ever left her mother's side. She admired Vicky and was distressed by her sad fate, but was also acutely aware of her shortcomings. To Alice she might have been more generous had she not been so afraid of being coerced and taken advantage of. Alice surprised her mother after her marriage by her forcefulness, which she had kept hidden when she lived at home.

There was a jealous trait in the Queen which surfaced whenever she believed that her daughters were enjoying themselves more than she was and 'leaving her out': Alice at Darmstadt in her happier days, Louise at Argyll House, the Christians at Buckingham Palace in her absence. As years went by there developed the inevitable estrangements caused by time and distance. Victoria became less German in her outlook, her daughters more so; even Beatrice, once called the 'British Rosebud', had pronounced German traits according to her ladies, as we have seen. Helena lived in England, but in the constant Teutonic presence of Prince Christian. Vicky was so assertively English in Germany that she defeated her purpose. Louise was more cosmopolitan, but her 'peculiar manner' and sharp tongue prevented her from being popular anywhere for any length of time.

None of Victoria's daughters possessed their mother's bewitching smile or disarming candour. *Elle était tout d'une pièce*: people always knew exactly where they were with her; she inspired trust, confidence and willing slavery from all who approached her, more so in her later years.

Vicky had brains; Alice and Helena benevolence; Louise taste and the gift of repartee; Beatrice was devoted and 'pure'. As a group, the five Princesses were each of them in their own way good examples of the best type of Victorian womanhood: imbued with high ideals, a strong sense of duty and altruism; talented and useful. Queen Victoria did her best to mould them from their cradles. For Vicky, Alice and Beatrice she was their beloved model.

This book deals solely with domestic issues, which was only one aspect of the Queen's very full life; it is amazing that she could have found so much time, in addition to her public duties and preoccupations, which she took so much to heart (chiefly in fulfilment of her vow to Albert's memory), to deal in such detail with her daughters' affairs.

'A Princess must do this – a Princess mustn't do that . . .': the Queen had firm ideas on the subject. She never forgot that she and her daughters were 'in harness'. But she did her best to make them flesh-and-blood, humanitarian Princesses, unlike so many aloof, extravagant and arrogant foreign royalties. It was – still is – a difficult profession, whose duties have never been properly defined and whose era has passed away with ermine-trimmed trains, diadems and rigid court etiquette, which became irksome even to the Queen. Victoria's daughters belonged to a world that has vanished.

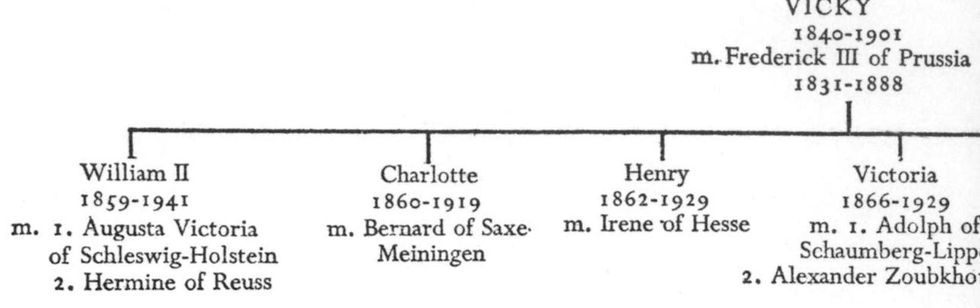
VICKY
1840-1901
m. Frederick III of Prussia
1831-1888
William II
1859-1941
m. 1. Augusta Victoria
of Schleswig-Holstein
2. Hermine of Reuss
Charlotte
1860-1919
m. Bernard of Saxe-
Meiningen
Henry
1862-1929
m. Irene of Hesse
Victoria
1866-1929
m. 1. Adolph of
Schaumberg-Lippe
2. Alexander Zoubkhov

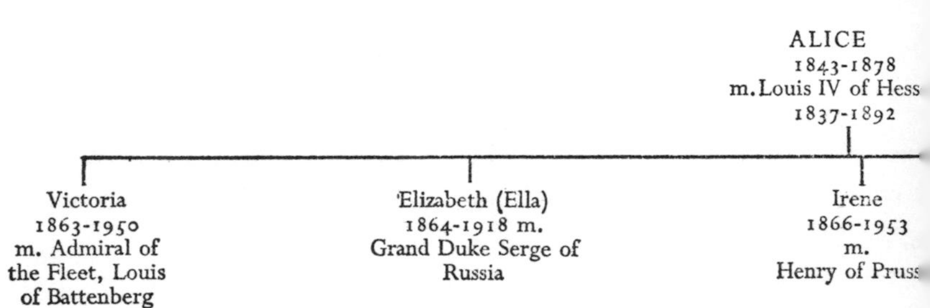
ALICE
1843-1878
m. Louis IV of Hess
1837-1892
Victoria
1863-1950
m. Admiral of
the Fleet, Louis
of Battenberg
Elizabeth (Ella)
1864-1918 m.
Grand Duke Serge of
Russia
Irene
1866-1953
m.
Henry of Pruss

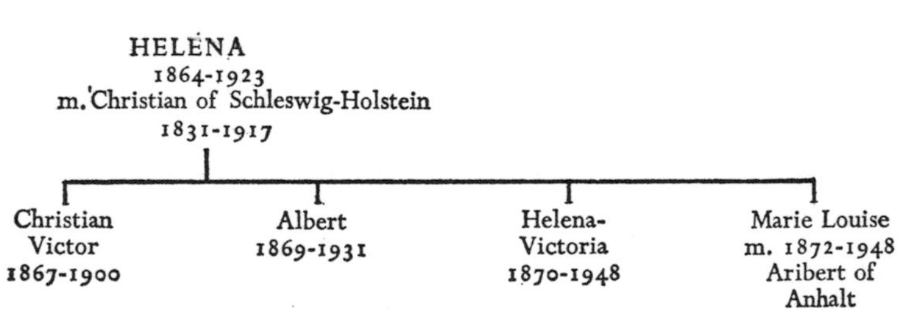
HELENA
1864-1923
m. Christian of Schleswig-Holstein
1831-1917
Christian
Victor
1867-1900
Albert
1869-1931
Helena-
Victoria
1870-1948
Marie Louise
m. 1872-1948
Aribert of
Anhalt

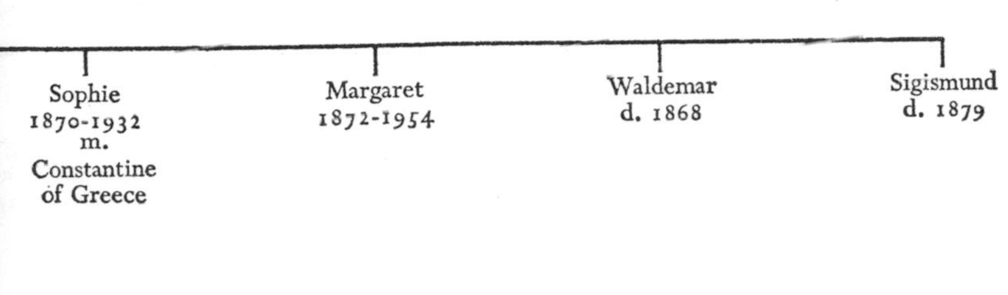


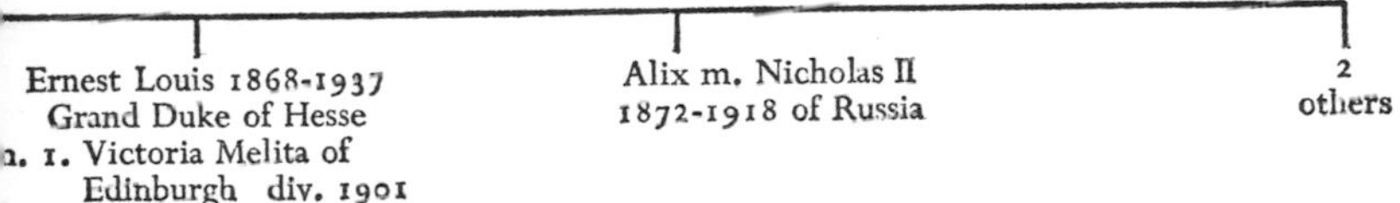


LOUISE m. 9th Duke
1848-1939 Argyll
(no issue)

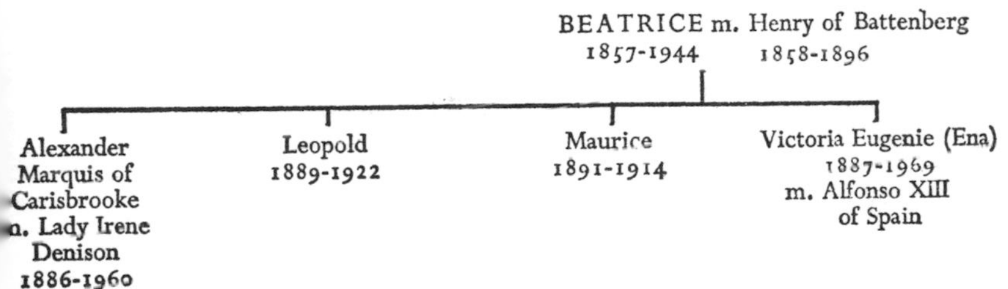

# *Select Bibliography*


Alice, Grand Duchess of Hesse, *A Memoir Compiled by Princess Christian* (1884).

Almedingen, E. M., *Unbroken Unity* (1964)

Balfour, Michael, *The Kaiser and His Times* (1964).

Barkeley, Richard, *The Empress Frederick* (1950).

Battenberg, Princess Marie of, *Reminiscences* (1925).

Benson, A. C. and Esher, Viscount (eds.) *The Letters of Queen Victoria*, (1st series, 3 vols), (1907).

Benson, E. F., *Daughters of Victoria* (1939).

Bolitho, Hector, *Albert the Good* (1932).

Bolitho, Hector (ed.) *Further Letters of Queen Victoria* (1938).

Bolitho, Hector and Baillie, A. V. (eds.) *Letter of Lady Augusta Stanley* (1927).

Bolitho, Hector and Windsor, Dean of (eds.), *Later Letters of Lady Augusta Stanley* (1929).

Buckle, G. E. (ed.), *Letters of Queen Victoria* (2nd Series), (1926).

Bunsen, Marie von, *The World I Used to Know* (1930).

Buxhoeveden, Baroness Sophie, *The Life and Tragedy of Alexandra Feodorovna, Empress of Russia* (1928).

Collier, Hon. E. C. F. (ed.) *A Victoria Diarist* (Extracts from the journals of Mary, Lady Monkswell), (1944).

Cowan, John, *Canada's Governor Generals* (1867–1952) (1961).

*The Correspondence of Sarah Spencer, Lady Lyttelton* (1912)

Crawford, E., *Victoria, Queen and Ruler* (1903).

Cust, Sir Lionel, *King Edward VII and His Court* (1930).

*Daisy, Princess of Pless. By Herself* (1928).

Disher, M. Willson, *The Greatest Show on Earth* (1927).

Duff, David, *Hessian Tapestry* (1967).

Duff, David, *The Life Story of H.R.H. Princess Louise, Duchess of Argyll* (1940).

Duff, David, *The Shy Princess* (1958).

Dyson, Hope and Tennyson, Charles (eds.), *Dear and Honoured Lady* (correspondence between Queen Victoria and Alfred Tennyson), (1969).

Elder, Smith, *Life and Letters of Sir Charles Hallé* (1896).

Esher, Viscount (ed.) *The Girlhood of Queen Victoria* (2 vols), (1912).

Fulford, Roger, *Dearest Child* (Letters from Queen Victoria to the Princess Royal), (1964).

Fulford, Roger (ed.) *Dearest Mama* (Letters between Queen Victoria and the Crown Princess of Prussia 1861–64), (1968).

Fulford, Roger, *The Prince Consort* (1949).

Graham, Harvey, *Eternal Eve* (1950).

Gower, Lord Ronald, *My Reminiscences* (1883).

Gower, Lord Ronald, *Old Diaries* (1912).

Hardinge, Major GI. the Hon. Arthur, *Sidelights on Queen Victoria* (ed. F. Ponsonby), (1930).

Houston, Major Desmond Chapman (ed.) *Behind the Scenes at the Prussian Court, H.R.H. Princess Friedrich Leopold of Prussia, Princess of Schelsvig-Holstein* (1939).

Huston, Major Desmond Chapman (ed.) *What I Left Unsaid. Daisy, Princess of Pless* (1936).

Jerrold, Clare, *The Early Court of Queen Victoria* (1912).

Jerrold, Clare, *The Married Life of Queen Victoria* (1913).

Kennedy, A. L. (ed.), *My Dear Duchess* (social and political letters to the Duchess of Manchester), (1956).

*Lady Lytton's Court Diary, 1895–1899* (1961)

Lee, A. Gould, (ed.), *The Empress Frederick Writes to Sophie* (1955).

Liddell, Georgiana, Baroness Bloomfield, *Reminiscences of Court and Diplomatic Life* (1883).

Lloyd, Alan, *The Drums of Kumasi* (1964).

Longford, Elizabeth, *Victoria R.I.* (1964).

Macdonnel, Lady, *Reminiscences of Diplomatic Life* (1913).

MacNutt, W. Stewart, *Days of Lorne* (1955).

Magnus, Philip, *King Edward VII* (1969).
Mallet, Victor (ed.), *Life with Queen Victoria* (Letters of Marie Mallet 1887 – 1901), (1968) and the Mallet Papers.
Manson, J., *Sir Edwin Landseer* (1902).
Martin, Sir Theodore, *Life of the Prince Consort* (1875).
Martin, Sir Theodore, *Queen Victoria as I Knew Her* (1902).
Masterman, Lucy (ed.) *Mary Gladstone; diaries and letters* (1930).
Maxwell, Sir Herbert (ed.), *Life and Letters of the 4th Earl of Clarendon* (2 vols), (1913).
Mortimer, Raymond, (intro.), *Queen Victoria: Leaves from a Journal* (1961).
Paget, Lady Walburga, *Embassies of Other Days* (1923).
Paget, Lady Walburga, *Scenes and Memories* (1903).
Pearson, G. Arthur, *The Private Life of the Queen by One of Her Servants* (1898).
Ponsonby, Sir F. (ed.) *Letters of the Empress Frederick* (1928).
Ponsonby, Sir Frederic, *Recollections of Three Reigns* (1951).
Ponsonby, Magdalen (ed.) *Mary Ponsonby, a Memoir* (1926).
Pope-Hennessey, James (ed.) *Queen Victoria at Windsor and Balmoral* (Letters from Princess Victoria of Prussia 1889), (1959).
Poschinger, Margaretha von, *Life of the Emperor Frederick* (1901).
Prothero, Rowland, *H.R.H. Prince Henry of Battenberg* (A private memoir), (1897).
Prothero, Rowland, *Whippingham to Westminster. Reminiscences of Lord Ernle* (1938).
Radziwill, Princess C., *The Empress Frederick* (1934).
Ribbesdale, Lord, *Impressions and Memoirs* (1927).
Rodd, Sir James Rennell, *Social and Diplomatic Memories* (1922).
Sara, M. E., *The Life and Times of H.R.H. Princess Beatrice* (1945).
Stockmar, Baron, *Memoirs* (1872).
Strachey, Lytton, *Queen Victoria* (1921).
Stuart, D. M., *The Mother of Victoria* (1941).

Stuart, Mrs (ed.), 20 *Years at Court* (from the correspondence of the Hon. Eleanor Stanley), (1916).

Tisdall, E., *She Made World Chaos* (1940).

Tooley, Sarah, *The Personal Life of Queen Victoria* (1897).

Victoria, Princess of Prussia, *My Memoirs* (1929).

Victoria, Queen, *Journal of our Life in the Highlands* (1868).

Victoria, Queen, *Leaves from the Journal of our Life in the Highlands* (1868).

Watson, Vera, *A Queen at Home* (1952).

Weigall, Lady Rose (ed.) *The Correspondence of Priscilla, Countess of Westmoreland* (1909).

Wemyss, Mrs E. (ed.) Memoirs and Letters of the Rt. Hon. Sir Robert Morier, *G.C.B.* (*1826–1876*), (1911).

Woodham-Smith, Mrs Cecil, *Florence Nightingale* (1950).

# Index

# Index